THE NEW ENGLAND GIRL

PAUL JOHN EAKIN

The New England Girl

Cultural Ideals in Hawthorne, Stowe, Howells and James

THE UNIVERSITY OF GEORGIA PRESS
ATHENS

46721

Library of Congress Catalog Card Number: 74–185–83
International Standard Book Number: 0–8203–0398–4

The University of Georgia Press, Athens 30602

Set in 10 on 12 pt. Linotype Caledonia Type
Printed in the United States of America

FOR MY PARENTS

PAUL JAMES EAKIN

JEAN GIBSON EAKIN

Contents

Acknowledgments

Kenneth S. Lynn created my interest in the American girl in his course on American realism at Harvard, and his ability to ask the right, the searching, questions about this project in its early stages invariably led to substantial improvements. Perry Miller introduced me to the literature of romantic individualism in a seminar at Harvard on American transcendentalism, and his thinking has had an important influence on my own understanding and formulation of the problems of that time. Alan Heimert read the original version and helped me to see the strength and weakness of the argument as it stood then.

David Levin gave the entire manuscript a careful and generous reading, as did David Smith the chapter on Stowe, and George Arms and Edwin Cady the chapter on Howells. I owe a special debt to Terence Martin, who helped me to resolve certain problems of design. It is a pleasure to acknowledge here the advice and encouragement given me by my colleagues at Indiana: Mary Alice Burgan, the late David Dickason, Robert Dunn, Rudolf Gottfried, Donald Gray, Kenneth Gros Louis, Robert Gross, Christoph Lohmann, Lewis Miller, David Nordloh, Melvin Plotinsky, Wallace Williams, and Paul Zietlow.

Preparation of the manuscript was assisted by a Grant-in-Aid of Research from Indiana University. I would also like to thank the Howells Center of Indiana University for permission to use the resources of their Howells collection.

Sybil Shepard Eakin was my best critic, and the most patient.

Introduction

Chapter 1

INTRODUCTION: HISTORY AND THE HEROINES OF FICTION

I

THIS BOOK has been intended from its inception as an investigation of the impulse behind the American fiction of the first two decades after the Civil War, the first phase of what is now commonly referred to as the movement toward realism. Criticism had drawn so negative a portrait of this period of literary history—its favorite labels were "The Gilded Age" and "The Genteel Tradition"—that Robert Falk, writing in 1964, called for "a more affirmative evaluation" of *The Victorian Mode in American Fiction, 1865–1885.* As a corrective to past errors of judgment, he aimed "to look at the Victorian age as nearly as possible through Victorian eyes," proposing to define the 1870s and the 1880s as "a self-contained unit of social, intellectual, and literary history," "a recognizable literary 'period.'" Determined to prove this thesis, he pursued a survey of these years which necessarily precluded any extended consideration of individual novels, although he emphasized the careers of John William DeForest, William Dean Howells, and Henry James. He himself observed, nevertheless, "It is, of course, the separate work of art and the individual writer which lend force and direction to an otherwise vaguely defined literary tradition."[1] This view has been fundamental to my own approach, and I have sought accordingly a means of restoring what has so often been an overly schematized discussion of the familiar ideas of the period—the reaction against sentimentalism, the revolt against romanticism—to its primary literary context, the fiction on which it is based.

A key group of the realists, James and Howells foremost among them, made precisely the kind of connection between literature and culture which could serve this purpose. The design of their fiction in these years consistently reflects a belief that the portrayal of women, especially young women, and the narration of a certain kind of courtship fable about them affords the best available opportunity to assess the national character, to grasp the quality of the moral life in America. Further, explicit statements by James, Howells, Henry Adams and others show that this testimony of the novels is anything but fortuitous.

Early and late none of them was more eloquent nor more extreme than Henry James in speaking of the preeminent place of women in American life. "The restless analyst" of *The American Scene* (1907) wrote: "The phenomenon may easily become, for a spectator, the sentence written largest in the American sky: when he is in search of the characteristic, what else so plays the part? The woman is two-thirds of the apparent life—which means that she is absolutely all of the social."[2] He could only conclude that the challenge of the American novel was to read aright this sentence in the sky.

Why did these writers connect their characterization of women with their ambition to comprehend the moral reality of American life? It may well be that this conception of their novels should be interpreted, following James's lead, as a literary manifestation of an historically verifiable social fact. This is the thrust of William Wasserstrom's argument in *Heiress of All the Ages: Sex and Sentiment in the Genteel Tradition*. Noting that women rather than men seemed best suited to preach genteel morality in nineteenth-century American literature, he proceeds in his review of the heroines of fiction "to connect the public life of society with the private life of the imagination."[3] The breadth of Wasserstrom's conception of this literature as a reflection of social history is exemplary; all too often studies of women in fiction have been limited to a consideration of the impact of feminist agitation on the novel.[4] Indeed it may be necessary to emphasize, in the wake of such recent books as Kate Millett's *Sexual Politics* (1970), that "the woman question" as such, while it is a prominent feature in several of the novels I shall discuss (*The Blithedale Romance, Dr. Breen's Practice, The Bostonians*), is finally only tangential to my own investigation. This study, in contrast to Wasserstrom's, concerns itself with intellectual rather than social history, with the peculiar features of New England consciousness in particular rather than American cultural currents generally, and it considers intensively the novels of four writers over a period of some forty years as opposed to a rapid survey of American fiction from the 1830s to the 1920s. It is offered nevertheless in a kindred spirit, in the conviction that the heroines of fiction have a great deal to teach us about the American character and its history.

Pursuing the origins of the realists' concern with women, one can turn from the public record left by the culture as a whole to the private history of the consciousness of the individual writer. Leon Edel has amply demonstrated the value of such an approach in the case of

Henry James; his moving account, for example, of James's youthful adoration of his cousin Minnie Temple illuminates the special place that women were to occupy in his fiction for the rest of his life. Erik Erikson's essay "Inner and Outer Space: Reflections on Womanhood" suggests that this predisposition of an individual or a culture to attribute to women an inner life of unusual significance may rest ultimately upon "the biological rock-bottom" of sexual fact, for he argues that women are to be defined by their possession of a "productive inner space." He writes moreover that "the inner life which characterizes some artistic and creative men certainly also compensates for their being biologically men by helping them to specialize in that inwardness and sensitive indwelling (the German *Innigkeit*) usually ascribed to women."[5] By extension, if an artist were endowed with a characteristically "female" personality (in Erikson's terms), one could read his affinity for the women in his fiction as a form of self-projection.

Fascinating as such speculations are, I have not been able to reach any final conclusion about the origins of the connection the realists made between the heroines of their fiction and their scrutiny of the national character. What I have had to come back to is this: the performance of James, Howells, and others in this regard drew upon a well-established assumption of nineteenth-century American society. Woman functioned as an all-purpose symbol of the ideals of the culture, the official repository of its acknowledged moral code, and she appears accordingly as a redemptive figure in the fiction of the era. The end of Harriet Beecher Stowe's *The Minister's Wooing* (1859) offers a classic instance: "The fair poetic maiden, the seeress, the saint, has passed into that appointed shrine for woman, more holy than cloister, more saintly and pure than church or altar, a Christian home. Priestess, wife, and mother, there she ministers daily in holy works of household peace, and by faith and prayer and love redeems from grossness and earthliness the common toils and wants of life."[6] The religion of womanhood celebrated here is one of the most characteristic phenomena of nineteenth-century American novels. The drive toward a literature of this kind, spurred by the demand for women's rights, seems to have sprung from the religious stirrings of the period, the outbreak of millenarian fever in the years before the Civil War, and the wave of mind-science and spiritualism that followed later on. The restless energies of a deeply ingrained tradition of revivalism and evangelical experience fed the hopes of an unending series of utopian communities and new religions. In particular the venerable belief that the Messiah would take the form of a woman at the Second Coming had quickened; such was the conception of Mother Ann Lee accepted by the Shakers, who engaged the attention of Hawthorne and Howells, while Mrs. Stowe's eccentric sister, Isabella Beecher Hooker, assigned this role to herself. As the country moved toward more secular ways, a fiction arose which explicitly proposed its heroines as cult objects. Mrs. Stowe, as we have seen, did not hesitate to make such claims for her heroines herself, while Hawthorne and James for example, preferring a more cautious stance of disengagement, left it to their characters to embrace what exalted views of women they would without benefit of any authorial sanction. The value of these young women was measured by their power to redeem the individual, to regenerate society, through love. Whether or not they possessed a moral vision of their own, they figured prominently in the millennial expectations of others. Not infrequently they were cast as messianic figures, glowing with the dream of a new dispensation. It is my hope that in recognizing the service to which such writing was dedicated I shall be able to place many of its more distinctive features, especially the conception of the heroine and her story, in a perspective that approximates the point of view of that period.

It is then the literary implications of the connection between young women in fiction and their moral role in nineteenth-century American culture that I wish to explore. So firmly entrenched was this exalted conception of womanhood that it easily became the touchstone of literary success. When William Dean Howells, then the acknowledged spokesman of the American literary establishment, arranged the *Heroines of Fiction* in a two-volume gallery of portraits at the end of the century, he elevated the characterization of women as the primary test of the truth of fiction to reality: "Apparently the ever-womanly refuses herself to the novelist who proposes anything but truth to nature; apparently she cannot trust him. She may not always be so very sincere herself, but she requires sincerity in the artist who would take her likeness, and it is only in the fiction of one who faithfully reports his knowledge of things seen that she will deign to show her face, to let her divine presence be felt. That is the highest and best fiction, and her presence is the supreme evidence of its truth to the whole of life."[7] The language of the moralist informed the analysis of the critic: the realist was identified as much by his "sincerity" and "trust" as by his "report" of the "evidence," "his knowledge of things seen." It was "the divine presence" of womanhood that conferred distinction upon the novel, the right to canonization in Howells's hall of fame, and he proceeded to construct a history of the novel in England and America to illustrate the superiority of the realistic mode over the romantic, that is, the triumph of "the ever-womanly" in literature. This retrospect of nineteenth-century literary history by a leading contemporary author and critic offers an instructive precedent for later students of the period. In my desire to achieve a fresh understanding of American realism in the work of Howells and James during the 1870s and 80s, I have followed his example but with an emphasis of my own, focusing on the characterization of *young* women and their role in a fable of redemptive courtship.

Given the aura of novelty surrounding such early heroines of Howells and James as Kitty Ellison and Daisy Miller, I was surprised to discover how extensively these authors had used the mind of the American girl as a medium for the revaluation of the past, convinced as they were of the survival of the past in the present. As they gradually stripped away the glamorous overlay of her stridently proclaimed contemporaneity, they laid bare the surviving prewar moral structure of their chosen symbol of the national character, the psychic anatomy of an earlier America. In particular it was the striking likeness between James's description of the consciousness of Isabel Archer in *The Portrait of a Lady* (1881) and his reconstruction of the inner life of Emerson and his contemporaries in his *Hawthorne* (1879) that brought this home to me. The meditations of his inexperienced young woman from Albany recapitulated the flawed ideals, the moral and aesthetic confusion, of New England thought before the Civil War. To dig into the moral archaeology of the nation in this way was in fact a characteristic proceeding for an artist of the time; not only James but Howells as well developed a particular type of New England heroine as a medium for pursuit of the past. They were not moreover the first generation of American artists to do so, and I have devoted the first part of this book to the heroines of Harriet Beecher Stowe and Nathaniel Hawthorne in order to place my account of the achievement of Howells and James in part two within the framework of a continuing native literary tradition.

When considered as a group, these four writers dramatize in the consciousness of their New England heroines the essential history of the New England mind in nineteenth-century American fiction. My investigation is by no means intended as exhaustive, omitting as it does any consideration of the contribution of Oliver Wendell Holmes, Mary Wilkins Freeman, and others to the literature of this subject. I feel nevertheless that the major developments and vicissitudes of New England spiritual life from its puritan origins through its transcendentalist flowering to its atrophy at the end of the century are amply documented in the novels of Stowe, Hawthorne, Howells, and James.

Many a practicing modern historian, whose pretensions to scientific objectivity are buttressed by computers and the statistics they feed on, will surely question the validity of the historical insight such fiction offers. Attacking the inveterate and unexamined prejudices which so frequently set history and literature at odds, David Levin begins his recent defense of historical literature by affirming the legitimacy of the literary criticism of history. He argues persuasively that "no historian can avoid using literary techniques," for "historians have to make a number of extremely important literary decisions."[8] By the same token, to dismiss a novelist's contribution to the understanding of history and the historical process simply because he expresses himself in fiction is certainly no less foolish than to attribute an unimpeachable objectivity to an historian because he deals ostensibly with facts. Levin shows that the usual distinctions between history and literature are arbitrary and misleading, for both often share a common concern with art and truth.

No one has explored the relationship between history and literature more suggestively than Hawthorne in "The Custom-House." As Levin has shown, Hawthorne the "romance-writer" presents himself here as an historian. Contemplating the accumulation of old papers in the Custom-House attic, he observes that the burden of the past is transmitted in two sorts of documents, in the "worthless scratchings" of "official" public records filled with "statistics of the former commerce of Salem," and "reams of other manuscripts" which express the private world of the inner life, "the thought of inventive brains and the rich effusion of deep hearts." Through his fiction of the discovery of a faded manuscript "containing many particulars respecting the life and conversation of one Hester Prynne," the author of *The Scarlet Letter* attributes to "the main facts" of his romance of the inner life a special significance. They are to be received in the spirit with which he "received" them himself. That is to say that they are not merely "authorized and authenticated" by history but that they provide as valuable an insight into history as if they were in fact what they appear to his discovering hand, "an official record of some period long past":

> Poking and burrowing into the heaped-up rubbish in the corner; unfolding one and another document, and reading the names of vessels that had long ago foundered at sea or rotted at the wharves, and those of merchants, never heard of now on 'Change nor very readily decipherable on their mossy tombstones; glancing at such matters with the saddened, weary, half-reluctant interest which we bestow on the corpse of dead activity,—and exerting my fancy, sluggish with little use, to raise up from these dry bones an image of the old town's brighter aspect, when India was a new region, and only Salem knew the way thither,—I chanced to lay my hand on a small package, carefully done up in a piece of ancient yellow parchment.[9]

Hawthorne's decision to treat the genesis of *The Scarlet Letter* in this passage as though it were an historical event is not simply a convenient metaphor for his conception of the creative process; the correspondence is deliberate, the analogy is functional, for the art of the historian and the art of the novelist could be one and the same. Thus if the monographs of the New History were to flower from the "heaped-up rubbish" of official documents in the Custom-House attic, as Hawthorne foresaw, so did *The Scarlet Letter*, and Hawthorne's romance deserves the admiration of historians for grappling so deeply with the most interesting and most elusive of all historical facts, the nature of the representative consciousness of a given place and moment in human time.

It does not matter finally whether or not there ever was such a thing as the New England mind; Hawthorne and his articulate contemporaries believed that there was, and their belief is incontestably factual. In the larger view, which Levin with good reason encourages us to take, the upshot of such a novelist's conviction, in respect at least to this belief, is really no different from that of such eminent modern historians as the late Perry Miller, Oscar Handlin, and the late Richard Hofstadter who, seeking to capture the life of the past, create for us typical characters—the puritan, the immigrant, the reformer—designed to express their intepretation of historical evidence.[10] Formulations of representative states of mind are legion in historical literature—the spirit of the age, the American character, the Renaissance man, the

Russian soul—and while it is sobering perhaps to regard them all as fictions, the persistence of such fictions is, I think, one of the most revelatory facts of the human condition. Even though there is always the possibility that to trace the life of the New England mind in the heroines of a series of nineteenth-century novels may be to read the history of a fiction recorded in fiction, the authority of these writers is such that I assent to the historical validity of their vision of the past. As Frank Kermode reminds us in *The Sense of an Ending* (1967), through fictions we learn to know ourselves.

Obviously Stowe, Hawthorne, Howells, and James did not regard themselves as intellectual historians in any strict modern sense of that discipline. Nevertheless a major and determining influence on the form and content of their fiction was an interest in what we would now call intellectual history. James might be speaking for any student of the American past—historian or novelist—when he wrote that the interest of the mind of Margaret Fuller resided in "the story it has to tell us of those for whom it flourished and whose measure and reflection it necessarily more or less gives."[11] If, in his biography of Hawthorne, James was pleased to see in the romancer a type of the New England artist, it is not surprising that he drew in his portrait of Isabel Archer a type of the Emersonian seeker after self-culture. It was altogether natural that his sense of the past should extend equally to fiction and to history. Freely acknowledging the historical dimension of literary experience in his own work, he prized it in that of others as well. Thus he valued Hawthorne for giving "the most vivid reflection of New England life that has found its way into literature,"[12] while Howells, to atone for any slight in his judgment of *Uncle Tom's Cabin* as the great New England novel manqué, asserted that "no one has felt more deeply than myself the value of New England in literature."[13] Although the approach of these writers to the matter of intellectual history was personal and intuitive rather than systematic and scholarly, it was precisely their familiarity with New England life that uniquely qualified them to recreate it authoritatively as a culture with a consciousness distinctively its own.

It would be a serious mistake, however, to treat such fictions, even those of Mrs. Stowe, as merely intellectual history in a literary disguise. The relationship between literature and history is far too complex to permit such a simplification; each shapes and is shaped in turn by the other. I shall try to respect artistic design in order to show how it expresses a sense of history; in particular I mean to show how these authors' development of the New England girl mirrors the unfolding of their preoccupation with the New England past.

This formulation of my primary objective has determined the scope of the study which follows. I have felt free to restrict myself to commentary only on those heroines who function significantly in this special historical perspective, rather than to commit myself to any more generalized survey of all the young women created by these writers. Further, while both Howells and James maintained a lifelong interest in New England, the intense and continuous attention they devoted to it in their fiction from the late 1870s into the 1880s—climaxing for James with *The Bostonians* and somewhat earlier for Howells with *A Modern Instance*—marks out a distinct phase of their literary development which squares with the received conceptions of their careers in these years. It has seemed to me quite natural then to limit my treatment of these writers in the second part of this study to their fiction of this time, taking it up at a point when the New England girl enters the stage and putting it down with her exit. There are of course some disadvantages to this period definition of my subject, especially in the case of Henry James. The American heroines of his "major phase," notably Milly Theale, automatically lie beyond the scope of this study, as does his great portrait of Lambert Strether, the leading male presence in his predominantly feminine gallery of New England types.[14] Still, I have been reassured by my sense that with *The Bostonians* James's exploration of the perversion of the Emersonian ideal of self-culture, the special province of his early phase, was virtually complete.

II

To speak of the history of a culture portrayed in the consciousness of the heroines of fiction may sound rather far-fetched, especially when the most celebrated native heroine of the nineteenth-century was such an apparently rootless and largely expatriated figure as the American girl of Howells and James. James, however, credited himself with just such an ambition in his New York prefaces on the American girl of "thirty and forty years ago." Speaking of "the general quaint sisterhood, perfectly distinguished then, but displaced, disfeatured, 'discounted' today, for all I know," he stressed his determination in his stories of that time to use however "slight" an anecdote of a heroine's career to map out the contours of American society. He maintained, however, that his "insuperably restricted experience," his "various, missing American clues," had forced him to rely on essentially "negative aspects" of the national scene to supply him with the revelation of the American character that he sought. Reviewing "the Francie Dossons and the Daisy Millers and the Bessie Aldens and the Pandora Days" who formed "the American branch" of his "international department," James beheld a veritable procession of "unprecedented creatures," haunting incarnations of the same "characteristic blankness" that had doomed Hawthorne to an exquisite provinciality.

Faced with such a predicament, James, and Howells as well, had a motive for discovering a heroine *with* precedents, a young woman with a distinctive consciousness and cultural background, a girl, in short, like Isabel Archer or Marcia Gaylord, who could become the subject of a major novel as a Daisy Miller or a Kitty Ellison, lacking such equipment, could not. In the second part of this book I shall trace the emergence of a *precedented* heroine, a girl with a history and an inner life that are largely New England in derivation, in the fiction of James and Howells from *Roderick Hudson* (1875) and *The Lady of the Aroostook* (1879) to *The Bostonians* (1886) and *April Hopes* (1888). If I begin, however, not with a Mary Garland or a Lydia Blood, but with Daisy Miller, it is precisely because her story conveniently serves to dramatize the problem facing not only James but any American artist proposing to read the complexity of American experience into the courtship of an innocent girl. Daisy is not, of course, a New England girl; she is wholly lacking in the kind of specificity that such an identification would require, and that is my point. She could be, and was, a compelling archetype of the national simplicity, but she could be nothing more. In the discussion of "Daisy Miller" that follows I hope to suggest why the development of some such heroine as the New England girl did in fact occur in the novels of James and Howells of this period, since the spectacle offered by the Daisies and the Francies was at best what James was ruefully to term "a minor exhibition."[15]

Again and again in the New York prefaces, James linked the heroines of "Daisy Miller," *The Reverberator*, "Pandora," and "An International Episode," treating their stories as variations on a common theme. In this group of tales the design of James's fable of the American girl clearly emerges, illustrating his notion that the courtship of an ideal young woman held out to a rootless young man the redemptive possibility of an entry into American reality. To state in this way the familiar nineteenth-century love story, the staple, as we shall see, of Stowe and Hawthorne, is to suggest how easily it could and did become for James an extended metaphor for a second story, the fable of the expatriate American artist and his ambivalent desire for the native American materials from which he hoped to create a truly national literature. The merging of these two stories, of boy-meets-girl with artist-confronts-national-scene, was something more than a marriage of convenience between a popular commercial formula and a deep-seated professional dilemma; for it not only proposed reassuringly that America was meetable and lovable, but it reflected as well James's conviction that American womanhood was somehow supremely the representative national fact.

"Daisy Miller: A Study" (June–July, 1878) has always been regarded as the classic version of James's fable of the American girl, and properly so. The tale itself, however, hardly justifies the notoriety it once enjoyed as a controversial portrait of the American girl, for of Daisy herself there is very little to say, and what the narrative says of her finally is said clearly enough to admit of no mistake. As a narrative quantity in her own right the girl is *pretty* and *little;* these are the adjectives James uses again and again to describe her appearance, her voice, her manner. He wisely refrained from any attempt to say more of her, to render her inner life, which could only have shown as a gratuitous violation of the mythic simplicity of his conception of her as "a child of nature and of freedom." One of the two terms of his courtship equation could hardly be said then to count for much as a representative national fact, as James himself acknowledged when he observed that his "supposedly typical little figure was of course pure poetry." The retrospective judgment of the New York preface to the story is unsparing: "Flatness . . . was the very sum of her story."[16]

It was left to the second term, the young man, to balance the symbolic equation of James's tale of courtship, and the reference to "A Study" in the title of the story suggests the extent to which the hero usurps the role of the heroine despite her featured billing. It is Frederick Winterbourne, after all, the eternal student, who studies Daisy Miller, and the portrait of the young man as observer explains his failure to make out the true likeness of the pretty American girl in James's canvas. The debate over Daisy's innocence, like that over the reality of the ghosts in *The Turn of the Screw,* has obscured the simple yet crucial fact that the primary subject of the narrative in each case is the point of view from which it is told. Nevertheless, in order not to slight the importance of the remarkable Daisy, it must in all fairness be pointed out that if the reader is dependent on Winterbourne for his knowledge of Daisy Miller, he is equally dependent on Daisy for his knowledge of "poor" Winterbourne. The negligible young man appears not to have any life of his own to speak of, or any that might yield narrative substance, aside from his abortive encounter with Daisy.

If the phenomenon of the American girl was without question highly charged with significance for Henry James, there is something perverse, suggestive of self-punishment, in his choice of so inadequate an individual as Winterbourne to study it. If the young man "was booked to make a mistake,"[17] it was James after all who "booked" him. Winterbourne's handicap is substantial, for the slim facts that serve to identify him promise nothing. An American without knowledge of America, a young man without an occupation in the American sense (he is reported to be "studying" in Geneva), he is an eligible bachelor with only a limited experience of young women. Against the blankness of this background, Winterbourne's connection with Geneva, "the little metropolis of Calvinism" (142), with its narrow morality based on a strict observance of social conventions, stands out as a solitary point of interest, however uninviting. James takes up Winterbourne's story at Vevey, a worldly resort (James likens it to an American watering place such as Saratoga or Newport) where one can approach pretty young girls without much interference from vigilant mamas. Here, poles apart from the puritanism of Geneva (an analogue, perhaps, for Boston) at the other end of the lake, Winterbourne is distinctly out of his element. Here he is destined to encounter a pretty American girl, and his relationship with her, if successful, contains the possible resolution of all of his problems through an initiation into experience which will achieve for him a contemporary American identity.[18] What James would wish for Winterbourne he would of course wish for himself, yet the form his imagination gives to this wish is, curiously, a story of early death and failure.

Winterbourne struggles in the opening scene to read aright the vision of a pretty American girl standing in a garden, always the native setting of this archetypal figure in James as in Hawthorne, Stowe, and Howells. His confusion here offers a paradigm of the limitations of his moral and aesthetic perceptions which is reenacted relentlessly throughout the tale. His first impression of Daisy Miller strikes the cool restraint, latent in his very name, that is to be his habitual note: "How pretty they are!" (144–45). Although the young man moves instinctively to classification by type—the "they" here refers to the entire category of American girls—his impulse is nevertheless to rise and greet her. Winterbourne cannot surrender to the pleasure of fresh experience, however, without disconcerting second thoughts: "Was she simply a pretty girl from New York State—were they all like that, the pretty girls who had a good deal of gentlemen's society? Or was she also a designing, an audacious, an unscrupulous young person? . . . He was inclined to think Miss Daisy Miller was a flirt—a pretty American flirt. He had never, as yet, had any relations with young ladies of this category" (151). The young man emphasizes that the American girl is to him an undiscovered country where Geneva scruples simply do not apply. The alternative interpretations of the American character before him are ridiculously exaggerated; the stilted formality of his interior discourse is entirely at odds with the artless young woman's colloquial ease. Clearly the expatriate's fastidious pretensions to a Continental mode of vision are hopelessly ill-equipped to cope with the self-reliant daughter of Emerson and Whitman. How to see her as she is? Significantly it is only the discovery of another "formula" for Daisy Miller that restores the young man's fragile self-confidence. All artifice, Winterbourne is constitutionally incapable of transcending his reductively conventional approach to reality. As the passage concludes, he pursues his dogged perversion of the creative process with a comic inevitability: "he wondered what were the regular conditions and limitations of one's intercourse with a pretty American flirt" (151).

The rest of the story unfolds as a series of such attempts to define the reality of the American girl. At stake in all of these confrontations is the possibility that, in opening himself to experience, the young American might move from the constraints of his European withdrawal and its sterile forms toward the freedom of the American girl and the experience of life and love which she represents. Her brief existence is devoted to a single principle, to enjoy life fully, and to a single important corollary, to persuade, even to provoke, Winterbourne to enjoy it with her. Faced with the inadequacy of Winterbourne's stale imagination, however, only once, at Chillon, does the generosity of Daisy's untamed spirit manage to quicken his perception, creating an entente, a "personal accent" (170), between them. The inconclusive idyl in Switzerland is followed in the second part of the tale by a group of scenes in Rome in which the obstacles preventing the es-

tablishment of a successful relationship between the two young Americans prove insurmountable. In these episodes the baffled student from
Geneva seeks to interpret correctly the meaning of the image initially
contemplated at Vevey: the haunting figure of a pretty American girl
in a garden. The limitations of the expatriate American observer show
now not as a comic incapacity but as a sickness which kills the American reality that has been his study, a reality too true to itself to admit
of any compromise he might seek to impose upon it.

In the moonlit Colosseum Winterbourne is given a final, fatal chance
to grasp the true value of the American girl and save himself in the
process. He succeeds, however, only in destroying the agent of his
redemption, sacrificing the living girl on the altar of his own dead
sensibility. Encountering Daisy and Giovanelli, a handsome Italian
adventurer, alone in the ancient arena, he concludes mistakenly that
"she was a young lady whom a gentleman need no longer be at pains
to respect" (202). On the strength of this erroneous estimate of her
character, Winterbourne tells Daisy that "it makes very little difference
whether you are engaged or not" (203). The development of the narrative ends here, for the hero has abandoned any desire for a new
life and the heroine through whom he might have achieved it has
received her death-blow at his hands. This the girl perfectly, instinctively, totally grasps: her overwhelming sense of an ending shines like
a small white light upon the young man's waste of consciousness. It
did not matter with the others, but when the man she loves fails to
accept or to understand her as she is, the very principle and value of
her existence is called in question. To the threat of malaria latent in
the tainted atmosphere of the arena which witnessed her failure to
free Winterbourne, she responds "in a little strange tone," "I don't
care . . . whether I have Roman fever or not!" (204). The timing of
Daisy's sudden death immediately following this episode in the Colosseum points to its cause. If her death symbolizes the high cost of an
uninhibited pursuit of experience, Winterbourne is nonetheless, in the
imaginative economy of the narrative, responsible for finishing her off.
Once he has definitely made up his mind to repudiate her, the girl
dies, fully revealing the destructive potential of his blindness.

James might have titled his picture of "poor" Winterbourne "A
Painful Case" with greater justification even than Joyce was to have
in his portrait of a similarly hopeless figure, for Winterbourne's comprehension of the American girl—or at least of his mistake—is achieved
after her death but not because of it. His complacent view of Daisy's

character is overturned only when Giovanelli tells him as they stand by the girl's grave that "she was the most innocent" (205). He has understood her love for him too late; not even the American girl has been able to liberate him, to engage him to contemporary American reality.

James's appraisal of the redemptive possibilities of American court-ship in "Daisy Miller" is doubly pessimistic, for the design of the story does not exempt the purity of the girl from the searching criticism which exposes the poverty of the young man. Winterbourne and the other observers of Daisy Miller, the Mrs. Walkers of the American reading public, made the character of this American girl the subject of a controversy which, despite her sterling simplicity, was nevertheless clearly envisaged by her creator's imagination. For if James could claim with justice that his young woman was "pure poetry," he could also dramatize for his readers the possibility that his heroine might in fact deserve to be assigned to "a vulgar place among the categories of disorder." The attitude toward this representative national fact was decidedly ambivalent: the other face of love for America, for all that was "pretty and undefended and natural" (196) was a very real hostility. There must always have been, even for James himself, the temptation to accept as fact the negative verdict in the fiction: if his heroine were truly as "common" as his disparaging dowagers would have her, then her want of novelistic substance would be her fault and not his own. Final responsibility for the characterization of the Ameri-can girl rested of course with James, and any hostility toward her on his own part would have been in some sort directed toward himself, any shortcomings of her character an index of his inability at the time to say more of a young woman very much worth bothering about. And she was indeed worth bothering about, for Winterbourne's decision not to trouble himself further to find her out stands in the tale as the leading ground for a moral judgment against him.

In any case, Winterbourne's story must have had a special resonance for James, for he allows it to envelop Daisy's. In fact, the young man's delayed and retrospective vision not only illustrates the inadequacy of conventional standards as a measure of novel kinds of experience, but his difficulties in a more general sense provide an analogue for those of the American artist who, nourished on expatriate traditions, would attempt to accommodate his art to an American reality. If "poor" Winterbourne seems an unlikely candidate for the role of the American artist, one need only think of James's portrait in the following year of

the marginal careers of Hawthorne and his contemporaries to be re-
minded that nothing could have been more likely in James's view at
the time than the unlikelihood of such figures. With a curious, perhaps
self-deprecating, certainly calculated inversion, James proceeded to
paint the story of his own success as an American artist in a series of
ironic pictures of incapacitated Americans who have failed in this role.

Lest such an extension of the significance of these courtship tales
seem unwarranted, consider *The Reverberator* (1888), as characteristic
of them all as any, in which James gives an explicit statement of the
connection, always present in his fables of the American girl, between
the twin stories of love and art. Like Winterbourne, Gaston Probert is
an expatriate American filled with an eloquent sense of his nonentity;
following the pattern of the earlier tale, the young man is granted the
opportunity to forge an identity for himself through a confrontation
with American reality in the person of an American girl, pretty Francie
Dosson. This time, however, James makes the familiar figure of the
observer of the national scene who haunts these tales not only a lover
but a would-be artist who in marrying the American girl finds at last
not only himself but the long-sought subject for his art as well. In
order to fire the weak-kneed swain to the achievement of this unabashedly happy ending, he inserts a lecture, delivered by the hero's
confidant and mentor, an American painter named Charles Waterlow,
on the issues at stake in the drama of Gaston's courtship. This episode,
a rather bald piece of exposition, spells out in unmistakable letters
James's conception of the redemptive mission of the American girl.
Urging his indecisive friend to marry Francie, Waterlow exalts their
union as an emblem of his achievement of manhood, of "individual
life" and "moral independence," of his choice for America and the open
air. With an Emersonian exuberance in his final tribute to the American girl as an irresistible fact with a limitless capacity for growth,
Waterlow makes it clear that in the emancipation of the man is contained the salvation of the artist as well, that marriage to the American
girl will work the metamorphosis of the wavering Gaston into the
American Scholar: " 'Lord, man, how can you be so impenetrably
dense? Don't you see that she's really of the softest, finest material
that breathes, that she's a perfect flower of plasticity, that everything
you may have an apprehension about will drop away from her like
the dead leaves from a rose and that you may make of her any perfect
and enchanting thing you yourself have the wit to conceive?' "[19]

Tales like "Daisy Miller" and *The Reverberator*—and there are others, "Pandora," for example—show the American girl as others see her, especially from the point of view of a young American expatriate who is potentially an artist and lover. Although this observer never manages to learn very much about her, his conviction in his quest for American knowledge that she possesses decisive significance as a type of the national character lends a certain urgency to his encounters with her. As he presents her, however, she verges on abstraction, either the soul of simplicity and innocence or quite the reverse. Clearly the American girl occupied a central yet unsettled place in James's imagination. The ambivalent reflections of Louis Leverett, the fastidious Bostonian aesthete in "A Bundle of Letters" (1879), concerning two young women staying in the same pension with him in Paris present a characteristic Jamesian meditation of this period on the value of his heroine: "These young girls are rather curious types; they have a certain interest, they have a certain grace but they are disappointing too; they don't go far; they don't keep all they promise; they don't satisfy the imagination. They are cold, slim, sexless; the physique is not generous, not abundant. . . . They are both specimens of the emancipated young American girl—practical, positive, passionless, subtle, and knowing, as you please, either too much or too little. And yet, as I say, they have a certain stamp, a certain grace; I like to talk with them, to study them."[20]

The drama of the hero's relationship to the American girl in these tales lies in the disparity between his interpretation of her and the reality which she represents, and James offers alternative explanations for the young man's imperfect vision, explanations that yield a critical commentary not only on the representation of American life in art but on his own uncertainties about his subject and his ability to handle it. At times the artist in these stories blames his failures on the intractable nature of American reality itself. His complaints concerning its mediocrity, its strident vulgarity, its aggressive flatness, are endless; baffled and defensive, he seeks in vain the means of giving these materials relief and dimension. James himself must have shared these misgivings, frequently choosing to focus the interest of these tales on the figure of this observer, the artist, and his problems; in this way he could make the most of apparently thin literary opportunities, capitalizing on the thorough knowledge of this character which he could draw from personal experience. The thinness, the blankness of the American scene were only apparent, however, as James well knew: the occasion for his famous dismay over the poverty of Hawthorne's note-

books was after all the writing of a biography which recognized the
legitimacy of Hawthorne's place among the English men of letters.
James's "provincial" Hawthorne, unlike his own "poor" young men, was
the kind of successful failure he himself might hope to be.

Study of his observer figure suggests in fact that the difficulty of
creating an American art lay not so much in the nature of the reality
itself as in the limited experience and fallible perception of the artist.
The seeming perversity of James's decision to make his literary alter
egos pathetically weak may have been a deliberate and even confident
piece of strategy designed at once to limit readers' expectations of his
present work without compromising those of his future. The claims
of the American scene as a subject worthy of art were not of course
disproved because inexperienced and fatuous young Jamesian males
were not clever enough to vindicate them, and the very ineptitude of
these "poor" young men implied the potential mastery of others. Yet
it is equally true that such claims could not be substantiated either,
perhaps conveniently so if James felt that he was not yet fully prepared to deliver an account of America with the kind of Balzacian
density and breadth to which he aspired. He might, quite simply, not
be altogether sure what the American girl, viewed from within, might
prove to be. These observations are of course speculative, but the
course of James's fiction in these years bears them out. As he grew
more certain of his native ground, he took upon himself the burden
of the role his "poor" young men could never handle. His conception
of the consciousness of the American girl expanded in direct proportion to the growth of his knowledge of the American mind, particularly, as we shall see, in its New England phase. Thus while the invariably remarkable heroine and her cautious expatriate observer
remain constant as the principal figures in his tales of courtship, the
girl increasingly displaces the young man as the dominant narrative
presence in these fictions, especially when they take on the dimensions
of the novel.[21] It is this shift toward a more exclusive concern with the
inner life of his heroine that constitutes the major area of significant
change in James's development of his fable of the American girl.

In his preface to the New York edition of *The Portrait of a Lady*
James located this shift at the core of his conception of this novel:
" 'Place the centre of the subject in the young woman's own consciousness,' I said to myself, 'and you get as interesting and as beautiful a
difficulty as you could wish. . . . Put the heaviest weight into *that* scale,
which will be so largely the scale of her relation to herself. . . . Place

meanwhile in the other scale the lighter weight (which is usually the one that tips the balance of interest): press least hard, in short, on the consciousness of your heroine's satellites, especially the male; make it an interest contributive only to the greater one.' " By the time of *The Portrait of a Lady*, then, James was prepared to transcend the limitations of "Daisy Miller," both the "flatness," the insufficiency, of his heroine's character and the inadequacy of his "poor" observer's vision. The "honest transposition of the weights in the two scales"[22] was indeed total: displacing the young man, the observer, as the primary member of the courtship pair, James made the drama of the young woman's consciousness, the center of his "centre," her observation of herself. Reserving the complete history of this shift in James's tales of the courtship of the American girl for part two of this study, I wish to show here through a brief consideration of "An International Episode" (December, 1878–January, 1879) that James was already moving at the time of "Daisy Miller" towards the solution of the difficulties of the American realist that, he felt, he achieved in his portrait of Isabel Archer.

While James does not present Bessie Alden as the controlling center of consciousness in "An International Episode," he nevertheless fore-shadows, in his rendering of this serious young woman with her New England idealism and her independent imagination, his most fully realized portrait of the American girl, Isabel Archer. She is in fact the first of the heroines discussed so far who can be said to have an inner life of any complexity, although James sketches only its barest outline in this tale. James to be sure grouped Bessie with his Daisies and Francies in his New York prefaces on the American girl, and there is much in "An International Episode" that recalls the familiar pattern of "Daisy Miller" and *The Reverberator*. Thus when others attempt to force Bessie's natural curiosity and imaginative enjoyment of Lord Lambeth, her hapless English suitor, to fit a more limited, rigidly defined code of manners, Bessie like her sister heroines holds to her belief that her behavior takes place in an open medium which she herself controls rather than one in which the significance of conduct is predetermined, governed by tradition, convention, and prejudice. While Bessie's intransigence may suggest her kinship with Daisy and Francie, her self-conscious introspection contributes to a motivation of her conduct more complex than that of the other two, whose spontaneity was perplexing only to observers lacking the experience to deal with the unconventional, baffling in its very simplicity and innocence. In order to understand Bessie Alden, James makes it necessary to witness the drama of her consciousness.

Although Lambeth first glimpses Bessie as she moves slowly across the lawn at Newport in a garden setting that recalls the opening of "Daisy Miller," the heroine of "An International Episode," for all her slimness and grace, her freshness and charm, is quite unlike the unreflecting girl from Schenectady with her decided preference for "gentlemen's society." Instead, as the narrative begins to reveal not only her innocence but her preoccupation with national character, her studied grasp for freedom, and her aesthetic sensibility, Bessie increasingly resembles the other member of James's courtship pair, the expatriate artist observer; here the twin stories of the girl and the artist in his fable are one. Using the most conventional materials—the wooing of an American girl by an English lord—James makes it clear that he is not concerned in his tales of courtship with a love story of the usual sort but rather with certain modes of consciousness which prove in fact to be incompatible with the life of the heart.

To begin with, Bessie is, in the words of her worldly sister, Mrs. Westgate, "what they call in Boston 'thoughtful' ";[23] her intellectual cast of mind, her gravity of manner, and her air of deliberation are linked repeatedly with her Boston background. James's innocent abroad is a bookish young woman who seeks literary pleasures in the landscape of Europe. Her romanticism, however, runs deeper than the literary taste of the sentimental tourist, for she has unbounded confidence in her imagination as a source of knowledge. She finds her greatest pleasure in allowing it to range freely over the field of her limited experience, manipulating these materials to form designs of its own. It is the fate of Lord Lambeth to find an established place in Bessie's gallery of generalizations if not in her heart, for the girl immediately identifies him as the type of the British aristocrat, and, in the manner of a Dorothea Brooke, she forms her expectations of him on the basis of the heroic opportunities which she attributes to an "hereditary legislator" (309), a term borrowed from her reading.

In his most extended presentation of Bessie's consciousness, her final appraisal of her conventional lover, James probes to its core, uncovering the workings of his heroine's imagination. Here, pursuing an orderly investigation of the ambiguous movements of her heart, the girl reveals that she is clearly not in love with the Englishman but with an image of her own creation, and with a vague, derivative ideal of heroic action which she associates with it. The "poor" young man serves only as an occasion for the restless activity of her imagination, bent on its own gratification and impatient of an intractable reality which impedes the freedom of its flight and constrains its art:

> She had a kind of ideal of conduct for a young man who should find himself in this magnificent position, and she tried to adapt it to Lord Lambeth's deportment, as you might attempt to fit a silhouette in cut paper upon a shadow projected upon a wall. But Bessie Alden's silhouette refused to coincide with his lordship's image; and this want of harmony sometimes vexed her more than she thought reasonable. . . . Then her imagination wandered away from him—very far away; for it was an incontestable fact that at such moments he seemed distinctly dull. (312)

To the perception of the New England girl, this license of her imagination raises a moral issue which calls her conscience into play: "she reflected that it was no more than fair that she should think as well of him as he thought of her" (313). Nonetheless when Lord Lambeth eventually proposes to Bessie, she refuses his offer because she is not in love with him, that is to say, because he fails to meet the requirements of her imagination.

Bessie's idealism proves to be the force that determines her behavior, but here James does not allow it to be seriously challenged, nor does he give much account of its origins. Boston, books, and especially the imagination, a New England identity and a heritage of romanticism— he advances all these as possible sources of her conduct and character. He did not require himself to go beyond these hints in 1878. By 1881, however, James was ready to present in the Albany chapters of *The Portrait of a Lady* an elaborate anatomy of Isabel Archer's transcendentalist meditations, her hyperactive imagination and her untried ideals, in order to prepare for her "no" to Lord Warburton, a rejection which is, perhaps, derived in part from "An International Episode." Henry James was not the first American artist to make his heroine's courtship an occasion to revaluate the spiritual history of New England in this way. James for one believed that Hawthorne had captured in his tragic portrait of Zenobia's "baffled effort to make a hero of Hollingsworth" the essence of "the romance of New England," "the secret play of the Puritan faith."[24] Similarly Harriet Beecher Stowe, convinced that only an acquaintance with the theology of Jonathan Edwards could permit her readers to comprehend *The Minister's Wooing*, obliged accordingly. James's biography of Hawthorne, published in 1879, the central document of his meditations on the history of the American mind, led to his identification of the consciousness of his heroine as somehow peculiar to New England life. Exploring the moral and aesthetic confusion of the age of Emerson, Hawthorne, and Margaret Fuller, he discovered (or rediscovered) a complex American reality, providing new resources for American fiction founded on a native literary tradition. The chapters on Stowe and Hawthorne which follow document the existence of this tradition, which embodied in the consciousness of its heroines the aspirations of the New England mind.

Part One

A Native Literary Tradition: Harriet Beecher Stowe & Nathaniel Hawthorne

Chapter 2

RENUNCIATION IN NEW ENGLAND:
HARRIET BEECHER STOWE
AND *THE MINISTER'S WOOING*

THE ENDURING POPULARITY of Henry James's irrepressible young woman from Schenectady has fixed in the national imagination the type of the American girl, so simple in her "audacious innocence" as to seem finally a peculiarly American enigma. When he wrote of Daisy Miller that "flatness . . . was the sum of her story," he might have been speaking of Hawthorne as well, for the notebooks of the American novelist were in his view as wanting in relief as the story of the American girl. In any case, his own designation of Daisy Miller and her kind as "unprecedented creatures" has encouraged the widely accepted interpretation of this archetypal figure as a classic manifestation of the blankness of the American scene. If the national character could justly be called blank, it proved nevertheless to be a blankness with distinctively American features which could be made the subject of fiction, for James was to discover that the American girl had origins and precedents after all. Only by an act of the imagination, however, could he recover a history for his heroines which those of Hawthorne and Mrs. Stowe had possessed as their birthright: a usable, indeed an inescapable, if not an ancient past, with at its heart a village culture at once narrow and strong, itself the embodiment of a certain striking queerness of the New England mind, angular and severe, predisposed to strange passages of moral ecstasy. This puritan heritage, which for James, standing at the farther edge of the gulf left by the Civil War, lay well behind him at the remove of an earlier generation, was for Hawthorne an ancestral legacy, the questionable gift of his "grave, bearded, sable-cloaked and steeple-crowned progenitors"; for Mrs. Stowe it lived on in her religion-centered family, especially in the formidable person of her own father, Lyman Beecher, the foremost Calvinist preacher of his day. It is this spiritual proximity that places the New England girls of Mrs. Stowe at the fountainhead of the inner history of the nineteenth-century American heroine.

Despite the passing of the taste for sentimental fiction, Vernon L. Parrington, Perry Miller, Edmund Wilson, Charles H. Foster and oth-

ers have managed to establish the critical reputation of Harriet Beecher Stowe on a permanent basis, stressing her contribution to our
understanding of moral psychology and intellectual history. In the attention that Mrs. Stowe now receives there is an unmistakable tendency
to set aside as unprofitable any serious consideration of her fiction *as
fiction;* instead her novels, taken as barely veiled autobiographical con-
fessions, have become documents for the study of a culture and its religious preoccupations.[1] In this way the characteristic design of all of
her work—rated at the value of her weakest productions, the fat, form-
less serials of her final years—is easily dismissed as simply a convenient
bag into which she stuffed her rich store of personal and at the same
time representative reminiscences of the New England past. While I,
too, value Mrs. Stowe's fiction for its vision of history, I seek to approach her achievement not in spite of the literary form in which she
sought expression but through it, for her treatment of her material is
as properly a kind of cultural evidence as that material in itself. My
study of Mrs. Stowe is focussed on an analysis of *The Minister's Wooing* (1859), not simply because it is a characteristic example of her art
but also because it is her most distinguished attempt in fiction to come
to terms with her culture on the subject of the moral life.[2]

　　To begin with, as even the barest outline of the fable of courtship
in *The Minister's Wooing* suggests, Mrs. Stowe's performance as a novelist encountering a novelist's problems reveals her willingness to vio-
late the conventional logic of the fiction itself. The plot is certainly a
curious one. Mrs. Stowe quickly establishes a natural, reciprocal love
between her heroine, Mary Scudder, and James Marvyn, the unregenerate boy next door, and then as quickly removes him from the scene
until the final chapters. She introduces this sentimental boy-girl romance only to redirect the reader's interest toward another love story
which she clearly intends as the primary matter of the novel, the minister's wooing. She proposes Dr. Samuel Hopkins, the minister of
Mary's religion, who boards with the Widow Scudder, Mary's mother,
as the proper hero for her heroine. The minister soon falls in love with
the exemplary girl, and Mrs. Stowe, seemingly determined to bring
about Mary's union with the eminent theologian, circumvents her heroine's unshakeable fidelity to her beloved James through the supposed
death of the young man in a disaster at sea. The shock sends Mary into
a grave spiritual crisis, and it is in the aftermath of suffering that the
girl, greatly changed, resigns herself to accept the minister's suit. At
the end of the novel, however, the author prevents the very union

which she has taken such pains to make possible. Safe after all, Marvyn returns, Hopkins manfully absolves Mary of her promise to him, and Mary is free to marry the man whom she and, obviously, Mrs. Stowe prefer. Mrs. Stowe alters her characterization of her heroine to accompany these shifts in the elaboration of her plot. Thus in a single career Mary Scudder traverses the complete cycle of Hawthorne's New England girls: she moves from the household poetry of a Phoebe Pyncheon to become first a sickly and spiritual Priscilla, then a Hilda, snow-maiden and virgin saint, to emerge finally as a Phoebe once more, only more mature, matronly, and maternal, more Stowe.

The changes in the direction of the narrative—the reversals in the plot and the circular movement in the characterization—would seem to suggest that Mrs. Stowe is pursuing two different stories simultaneously. This is in fact the case. Exploring alternative destinies for her heroine, Christian matron or New England nun, Mrs. Stowe dramatized in the double courtship of Mary Scudder by James Marvyn and Dr. Hopkins the two disparate moral traditions which engaged her imagination throughout her literary career: on the one hand the domestic sentimentalism of feminine fiction which proposed marriage and family life as the reward of life's tearful trials, and on the other the Calvinism of the New England fathers which led, she believed, towards solitude, suffering, and renunciation. In the minister's wooing of Mary, Mrs. Stowe entertained a marriage of the way of thought to the way of feeling only to stand up herself and say why the twain might not be joined together. In studying her divided allegiance to these two ideals and her working out of the two love stories in which they find expression, I hope to capture something of the complexity of Mrs. Stowe's attitude towards her New England heritage.

I

In the opening pages of *The Minister's Wooing* Harriet Beecher Stowe turns from the contemporary American girl, an unregenerate, frivolous, decadent individual whom she pictures "lying in a rustling silk *négligée*, and, amid a gentle generality of rings, ribbons, puffs, laces, beaux, and dinner-discussion, reading our humble sketch,"[3] to reach backward into the past to recapture in her ancestor and prototype the former rectitude of this now reclining figure. The Newport of her story is not the cosmopolitan watering place of her own day (a favorite setting for the young women of James and Howells), but the New England village of the previous century. The initial glimpse of Mary is an auspicious one, a seemingly Arcadian moment brimming with a millennial promise never to be redeemed in the procession of nineteenth-century American heroines who were to follow her: dressed in white, she stands amidst apple blossoms in the doorway of a perfect country home, transfigured in the streaming sunshine of a springtime afternoon. This numinous vision of purity, sanctified by the presence of a dove perched on the girl's finger, reminds Mrs. Stowe of "some old pictures of the girlhood of the Virgin" (2:14).[4]

The sources of the distinction of this holy girl are twofold, domestic and religious, derived respectively from her mother and from her father; each strain of her double inheritance shades imperceptibly into the other in this charmed moment of equilibrium in the village culture of which she is the flower. Like her mother, Mary Scudder has "faculty," the New England term for an art of housekeeping raised to the perfection of a virtue; it is "faculty" that makes of the humblest task a moral exercise. Were it not for a second gift, Mary would be nothing more than one of a bland, not particularly memorable, but enduring line of heroines, the little homemaker, the perfect wife who saves the soul of the boy next door by creating the blessed home-sweet-home of the sentimentalists, where "grandmother nodded over her knitting-work, and puss purred, and old Rover lay dreamily opening now one eye and then the other on the family group!" (2:13).

From her father, however, Mary has inherited "a deep and thoughtful nature, predisposed to moral and religious exaltation" (2:16), and it is this spiritual capacity, the peculiar constitution of her inner life, that makes her display for a time a closer affinity to the lonely martyr Olive Chancellor, the morbid heroine of James's *The Bostonians* (1886), than to sweet Phoebe Pyncheon, the cheerful household divinity of Hawthorne's *The House of the Seven Gables* (1851), whom she resembles at the last. Despite her desire to locate her heroine in a pre–nineteenth-century paradise—"Oh, that kitchen of the olden times, the old, clean, roomy New England kitchen!" (2:13)—Mrs. Stowe is the first to recognize that the life of Mary Scudder is darkened by a "great sorrow, which lay ever on her heart" (2:19), her troubled but as yet uninitiated awareness of the place of sin and suffering in the creation: Mary's world lies after the Fall. Although the girl is endowed with the sensibility of an artist, the movements of her heart are determined by "the keen New England air" that "crystallizes emotions into ideas" (2:

17). At the very center of her consciousness is her conviction of the beauty of the somber Calvinist doctrine of the election: "It was easy enough for Mary to believe in *self*-renunciation, for she was one with a born vocation for martyrdom; and so, when the idea was put to her of suffering eternal pains for the glory of God and the good of being in general, she responded to it with a sort of sublime thrill, such as it is given to some natures to feel in view of uttermost sacrifice" (2:19). Planted in Mary by her father's religion and fostered no doubt by her reading of Jonathan Edwards, whose works are well represented in her select collection of improving books, are the seeds of that confusion of aesthetic and moral experience, of thought and feeling, which were to bear strange and bitter fruit in many another heroine of nineteenth-century American fiction.[5] In the "sublime thrill" to be derived from the contemplation of moral ideas, which in Calvinist belief so often involved a curious linkage of joy and pain, lay for the New England girl an ambiguous opportunity for spiritual experience, which might lead either to a saving self-transcendence or else to an unregenerate and even masochistic self indulgence. The sublimity of the thrill itself might cast "the glory of God and the good of being in general" into eclipse.

"Faculty" and ecstasy, a talent for the domestic beautiful and a genius for the religious sublime—these then are the gifts of Mary Scudder. Presently I shall focus upon Mrs. Stowe's portrait of Mary as the priestess of self-sacrifice in her relationship with Dr. Hopkins, for it is here, in the minister's wooing, that the author probes the dynamics of moral action, the psychology of the puritan consciousness. First, however, I would like to consider her conception of her heroine as domestic savior, which serves as a frame for the girl's critical experience of renunciation, her highest calling, in the central chapters of the novel. In her presentation of the courtship of Mary by James Marvyn, her dashing, dark-eyed, raven-haired, restless cousin, Mrs. Stowe exploits the conventions of a religion of love codified by the practice of a century of sentimental fiction. The prototype of her heroine's story—and of Hawthorne's in *The House of the Seven Gables*, of James's in "Daisy Miller," of Howells's in *The Lady of the Aroostook*—is a drama of salvation in which the wayward hero is returned to the fold through his ennobling love for a pure and beautiful young woman.[6] It is a nice touch for Mrs. Stowe to attribute to the young man himself a familiarity with the outline of this moral design, for James shrewdly recognizes that the way to the heart of such a girl as Mary is through her religion:

"Now I confess I never did care much about religion, but I thought, without being really a hypocrite, I'd just let you try to save my soul for the sake of getting you" (3:29).

Mrs. Stowe gives an explicitly religious formulation of this redemptive process in the love of Mary and James, and she reshapes each phase of the traditional boy-girl romance accordingly. Thus the inevitable chapter called "The Interview" and the "declaration" which it contains eventuate not in a lover's engagement but in a pilgrim's progress. On the eve of his departure for a voyage at sea which will mean years of separation from his beloved, James receives the gift of Mary's Bible, the moral equivalent of her love. She is, he believes, "a living gospel" (3:29). In "The Letter" he asserts the efficacy of her "image"— which he presently defines as an incarnation of the difficult Calvinist doctrine of "the beauty of holiness" (5:54)—in aiding him to resist the manifold temptations of a sailor's life. Later in a second letter, "Jacob's Vow," he relates that the reading of her Bible, especially the New Testament, brought about the spiritual regeneration that he achieved during his years of absence. Finally in "The Wedding," James's account of his "evidences" to Dr. Hopkins, solemnizing his triumphant embrace of Mary's Christianity, is given an importance equal to his marriage to the girl herself that symbolizes his redemption. Mary has become her lover's religion, indeed, his Holy Ghost; her spirit, "brooding peacefully with dove-like wings over his soul," inspires in him "the higher conception of an heroic and Christ-like manhood" (42:410).

Eager to clothe her heroine in the mantle of Calvinist orthodoxy, Mrs. Stowe defined Mary's "vocation," her "ministry," as that of the "soul-artist" (8:97), a term which not only recalls the traditional conception of the puritan divine as "soul physician" but which suggests as well the release of aesthetic energy into a distinctly moral sphere. In her lover Mary worships "the divine ideal" (8:96) of his nature, the Christian hero that he might become, and she is willing, so great is her devotion, that his salvation be won at the sacrifice of her own. Worship and sacrifice—for Mrs. Stowe these were the noblest acts in which woman's capacity for redemptive love was expressed, yet her analysis of them revealed that woman's very strength might prove to be her weakness, that the fulfillment of her heroic nature might yield her self-destruction.[7]

When Mrs. Stowe introduced Colonel Aaron Burr and Madame Virginie de Frontignac into the tranquil village sphere where Mary Scudder dwelt, she displayed to be sure the respect of a professional writer for the taste of her popular audience. She meant, however, not only to enliven the prosy materials of Mary's world with the glamorous aura of a more sophisticated milieu of fashionable manners and questionable morals, but to explore an issue closely related in theme and in psychology to the wooing of Mary herself: the perversion of the religion of love which Mary incarnates. In Burr's unscrupulous pursuit of the innocent and susceptible Virginie, she showed that a woman's instinctive veneration of the ideal in the character of her beloved placed her in a particularly vulnerable position, for it necessarily involved her participation in an experience of hero worship, a morally ambiguous relationship with the power at once to uplift the soul or to betray forever its hope of salvation.[8] The object of Virginie's mistaken devotions is not the unregenerate young man with a heart of gold but the heartless seducer, the handsome, unprincipled aristocrat of the epistolary novel. But for Mary's blessed intervention, the wiles of Burr would have found in Madame de Frontignac an easy prey, leading her to the dishonor of the fallen woman, the lamentable destiny that awaited those who forsook woman's highest calling as "the pure priestess of a domestic temple" (14:168).

To Mrs. Stowe, however, Aaron Burr stood for something more than simply the American Lovelace which she made him; he was in his own right the grandson of Jonathan Edwards. Curiously, at the moment when we seem most to enter the theater of the conventional we pass at the same time into the realm of history. As the grandson of New England's greatest theologian and his wife, the saintly Sarah Pierrepont, Burr was in fact what Mary Scudder was in fiction, the heir to the greatest of New England's moral gifts of mind and soul. The lesson of history as Mrs. Stowe read it, however, was disturbing, offering as it did a counterpoint in shadows to the radiant union of her story of the minister's wooing. The double strains of Burr's spiritual inheritance led not to that life-giving harmony which prevailed—if more precariously than Mrs. Stowe might have wished—in the moral consciousness of the obedient girl, but to open rebellion against Calvinism, a death-struggle between forces unalterably opposed.

In order to account, however, for Burr's failure to respond to the "redeeming power" (19:220) of "God's eternal sacrament of love" (14: 170), an insensibility which might otherwise seem to discredit the efficacy of her religion of the heart, Mrs. Stowe gives the sentimental stereotype of his character a romantic elaboration. She asserts that his was a divided nature in which a generous capacity for genuine feeling was

sacrificed to a proud and indomitable will. In his cold, artistic experimentation with his own emotions and those of the women he ruins,
Burr resembles the Hawthornian seeker, or the Goethe whose lawless
genius filled the transcendentalists with dismay. The logic of her conception of Burr as the archenemy of her gospel of love requires a confrontation with Mary Scudder, the apostle of her faith. Burr, seeking the
sources of Mary's moral strength, a power immune to the blandish-
ments of his usually irresistible egotism, recognizes in her image the
purity and grace that he associates with his mother, Esther Burr, and
especially with his grandmother, Sarah Pierrepont. Mrs. Stowe here
quotes in full Edwards's well-known description of his future wife. To
the creator of Mary Scudder the appeal of Edwards's tribute was fundamental: distinguished by the beauty of its language, his prose portrait was perhaps the earliest celebration of an ideal womanhood in
American letters.[9] Recalling the words of this passage of celestial courtship with its vision of a holy young woman, the chosen "beloved of
that Great Being who made and rules the world," uplifted in gracious
communion with her God, even the seducer pauses to wonder at Sarah-
Esther-Mary, the saint:

> Was there, then, a truth in that inner union of chosen souls with
> God, of which his mother and her mother before her had borne
> meek witness, their souls shining out as sacred lamps through the
> alabaster walls of a temple?
>   But then, again, had he not logically met and demonstrated, to
> his own satisfaction, the nullity of the religious dogmas on which
> New England faith was based? There could be no such inner life.
> (16:194)

As for Mary, from the moment of her first meeting with Edwards's
grandson she prayed for the conversion of the great New England
apostate. The decisive encounter between the two, which brings the
history of Burr's downward progress to a climax, is strategically placed
shortly before word reaches the girl of James Marvyn's conversion. In
one of those storms of opposing wills that were the staple of romantic
drama, in which rhetoric supplies the thunder and eye-flashes the light-
ning, the little puritan saint bids for the salvation of the seducer, the
egotist, the lost soul, a Lucifer figure with an overlay of Byronism.
Mary's display of "the religious sublime"—"the true Puritan seed of
heroism" (32:343)—raises her in the eyes of Mrs. Stowe to a Miltonic
stature. Although the New England girl elicits tears of contrition from

the sinner, she presently beholds the failure of her hopes for his soul; she is powerless to prevent the death of the heart in which Burr's misguided genius consents and conspires.[10]

II

In her rendering of the redemptive possibilities of woman's love, fulfilled in Mary Scudder and perverted in Virginie de Frontignac, Mrs. Stowe was following the conventions governing courtship in the sentimental fiction of an imported tradition. In the minister's wooing of her heroine, however, the primary subject of her narrative, she drew mainly on her own experience of native American materials, presenting a curious New England version of the archetypal sentimental relationship which confers on her novel a homely yet distinctive originality. Conscious of the oddness of this second love story, which features a middle-aged clergyman as the hero of a romance, Mrs. Stowe anticipates the objections of her popular audience, who were "particularly set against the success of our excellent orthodox hero, and bent on reminding us of the claims of that unregenerate James, whom we have sent to sea on purpose that our heroine may recover herself of that foolish partiality for him" (12:132). She makes it clear that she is willing to disappoint her readers, manipulate her plot, and provide Dr. Hopkins with an opportunity to press his suit. In the recurring image of this New England love story the bookish divine, seated in his study, looks up from the tangled manuscript of his "system" to behold in an innocent white-clad girl, warbling a hymn, his thoughts completed and published, the fulfillment of all that he has endlessly labored to express.[11] Surely Mrs. Stowe experienced a similar satisfaction when she created Mary Scudder. In such passages her imagination voiced a preference for the way of feeling independent of the claims of her education and her filial piety for the way of thought, claims which she sought to satisfy, to exorcize, in lengthy passages of exposition and apology.

Just as Henry James's presentation of the idealism that informs Isabel Archer's meditations in the old house in Albany is necessary to an understanding of her remarkable behavior toward her suitors, Mrs. Stowe similarly argues that comprehension of Mary Scudder's response to the minister's wooing requires a familiarity with the "systems" of puritan theology. Before those chapters in which the Doctor courts Mary, she places a crucial pair of chapters entitled "Views of Divine Government" and "Mysteries." The account of Mary's crisis of belief in these chapters is introduced by an excursus into Calvinist doctrine designed to point up the representative nature of the girl's religious experience. Boldly cutting through the intricate theology of the New England fathers, Mrs. Stowe summarizes her argument by rehearsing in a single unwieldy sentence, a maze of dependent clauses which reflects the labyrinthine turnings of their thought, the immutable design of God's government of the universe:

> The human race, without exception, coming into existence "under God's wrath and curse," with a nature so fatally disordered that, although perfect free agents, men were infallibly certain to do nothing to Divine acceptance until regenerated by the supernatural aid of God's Spirit,—this aid being given only to a certain decreed number of the human race, the rest, with enough free agency to make them responsible, but without this indispensable assistance exposed to the malignant assaults of evil spirits versed in every art of temptation, were sure to fall hopelessly into perdition. (23:244)

In this fearful sequence—innate depravity yet free agency, predestination leading possibly to regeneration but probably to damnation—she maps out the narrow confines of the puritan consciousness, the inexorable dimensions of that drama of salvation which was the subject of everything she ever wrote.

The two focal points of the system, according to Mrs. Stowe, were the certainty of the doctrine of the election and consequently the decisive importance and rarity of the gift of grace, of "true regeneration"; indeed, "evidences" of the latter were sought in an acceptance of the truth *and the beauty* of the former. She cites the case of Edwards as a classic paradigm of puritan religious experience, the progress from enmity towards "the facts of the Divine administration" to what he called his "'inward and sweet sense'" of them (23:246), a manifestation of his gracious submission to God's will. The exemplary Edwards, however, who finally accepted the rigors of theology with joyous exaltation, stood for an ideal of Calvinist piety rarely achieved. In fact, discerning a double strain in the annals of puritan inner life, Mrs. Stowe distinguished between two fundamentally different types of believers: those preoccupied with the theory of religious experience and those for whom the experience itself transcended any concern with theory. She defined the first type as the individual governed by reason and intellect, usually a man, identified especially as the minister, the system-maker himself; while she recognized in the second type the individual living from intuition and the heart, almost invariably a woman (with the notable exceptions of Christ himself and the Christ-like Uncle Tom), often, like Sarah Pierrepont (a favorite example), the minister's wife. When Mrs. Stowe portrayed these two types as the protagonists of a New England love story in *The Minister's Wooing* she explored the possibility of a symbolic union between the two which might lead to an accommodation of the way of thought to the way of feeling. She clearly meant moreover to extend the significance of her drama beyond the confines of fiction by rendering in her hero, Samuel Hopkins, a version of the historical figure of that name who had been an eminent eighteenth-century theologian, a follower of Edwards.

Appropriately, it is in the chapter called "Evidences" that Mrs. Stowe most clearly dramatizes the distinction between these two modes of apprehending spiritual truth which Dr. Hopkins and Mary Scudder respectively represent. If the favorite themes of the minister's meditations—disinterested benevolence, the millennium, and above all the purification of the soul through gracious affections—link them with Mary's creed of love, his devotion to his system and especially to a clinical analysis of the movements of the spirit which it inspires mark him as the believer acting from the head rather than the heart. Overturning the source of the girl's trust, the Doctor is convinced of the deceitfulness of the human heart, transforming it into the motive of all his doubts. Questioning Mary closely about her "evidences" in the most orthodox fashion, he chooses inevitably the doctrine of the election as the supreme test of her faith: "Say, my dear friend, are you sure, that should you discover yourself to be forever condemned by His justice, you would not find your heart rising up against Him?" (18:212). Mrs. Stowe's description of the anatomy of feeling performed by the soul physician shows the Doctor's healing art as an act against spontaneity and nature, possibly profane and potentially destructive, a threat to the spiritual well-being of her heroine, the soul-artist:

> The Doctor had practiced his subtile mental analysis till his instruments were so fine-pointed and keen-edged that he scarce ever allowed a flower of sacred emotion to spring in his soul without picking it to pieces to see if its genera and species were correct. . . . Mary, on the contrary, had the blessed gift of womanhood, that vivid life in the soul and sentiment which resists the chills of analysis, as a healthful human heart resists cold. (18:211)

Although she surely acquiesced in the confidence of Mary's considered reply, "Could any real Christian rejoice in this?" (18:214), Mrs. Stowe soon puts the girl's "evidences" to a severer trial: when "Tidings from Over Sea" bring her heroine word of her lover's death in a shipwreck, the "vivid life" of her "blessed gift of womanhood," numbed by grief, is nearly extinguished by an attack of the Doctor's Calvinist "chills."

To insist too much on such paired types of believers as these, however, setting one character against another, is to scant the interest of Mrs. Stowe's novel, to oversimplify the considerable depth of some of her characterization. In the most arresting figures in her gallery of New England portraits—especially in Mary Scudder and Mrs. Marvyn (as we shall see) and to a lesser extent in Dr. Hopkins and Aaron Burr —she has internalized both of these alternative capacities. It is precisely in the interaction between these forces, sometimes complementary, sometimes antagonistic to each other, that she sought the key to the design of the moral life.

III

Mrs. Stowe's most sustained and serious thought concerned the impact of belief upon the consciousness; this subject, more than any other, kindled her imagination, inspiring her most rewarding contribution to literature. *The Minister's Wooing*, and indeed all of her novels, reflect her conviction—of which she was perhaps only partly aware—that the energies of New England puritanism, dedicated in theory to the achievement of eternal life, became paradoxically, in the daily experience of the believer, directed towards death. Death posed the irrevocable alternatives of the puritan drama of salvation in a single awesome question: "Where?" (23:248)—Heaven or Hell? When he learns that James Marvyn has drowned at sea, Dr. Hopkins dutifully raises this very question at the earliest opportunity: "Have you been at all conversant with the exercises of our young friend's mind on the subject of religion?" Mary Scudder draws back in shock from this spiritual inquest which the minister instinctively initiates; his words fall on her soul "like the sound of clods falling on a coffin to the ear of one buried alive" (22:239).

Mrs. Stowe suggests not only that the Doctor's theology defines the significance of death but that it even partakes of the principle of death itself. Her narratives, peopled with the dying, studded with deathbeds, haunted by memories of the dead, set often in a somber landscape in which "the tolling bell in green hollows and lonely dells . . . shook the soul and searched the heart with fearful questions" (23:248), owe their inspiration directly to this death-centered religion rather than to an ancillary tradition of sentimentality which was itself descended from it. Revisiting Mrs. Stowe's New England in *The Europeans* (1878), Henry James was to have his expatriate hero observe of its sober inhabitants: "I think there is something the matter with them; they have some melancholy memory or some depressing expectation."[12] Mrs. Stowe held the clue to the mystery that puzzled Felix Young: the New England character had received its distinctive identity, its brooding moral seriousness, from two centuries' worship of a religion of death. In *The Minister's Wooing* it is the fact of death itself which precipitates the ultimate comparison between the way of thought and the way of feeling: what Mrs. Marvyn and Mary Scudder undergo as they face the supposed death of son and lover dramatizes the respective capacity of two fundamentally different kinds of belief to sustain faith at the moment of spiritual crisis.[13] The requirements of the plot at this point in the novel elevate Mrs. Marvyn to a role of primary importance for several chapters, representing as she does one member of Mrs. Stowe's inevitable pair of believers, a stand-in, as it were, for the Doctor, who operates in this sequence from the sidelines as a spiritual adviser to those more intimately related to the unfortunate James.

Mrs. Marvyn is as easily identified as one of Mrs. Stowe's first class of believers as Mary Scudder is of the second. An intellectual by temperament, with a taste for ideas and abstractions, she seeks to satisfy her hunger for the life of the mind on the austere diet offered by her limited world, mathematical treatises and works on systematic theology. From the sermons of Dr. Hopkins, in which he expounded the logical intricacies of his imposing system in weekly installments, she had imbibed "a slow poison, producing life habits of morbid action" (23:247). Indelibly stamped with that peculiarly Calvinistic melancholy of those resigned to a belief in their unregeneracy, Mrs. Marvyn rebels at the thought that her son, whose spiritual state at the moment of his death lies shrouded in uncertainty, might be similarly consigned to perdition. Fleeing the unforgiving reasoning of Dr. Hopkins, which has filled her with killing doubts, fever, agony, and hysteria, the distraught mother takes shelter in the arms of her Negro slave, the maternal Candace, whose simple faith in Jesus' love permits a liberal, reassuring construction of the doctrine of the election which threatens to drive her white mistress into unbelief altogether: "I'm clar Mass'r James is one o' de 'lect; and I'm clar dar's consid'able more o' de 'lect dan people tink" (23:254). Always filled with compassion for the personality warped by moral ideas, for the gifted individual thwarted in his development—a classic theme in the literature of New England, the locus of its tragic possibilities—Mrs. Stowe indicts the theology that has marked Mrs. Marvyn for its victim: "They [the systems] differ from the New Testament as the living embrace of a friend does from his lifeless body, mapped out under the knife of the anatomical demonstrator; every nerve and muscle is there, but to a sensitive spirit there is the very chill of death in the analysis" (23:247). The systems, which she regarded as the most characteristic expression of the New England mind, indeed the very principle of heroic action which she was presently to celebrate in Dr. Hopkins and Mary Scudder, made the Redeemer's promise of resurrection and life (inevitably, for Mrs. Stowe with her mother's heart, "a living embrace") the subject of the theologian's autopsy.

Nineteenth-century survivors of the tenacious grasp of Calvinism on the soul in New England, Mrs. Stowe and Hawthorne reenacted in their major novels the familiar pattern of so much latter-day puritan experience, the flight from the bondage of law to the freedom of love. The design of their fiction, however, the striking contrast for example between their respective versions of the story of a minister's wooing, reflects the relative distance of each of them from their fathers' religion. Mrs. Stowe defers to the close of the eighteenth century the breakup of the New England faith which Hawthorne—not, surely, without a certain satisfaction—projects into the lifetime of the first and founding generation. She treats at one remove in her story of Mrs. Marvyn the rebellious and subversive impulse which Hawthorne had placed more boldly at the very center of the stage in his drama of Hester Prynne. In the representative career of her New England heroine she sought to stay the course of history, steering precariously between "the Doctor's dreadful system" (24:259) on the one hand and the scarcely orthodox content of "Candace's way" (24:260) on the other.

Moving as she does from a conviction of her own regenerate state, Mary undergoes an attenuated but nonetheless severe attack of Mrs. Marvyn's sickness. Her religion of redemptive love badly shaken by Mrs. Marvyn's obsession with the orthodox construction of her son's death, the girl cries out in anguish, "*My* God! *my* God! oh, where art Thou?" (23:251). Yielding in her sorrow and suffering to the sway of system, Mary becomes a pale and weeping figure, her head drooping like "a snowdrop over a grave" (23:255). After a time, however, she emerges from the valley of the shadow of system, entering into "an ineffable union in Christ" (24:266). The girl's doubts of her lover's salvation are finally allayed and her faith renewed in a mystical experience of love. Basing her version of this moment of illumination, the resolution of Mary's crisis, on the standard romantic conception of the communion of the soul with the oversoul,[14] Mrs. Stowe shapes this visitation to express a maternal vision peculiarly her own. At such a time, she writes, "The All-Father treats us as the mother does her 'infant crying in the dark'; He does not reason with our fears, or demonstrate their fallacy, but draws us silently to His bosom, and we are at peace" (28:309). Mrs. Stowe's religion of love receives its apotheosis in this feminization of the godhead, the natural extension of her cardinal belief in the divine calling of women to the work of regeneration.[15] The doctrinaire Hopkins lends his support to this position when he observes, "If we consider that the Son of God, as to his human nature, was made of a woman, it leads us to see that in matters of grace God sets a special value on woman's nature" (24:265). Confirming Mary's vocation, the minister identifies her "uncommonly gracious exercises" (24:264) with those of Sarah Pierrepont, the prototype of the puritan saint. His recognition of the purity, the correctness, of her spiritual history is absolute: willing "to yield his soul up to her leading," the theologian defers to the holy girl as an authority on "all questions of internal experience" (25:276). The "pure priestess of a domestic temple" has become the "sanctified priestess of the great worship of sorrow," a sister of mercy interceding for those in tribulation, who find "in her bosom at once confessional and sanctuary" (25:277).

Mrs. Stowe no longer beholds in her heroine an image of the girlhood of the Virgin, "the childlike loveliness of early days, looking with dovelike, ignorant eyes on sin and sorrow," but an altered, more mature Mary, the mater dolorosa, a "Sistine Madonna [whose] eyes . . . have measured infinite sorrow and looked through it to an infinite peace" (24:264). As she accepts this new role, in which her heart takes on the status of a religious institution, the girl's orientation is unmistakably towards death. Hers is a "dying grace" (24:267), a "state of self-abnegation . . . not purely healthy," resembling "the hours that often precede dissolution" (25:273).

It is at this moment, when the youth and womanhood of her New England heroine lie "as still as the grave" (25:273), that Mrs. Stowe inaugurates the minister's wooing. Within the dry and intellectual divine she postulates the existence of a "dormant nature," "a whole mine of . . . artistic feelings and perceptions" (6:69), to be awakened by Mary's beneficent influence. Persuading herself at least of the possibility of such a transformation, she eventually refers to Hopkins no longer as "simple old soul" (27:303) but as "that great heart" (40:399). In any case the point of the relationship is clear: the Doctor's system is to be wedded to love, to be tempered, persuaded, and humanized; conversely, Mary's "way" is to receive the blessing of orthodoxy. In the minister's symbolic conversion Mrs. Stowe marked a decisive moment in her reading of the history of the New England mind, the unfolding of a new dispensation: the power of Christian womanhood, of a girl's gentle heart welling with New Testament love, supplants the waning Calvinism of the puritan fathers, the strenuous masculine intellect governed by Old Testament law. It was the love of Mary Scudder after all, rather than the theology of Dr. Hopkins, which had worked the salvation of James Marvyn.

Against the wishful moral symbolism of the minister's wooing, however, Mrs. Stowe projects the disturbing psychological reality of this courtship. Having passed her novitiate of sorrow which has made of her cottage a convent, having survived her confrontation with death which has laid her girlhood to rest, Mary Scudder has become a New England nun. Curiously, as the minister's wife the girl would remain a nun; this Madame de Frontignac understood when she observed of her friend's betrothal to Dr. Hopkins, "But, Mary, it is like a marriage with the altar, like taking the veil, is it not?" (28:313). It is a figure "pale as sculptured marble" (26:295), believing her earthly lover lost at sea, who receives from her mother the declaration of the man "for whom her reverence was almost like that for her God" (18:210) with these words of resignation, the response required by her puritan catechism: "Well, mother, I will do whatever is my duty" (26:296). In the passage of introspection which follows, standing alone before her mirror, gazing at the ghostly image of the nunlike version of her personality, the girl seems to hear in its urging of the iron commandment of the Doctor's creed—"Fulfill thy mission; life is made for sacrifice" (27:298)—the seductive promptings of a death-wish. Mary is never closer to death than at the moment of her surrender to this ideal of renunciation, when she resolves in "an act of uttermost self-sacrifice" (27:299) to marry Dr. Hopkins: "Only the gentlest heaving of the quiet breast told that the heavenly spirit within had not gone whither it was hourly aspiring to go" (27:300).

Mrs. Stowe betrayed her ambivalent feelings towards the religion of self-sacrifice in the highly contrived final section of her novel when young Marvyn, miraculously alive after all, returns just before Mary's marriage to Dr. Hopkins to resurrect in his beloved all her buried feelings for him. Pursuing her insight that the New England heroism which she admired was founded on a principle of repression which she abhorred, Mrs. Stowe executes an abrupt about-face, proposing an alternative interpretation of Mary's noble gesture. She now reads the girl's determination to keep her promise to the Doctor in spite of her love for Marvyn not as a saint's fidelity to a holy covenant but as a victim's perverse devotion to duty. The sailor's sudden reappearance completes the transformation of the ideal of self-sacrifice which Mary's spiritual crisis had begun: no longer the instinctive movement of a woman's heart, the highest expression of her sacred power of love, renunciation shows instead as unnatural behavior proceeding from the intellect, a self-destructive allegiance to a moral code that dares to exact a double tribute, that a self-sacrificing love itself be sacrificed. When spontaneity yields to indoctrination, the way of feeling to the way of thought, Mrs. Stowe rebels. In her simultaneous attraction and repulsion towards her heritage, in her anguish and compassion for an individual in the grips of its flawed ideals, she might have said of her New England as Faulkner's Quentin Compson, in the final line of *Absalom, Absalom!* (1936), was to say of the South: "*I dont. I dont! I dont hate it! I dont hate it!*"

Under the aegis of self-sacrifice Mrs. Stowe sought to reconcile two essentially incompatible moral traditions. Recognizing the impossibility of the union of Calvinism and sentimentalism which she wished to consummate, she attempted nevertheless to satisfy the claims of both. Thus in the chapter called "The Sacrifice" it is Dr. Hopkins, acting as a surrogate for Mary, rather than the girl herself, who performs the heroic gesture required by the puritan code, rescuing the New England heroine from the living death of her intended renunciation. Learning of Mary's love for Marvyn only three days before his own marriage to her is to take place, the minister suppresses the rebellion of his lover's heart and releases the girl from her vow. Mrs. Stowe's presentation underlines the double face of this act of renunciation which terminates her archetypal New England love story: the occasion of dismay threatened by the heroine's submission becomes in the hero's surrender the matter for edification. In "The Transfigured," as the girl and her lover attend one of the Doctor's Sunday services, it is the agency of her deathless romantic passion for Marvyn rather than her worship of Hopkins's religion which raises Mary Scudder to a transcendent vision of eternal life. When she marries her lover with the minister's blessing, Mary undergoes the last of a long series of transformations, passing from cold martyrdom to warm domestic womanhood. Through the freedom of her fiction Mrs. Stowe wished to demonstrate conclusively that Mary was all that the orthodox drama of salvation and sacrifice could make her and more when she embraced at the last what was for Mrs. Stowe a woman's true vocation, the religion of heart and home:

> The fair poetic maiden, the seeress, the saint, has passed into that appointed shrine for woman, more holy than cloister, more saintly and pure than church or altar, a Christian home. Priestess, wife, and mother, there she ministers daily in holy works of household peace, and by faith and prayer and love redeems from grossness and earthliness the common toils and wants of life. (42:410)

IV

Mrs. Stowe's difficulties as a writer are best understood in the light of the urgency of her relationship to her heritage; her manipulation of the strategies of fiction serves thus as a measure of her struggle to meet the challenge of intellectual history. She must be given credit in *The Minister's Wooing* for telling the essential truth about renunciation, the classic form of puritan heroism, at the price of a certain falseness in the design of her narrative. Her performance here shows that her effort to fashion a model for contemporary womanhood by updating an earlier ideal was doomed to failure from the start, for Calvinism itself and time were against her. If we glance at several of her other novels, we shall see that this impossible undertaking is pervasive in her fiction. As we examine its most distinctive features, her mother-focussed conception of family life, the curiously arrested development of her characters, her preoccupation with the past, it will be clear that hers was a conservative, indeed an embattled position, for all her ties to the party of reform.

Seeking to restore a vision of order to a generation of wayward

Americans whom she regarded as lapsed puritans, Mrs. Stowe selected as the institutional underpinning of her program not the church but the family, a tacit admission that the theology of Calvinism had become an unpromising option for her own day. If the quest for salvation, the acknowledged purpose of courtship in her novels, governed relations between the sexes to such an extent that she could consent to the heroine's death to save the hero's soul (Mara for Moses in *The Pearl of Orr's Island* [1862], Nina Gordon for Clayton in *Dred: A Tale of the Great Dismal Swamp* [1856]), Mrs. Stowe regarded both courtship and salvation as distinctly family affairs. Hero and heroine usually meet not in the fluid, open-ended situations preferred by James and Howells, the world of travel which struck them as the appropriate symbol of a society in dislocation, but in the clearly defined circumstances—religious, social, economic, domestic—of the traditional family center back home. Doubtless drawing on her own formation in the Beecher clan, she frequently patterned the relationship between the lovers on a brother-sister analogy, with the father-daughter tie a characteristic variation. In a favorite plot a brother and sister, for example, will be very close and the brother, interestingly, will marry; this disturbance of the family equilibrium, one of the most important sources of drama in her work, generates tension between the new wife and the adored sister, who is usually a paragon of womanhood; harmony is reestablished when the new wife grows spiritually to resemble the exalted sisterly image.[16] In such dealings it is the outsider, outside the home, the church, or the community, who must accommodate himself to the family ideal. Family loyalties, filial piety, are counted on to check the progress of any dangerous innovations and new allegiances that an undisciplined courtship might set in motion. Furthermore as courtship consolidates family connections it strengthens the structure of society, laying to rest the spectre of a house divided.

In the Stowe novel the family circle functions quite simply as an extension of the maternal embrace. Preferring for her characters the set of relationships into which they were born rather than any alternative and hence competitive series that they might independently create, Mrs. Stowe relished especially the rescue and adoption of the orphan, a surrogate for all the dispossessed, wandering beyond the pale of hearth and home, whom she would redeem to their birthright. Fleeing the destructive power of the masculine ego, suppliants seek out the sanctuary of a woman's world of love. The characters of the women who govern this matriarchal refuge are defined in terms of their fam-

ily roles rather than by any idiosyncratic elements of personality irrelevant to the decidedly domestic conception of Mrs. Stowe's moral design, which finds its center in the kitchen. There around the axis of the
mother, the omphalos of this village universe, revolve in their un-
changing orbits the enduring aunts who can never have been young,
the sisters, eternal sisters, and the saintly girl children so often claimed
by death before they cross the threshold into maturity.

The arrested development of these women, fixed in their allotted
roles, provides an index to Mrs. Stowe's desire to preserve the family
intact. The essentially defensive strategy which informs her characterization of women was crystallized in her attraction to the Virgin
Mary. Besides the authoritative precedent which the worship of the
Mother of God supplied for her own cult of womanhood, the very paradox of the virgin mother must have seemed to hold the solution to
the vexed problem of the perpetuation of an immutable world, for
Mary spanned the gulf between childhood and adult life without passing through the great initiation into womanhood, through sexuality
with its taint of impurity, that is, of change. In the Virgin the dual nature of her ideal woman had received a single incarnation: the innocence of the child which was the sign of woman's holiness, and the
knowledge and love of the mother which were the source of woman's
strength. Significantly, Mary Scudder, who in her survival to woman's
mature estate escaped the familiar destiny of many a short-lived Stowe
heroine, is explicitly modeled on the Virgin, while even little Eva, the
peerless type of all the ethereal girls elected to the company of death in
order that their sacred girlhood may last forever, assumes a distinctly
maternal authority in her final hours.

In the careers of the men in her fiction Mrs. Stowe reversed the pattern she had fixed on for the spiritual development of her women, the
leap with little or no transition from child to mother. In her work the
child is truly father of the man, and the child is a mama's boy. When
woman's maternal love accomplishes man's regeneration, he becomes as
a child once more. A man's life is largely determined by his relationship
with his mother, and it is the dormant recollection of this crucial phase
of his moral progress which the woman—girl, sister, friend, or wife—
proceeds to resurrect. The working out of such a conception as this
accounts for the improbable transformation of the worldly Augustine
St. Clare in *Uncle Tom's Cabin* into a long-lost orphan at the moment
of his death when, finally glimpsing the goal of his retrograde pilgrimage, he cries out, "Mother!" Again, when the hero is cast at the outset

of a novel as the heroine's spiritual adviser, a reversal of roles occurs during his courtship and he learns to reverence, with the respect of a boy for his mother, the moral authority of the holy girl he loves. Such is the pattern of the relationships between Clayton and Nina in *Dred*, Angie (Angelique) Van Arsdale and the minister, St. John, in *We and Our Neighbors: Records of an Unfashionable Street* (1873), and Dr. Hopkins and Mary Scudder in *The Minister's Wooing*. Conversely, eschewing the stage villain, the essentially evil man (except, notably, several characters of secondary importance in her most polemical works, *Uncle Tom's Cabin* and *Dred*), Mrs. Stowe was fascinated by the Lucifer figure, Simon Legree, for instance, or Aaron Burr, the potentially good man whose indomitable pride prevents submission to his mother's redemptive influence.

The determination with which Mrs. Stowe fitted her characters to the fixed dimensions of primordial family roles—especially her attribution of magical powers of moral agency to the figures of mother and child—betrays a perhaps unconscious sense of the vulnerability of her cherished ideals, a fear of the change which loss of innocence would necessarily bring. For all her preachments concerning the growth of the soul through initiation into the mysteries of suffering and sorrow, the arrested development of her characters and their commonly regressive route to salvation suggest their latent sterility, a fundamental inability of the personality to achieve a convincing maturity. Her vision of the individual and of his community moved instinctively backward in time. Mining her own generous reserves of reminiscence, supplemented by those of her husband, she devoted the major part of her creative energy to the preservation in literature of the world of her childhood. What might have been merely a sentimental exercise in nostalgia, however, became the occasion for an ambitious reconstruction of the life of the past. Turning from a disordered present she chronicled the establishment of homes in a series of historical novels; the celebration of these islands of security in villages like Newport, Oldtown, and Poganuc was always central to her fiction. Yet even as she granted in the work of her imagination the wish to stay the irrevocable passage of time, she placed at the heart of her idealized village world an ambiguous symbol of moral greatness. The very heroism of the New England girl, the capacity for the religious sublime, she recognized as a kind of sickness and bondage.

Entrenched in her retrospective bastion, Harriet Beecher Stowe was content to measure the moral value of her heroines in their degree of proximity to the culture of the puritan community. Beyond the confines of the world of Mrs. Stowe, however, there were heroes who, preferring to make their way abroad, failed to come home to marry the girl next door; there were heroines—Isabel Archer, say, or Margaret Fuller—who, tiring of the closed round of village life, of a covenant with a dying past, took the road to Rome.

Chapter 3

SELF-CULTURE:
MARGARET FULLER
AND HAWTHORNE'S HEROINES

THE PRINCIPAL VARIETIES of spiritual experience in the New Engand mind of the nineteenth century were derived from Calvinist and transcendentalist conceptions of the moral life, clustering respectively around the ideals of renunciation and self-culture. Students of New England culture from Henry James to Perry Miller have recognized in the Emersonian philosophy the original energy of the puritan consciousness freed from the grasp of the Calvinist theology. In his seminal essay on this passage of intellectual history, "From Edwards to Emerson," Miller demonstrated the truth of his sense that "certain basic continuities persist in a culture   which underlie the successive articulation of 'ideas.'" Thus he saw Edwards and Emerson linked by a persistent strain in the New England mind, "a piety, a religious passion, the sense of an inward communication and of the divine symbolism of nature." Quoting Emerson, he emphasized that Emerson himself was always aware of the great debt owed by his generation "to that old religion which, in the childhood of most of us, still dwelt like a sabbath morning in the country of New England, teaching privation, self-denial and sorrow!"[1] We have seen how Mrs. Stowe nurtured "that old religion" in her New England novels, expressing its legacy in the selfless devotion of her heroines to a sublime ideal of renunciation. To this classic form of puritan heroism, which Mrs. Stowe commemorated in Mary Scudder, Emerson and his contemporaries added another, the life of self-culture, which Hawthorne crystallized in the tragedy of Zenobia in *The Blithedale Romance*.

The inspiration for Zenobia, whom Howells and James praised as the greatest of Hawthorne's heroines, has been traced invariably since Hawthorne's day to Margaret Fuller. In the foreword to his anthology of her writings, Miller defined the enduring appeal of Margaret Fuller for the American imagination as follows: "In Margaret Fuller, daughter as she was of Puritan New England, we have virtually the only candidate—and in her case an authentic one—for the role of a native champion of the Romantic heroine in the grandiose (and so, for an

American, dangerously close to the ludicrous) operatic manner."[2] Miller pointed out that Fuller's contemporaries were amazed by the parallel between her life and that of the turbulent Madame de Staël and that she was universally identified—by Emerson, by James later on, and always by herself—with "the raven-haired" heroine of Madame de Staël's *Corinne* of 1807, a "sensuous *improvvisatrice*" (MF, xxi). While Miller was careful to state that "in no mechanical sense was Margaret Fuller the 'original' of Zenobia" (MF, xxiv), he urged nevertheless that in her role as a New England Corinne she served as "a provocation" for the Corinne-figures of Hawthorne and James in *The Blithedale Romance* and *The Bostonians* (MF, xxvii). No one has stated more suggestively the implications of the life of Margaret Fuller as a source for the heroines of Hawthorne and James. The difference finally between Miller's interpretation of this connection and my own turns on a question of emphasis, whether, as he would have it, we are to behold in Fuller and these heroines of fiction a domestication of Continental romanticism, or, as I would contend, an expression of the New England mind in romantic dress. "Daughter as she was of Puritan New England"—the concession is indicative of the thrust of Miller's portrait of Margaret Fuller. In his eagerness to establish the outlines of Continental romantic experience in the pattern of Fuller's biography, to confirm her as "a native Madame de Staël" (MF, xxii), he slighted the American elements in her story.

I shall argue that the heroines of Hawthorne and Henry James owe still more to Fuller as an Emersonian seeker after self-culture than to Fuller as a New England Corinne. Hers was a drama of the inner life, of thwarted self-development, and in this sense Margaret Fuller resembles Olive Chancellor of *The Bostonians* much more closely than she does Verena Tarrant of that novel. Beneath the conventional exotic attributes of the romantic heroine, James and Howells discerned in Zenobia a familiar type of nineteenth-century New England womanhood. In words that recall Hawthorne's final estimate of Margaret Fuller, Howells wrote of Zenobia: "The history is always without the concealment of the fact that from first to last her fineness was intellectual, and that emotionally, spiritually, she was of a coarse fibre, with even a strain of vulgarity. A certain kind of New England woman, to specialize a little more than to say American woman, has never been so clearly seen or boldly shown as in Zenobia; and in her phase of tragedy she stands as impressively for the nineteenth century as Hester Prynne for the seventeenth in hers."[3] Margaret Fuller was indeed, as Miller maintained, an American romantic, but to be a romantic in New England was to pass for a time under the Emersonian spell. The conclusion of Emerson's *Nature* (1836) sounded the clarion call to action: "Build, therefore, you own world. As fast as you conform your life to the pure idea in your mind, that will unfold its great proportions."[4] Fuller's generous, glowing tribute to Emerson for the religious inspiration that she derived from his gospel of the inner life captures the impact of his message for a generation of aspiring Americans: "You question me as to the nature of the benefits conferred upon me by Mr. E.'s preaching. I answer, that his influence has been more beneficial to me than that of any American, and that from him I first learned what is meant by an inward life. . . . That the 'mind is its own place,' was a dead phrase to me, till he cast light upon my mind. Several of his sermons stand apart in memory, like landmarks of my spiritual history."[5]

Nowhere in the annals of nineteenth-century American culture do the burden of its intellectual history and the destiny of the heroines of its fiction converge more strikingly than in the career of Margaret Fuller. In the facts of her life she sought deliberately, self-consciously, to enact the most compelling contemporary patterns of spiritual autobiography, whether the flamboyant romantic drama of a Madame de Staël with its attendant fictionalization in *Corinne*, or, closer to home, the more sober transcendentalist program of self-culture, the great theme of Emerson's inspirational lectures. Her life became accordingly a representative fiction of the time. She herself initiated this process in "Mariana"; continued by Emerson, William Henry Channing, and James Freeman Clarke, the editors of her *Memoirs*, it culminated with her metamorphosis into the New England heroines of Hawthorne and James. Self-culture became in the age of Emerson, Thoreau, and Whitman the most important model for the conception of the inner life in nineteenth-century America.

I

Margaret Fuller dedicated her life to the pursuit of self-culture, which her close friend and disciple, James Freeman Clarke, interpreted as her "profound desire for a full development of her whole nature, by means of a full experience of life" (Mem, I, 132). Self-culture, the subject of her most influential book, *Woman in the Nineteenth Century* (1845), and the major theme of the urgent personal revelations collected in her posthumous *Memoirs* (1852), represented Fuller's attempt to practice in her living an ideal of romantic individualism, which she imbibed principally from Emerson and Goethe. Her concept of self-culture was founded upon her belief that a law of growth was the fundamental principle of man's existence: *"Very early I knew that the only object in life was to grow."* In his commentary on this passage in her *Memoirs*, Clarke emphasized that the moral nature of this potentially anarchic, mechanistic, egoistic law lay in its recognition of "something divine in outward nature and providence, by which the soul is led along its appointed way" (Mem, I, 133). Fuller herself explicitly stated the religious quality of her belief: "I believe in a God, a Beauty and Perfection to which I am to strive all my life for assimilation" (Mem, I, 136).

Discussions of self-culture as an ideal never yield greater clarity of definition than in these characteristic statements of Clarke and Margaret Fuller; they seem designed to confer a moral sanction upon the development of character which was believed in for its own sake as an elevating experience. Characteristic accounts stress instead the role of exemplary figures encountered in literature or in life who are devoted to the same spiritual quest and serve as models of conduct, as sources of inspiration. A typical version of this relationship is this statement of William Henry Channing's, in which he speaks solemnly of Fuller's vocation as the ideal friend: "To how many was the forming of her acquaintance an era of renovation, of awakening from sloth, indulgence or despair, to heroic mastery of fate, of inward serenity and strength, of new-birth to real self-hood, of catholic sympathies, of energy consecrated to the Supreme Good" (Mem, II, 40). The corollary of the belief in self-culture was in fact a fascination with individuals of remarkable powers or genius. Contemporary critics, including Clarke, Emerson, Hawthorne, and later James, accepting Margaret Fuller as the leading American representative of self-culture, founded their evaluation of her ideal precisely upon a reading of the dynamics of these relationships. Moral influence exerted in such a personal context revealed itself to them as a highly ambiguous force, with a potential either to ennoble or to corrupt and destroy. The individual seeker seemed inevitably to become involved in an experience of hero worship which threatened his spiritual freedom with psychological or sexual domination.

This mixed view of the experience of self-culture—what Emerson himself termed its "pernicious ambiguity"[6]—is set forth with the clar-

ity of a paradigm in Margaret Fuller's account of her relationship to
Goethe. Only a generation after the time of Mary Scudder, the traditional sources of guidance in New England, particularly the church
and its heritage of Calvinism, which had been all in all to the saintly
heroine of *The Minister's Wooing*, had become meaningless to Margaret Fuller. In her *Memoirs* she dwells on her acute sense of spiritual
dislocation, and her earliest writings show her already in a state of
moral crisis:

> From a very early age I have felt that I was not born to the
> common womanly lot. I knew . . . I should be a pilgrim and so-
> journer on earth, and that the birds and foxes would be surer of a
> place to lay the head than I. . . . This destiny of the thinker, and
> (shall I dare to say it?) of the poetic priestess, sibylline, dwelling
> in the cave, or amid the Lybian sands, lay yet enfolded in my
> mind. (Mem, I, 98–99)

Clearly Fuller dreamed of being a priestess of quite another sort than
Mrs. Stowe's humble New England nun with her gracious affections,
for she believed that she possessed genius, which could only be fulfilled in a grand and special destiny. In the era of self-culture genius
looked to genius for salvation. Determined to break out of her crush-
ing moral isolation, Fuller prayed accordingly for the coming of a great
teacher, a messiah, to serve as "a centre, round which asking, aimless
hearts might rally" (Mem, I, 70). She turned at one time to Harriet
Martineau, at another to Emerson, but to no one did she turn with
greater abandon than to Goethe for the answers to her questions.
Given the uncompromising nature of her idealism, it is not surprising
that she was to find for a time in literature, in the work of a man she
was never destined to meet, the soul communion that seemed always
to elude her in life.

Fuller turned to Goethe not only as the man whom all of the transcendentalists acknowledged as *the* representative genius of the age,
but also as the great apostle of her own ideal of self-culture. Because
of the strong affinities between her own thought and Goethe's, Fuller
soon entered into an intellectual relationship with him, an exalted
form of hero worship, which was fraught with dangers for her own
survival as an independent personality. She has this to say of her first
reading of Goethe in 1832: "He comprehends every feeling I have ever
had so perfectly, expresses it so beautifully; but when I shut the book,
it seems as if I had lost my personal identity" (Mem, I, 119). In her

desire for self-development she had turned for inspiration to a man whose overpowering genius threatened her for a time with complete loss of self.

Although Fuller's initial acceptance of Goethe as an embodiment of her ideal was total, she eventually judged him unworthy of the role of hero and priest. In a lengthy article on him in the July number of the *Dial* in 1842, Fuller expresses not only her mature understanding of the limitations of his spiritual progress but a new insight into the difficulties of her own development as well, her intractable egoism and her determined struggle for self-transcendence. She traces his early career as a genius and seeker, impelled by the heart, until he abandoned his quest and assumed the role of resident sage at Weimar. There is something sinister in her rendering of the triumph of the head over the heart in the later Goethe: "Obliged to economy of time and means, he made of his intimates not objects of devout tenderness, of disinterested care, but the crammers and feeders of his intellect" (MF, 90–91). Like Ethan Brand, Hollingsworth, and many another of Hawthorne's seekers, the great German Prometheus had committed the Unpardonable Sin; he had cut himself off from nature, and his heart had turned to marble. Fuller's dismay at the dominance of the intellect in Goethe was undoubtedly deepened by her belief that she herself had barely escaped a similar fate in her childhood. In the opening pages of her *Memoirs* she claimed that her father (who resembles Goethe's father as he is described in the *Dial* article) had driven her to an overdevelopment of the intellect through the enormous amount of reading and study he required of her as a child, and she believed that her emotional and spiritual life had been repressed and retarded as a result.

Matching her insight into the miscarriage of self-culture in the career of a great genius was Fuller's full realization of the dangers of the hero worship in which she had indulged, at once the most characteristic, striking, and ambiguous manifestation of her ideal. When she portrays in the *Dial* the master-disciple relationship which existed between Goethe and Bettina Brentano, she writes with the authority of firsthand experience. "Idolatries," she says, "are natural to youthful hearts noble enough for a passion beyond the desire for sympathy or the instinct of dependence, and almost all aspiring natures can recall a period when some noble figure, whether in life or literature, stood for them at the gate of heaven, and represented all the possible glories of nature and art." She proceeds with a penetrating analysis of hero worship as a surrogate religion. Fully aware of the benefits which she herself has received from it, she endorses it only with great reservations: "When this worship is expressed, there must be singular purity and strength of character on the part both of Idol and Idolater, to prevent its degenerating into a mutual excitement of vanity, or mere infatuation."[7] Fuller might plead for a love "purely ideal, beholding in its object divine perfection, and delighting in it only in degree as it symbolizes the essential good" (Mem, II, 140–41), yet her conviction that the way toward moral regeneration lay through the self seemed to others fatally tainted with egotism. Even Clarke, who shared so much of her enthusiasm for self-culture, observed candidly in the *Memoirs* that her ideal had "at its core a profound selfishness," which betrayed itself in "an idolatrous hero-worship of genius and power" (Mem, I, 133–34).

Critics of the friendships and particularly of the "Conversations" in which Margaret Fuller sought to realize her program of self-culture saw in these relationships precisely the "mutual excitement of vanity" and the "infatuation" that Fuller herself criticized in her discussion of Bettina's hero worship of Goethe. The celebrated series of "Conversations," which Fuller conducted in Boston from 1839 to 1844, was construed by more than one observer as the occasion of a fervid cult of personality with Fuller as its priestess. On these occasions Fuller apparently attempted to incarnate what she later described in *Woman in the Nineteenth Century* as "the especial genius of Woman," "electrical in movement, intuitive in function, spiritual in tendency" (MF, 171). She identified two principal varieties of genius in women: the intellectual, represented by the courageous "self-reliance" of a Minerva, and the intuitive, represented by the inspired "self-impulse" of the Muse (MF, 188). It was the power of the Muse figure, of the actress, the singer, and the prophetess, however vulnerable to betrayal by an "impassioned sensibility" (MF, 168), that captured Fuller's imagination. There is substantial evidence in the contemporary accounts of the "Conversations" to suggest that the influence that Fuller exerted on these occasions involved a force more distinctly personal in nature than the disinterested moral suasion which was her declared intention. Frequent reference is made to her queenly manner and the complete submission to her will which she demanded of her followers. Emerson observed of Fuller that "there is almost an agreement in the testimony to an invariable power over the minds of all" (Mem, I, 312).[8] She possessed a seemingly irresistible magnetism which elicited confessional responses in others, drawing from them, even against their will, a revelation of their inmost consciousness.

The public manifestations of self-culture in Margaret Fuller's "Conversations" seemed to present something of the ambiguities of the more personal, private relationships devoted to its pursuit which troubled Emerson and which Hawthorne and James were to recognize as explicitly sexual in nature. Emerson acknowledged, with reservations, the "overstrained affections" in Fuller's circle: "Her friendships, as a girl with girls, as a woman with women, were not unmingled with passion, and had passages of romantic sacrifice and of ecstatic fusion, which I have heard with the ear, but could not trust my profane pen to report" (Mem, I, 281–82). As a measure of Fuller's "strong affections" Emerson proceeds to include the following excerpt from her journal, in which she describes just such a friendship as those to which he alludes. Deliberately identifying her own relationship with celebrated examples of the ennobling power of love drawn from the range of history, she reads in her attraction for another woman a glowing manifestation of idealism. It is worth noting that she finds her occasion for this effusion in an engraving of Madame Récamier, which engaged her attention in the boudoir of her friend and which led her to reflect on the "intimacy" between Madame Récamier and Madame de Staël:

It is so true that a woman may be in love with a woman, and a man with a man. I like to be sure of it for it is the same love which angels feel, where—

'Sie fragen nicht nach Mann und Weib.'

It is regulated by the same law as that of love between persons of different sexes; only it is purely intellectual and spiritual. Its law is the desire of the spirit to realize a whole, which makes it seek in another being what it finds not in itself. Thus the beautiful seek the strong, and the strong the beautiful; the mute seeks the eloquent, &c.; the butterfly settles always on the dark flower. Why did Socrates love Alcibiades? Why did Körner love Schneider? How natural is the love of Wallenstein for Max; that of De Staël for De Recamier; mine for ———. I loved ———, for a time, with as much passion as I was then strong enough to feel. Her face was always gleaming before me; her voice was always echoing in my ear; all poetic thoughts clustered round the dear image. This love was a key which unlocked for me many a treasure which I still possess; it was the carbuncle which cast light into many of the darkest caverns of human nature. She loved me, too, though not so much, because her nature was 'less high, less grave, less large, less deep.' But she loved more tenderly, less passionately. She loved me, for I well remember her suffering when she first could feel my faults, and knew one part of the exquisite veil rent away; how she wished to stay apart, and weep the whole day. . . .

I do not love her now with passion, but I still feel towards her as I can to no other woman. I thought of all this as I looked at Madame Recamier. (Mem, 1, 283–84)

So much for self-culture! The passion to which the *Memoirs* testify must necessarily qualify any judgment upon Margaret Fuller's claims for the transmission of moral influence through a purely spiritual love.

This brief review of Margaret Fuller's pursuit of self-culture is designed to prepare us to evaluate the literary versions of such experience and their fidelity to the historical record. Fuller and her transcendentalist contemporaries themselves helped to create the form this literature would take. To begin with, the belief in an ideal of self-culture determined their preference for spiritual autobiography as a means of self-expression. In addition to the journals they kept so faithfully, they admired such novels of moral quest as Goethe's *Wilhelm Meister* and De Wette's *Theodore*. Fuller saw in Goethe's *Faust* the great prototype of the drama that she sought to enact in her own life, "the progress of a soul through the various forms of existence" (MF, 91). The editors of Fuller's *Memoirs* clearly shaped their materials with an eye to just such a narrative form, creating in effect an American version of Goethe's *Dichtung und Wahrheit*. Even when Fuller sought material for fiction in her well-known sketch "Mariana," she drew instinctively on her own experience to provide a dramatic structure—here hardly more than an outline—for the play of her consciousness. More often than not, ironically, the very work designed as an apology for the life of self-culture documented its flaws instead.

"Mariana," a characteristic if minor example of the literature of self-culture, is particularly interesting because it offers a number of striking parallels to *The Blithedale Romance*. Hawthorne certainly had an opportunity to read Fuller's piece when it was first published in her travel book *Summer on the Lakes* in Boston in 1844, and he was probably familiar with it. In "Mariana" Fuller presents the portrait of a young woman of unusual powers whose spiritual development was thwarted because she failed to find in her relationships, first with a

circle of young girls and later with a lover, the quality of love necessary to forward a harmonious unfolding of her genius. Her description
of Mariana as "a mind whose large impulses are disproportioned to
the persons and occasions she meets, and which carry her beyond those
reserves which mark the appointed lot of woman" (MF, 23) resembles
Hawthorne's conception of Zenobia. At boarding-school Mariana undergoes the turbulent experience of the romantic cult of friendship at
peak psychological intensity: at first she is worshiped by the other
girls as a kind of inspired priestess; later she is defied and humiliated
by them, and she takes proud refuge in her position as scorned out-
cast. The narrator of these events is a timid, sickly, sentimental, idealistic girl, much like Hawthorne's Priscilla, whose hero worship of
Mariana meets with condescending laughter and rejection. She observes
with dismay in Mariana what Miles Coverdale was to fear in Zenobia,
the perversion of redemptive love into a force of destruction directed
not only against those who betrayed her but against herself as well.

Love is the force that determines the outcome of Mariana's quest for
self-development. When she discovers in her marriage to Sylvain
"that there was absolutely a whole province of her being to which
nothing in his answered" (MF, 17) the downward course of her destiny becomes irrevocable. In like manner Coverdale was to observe of
Zenobia's disastrous union with Westervelt, "Her deepest voice lacks
a response; the deeper her cry, the more dead his silence."[9] Fuller
recognized in the traditional relationship between the sexes the central
obstacle to the fulfillment of her ideal of self-culture, while Hawthorne
was to write of Zenobia's feminism, "A female reformer, in her attacks
upon society, has an instinctive sense of where the life lies, and is inclined to aim directly at that spot. Especially, the relation between the
sexes is naturally among the earliest to attract her notice" (6:44). In
Woman in the Nineteenth Century Fuller defined the most perfect
form of marriage as a communion of souls united in a religious "pilgrimage toward a common shrine" (MF, 162). Her anguished protests
invariably singled out incompatibility in marriage as the major source
of spiritual dislocation in women: "How terrible must be the tragedy
of a woman who awakes to find that she has given herself wholly to
a person for whom she is not eternally fitted!" (Mem, ii, 140). James's
Isabel Archer was destined to prove the truth of Fuller's prophecy,
awakening before her dying fire in Rome to the bitter knowledge that
she herself had helped to betray her glorious dreams of self-culture.

In looking to the life of the heart as central to the experience of self-culture, Margaret Fuller approached the insight with which her discerning contemporaries interpreted the drives of her own career. For Channing, knowledge of Fuller's "ardent nature" provided the key to an understanding of her complex inner life:

> The tragedy of Margaret's history was deeper yet. Behind the poet was the woman,—the fond and relying, the heroic and disinterested woman. The very glow of her poetic enthusiasm was but an outflush of trustful affection; the very restlessness of her intellect was the confession that her heart had found no home. A 'bookworm,' 'a dilettante,' 'a pedant,' I had heard her sneeringly called; but now it was evident that her seeming insensibility was virgin pride, and her absorption in study the natural vent of emotions, which had met no object worthy of life-long attachment. At once, many of her peculiarities became intelligible. Fitfulness, unlooked-for changes of mood, misconceptions of words and actions, substitution of fancy for fact,—which had annoyed me during the previous season, as inconsistent in a person of such capacious judgment and sustained self government,—were now referred to the morbid influence of affections pent up to prey upon themselves. (Mem, ii, 37)

No one has captured more succinctly than Channing the tragedy of Fuller's New England years. His crucial reading of the affective design of her highly intellectual personality, formed by the "morbid influence" of frustrated desires, confirms the authenticity of Hawthorne's Zenobia and, still later, of James's Olive Chancellor. Hawthorne and James, devoted alike to "the deeper psychology," detected in the exalted discourse of reform the unmistakable accents of the heart in pain. "Behind the poet was the woman." Behind the spiritual identity, which sought to display its ascendency, its freedom, in a grandly independent course of heroic action, stood the sexual identity, which refused to be denied. Although the likeness of the heroine of *The Bostonians* to the historical Margaret Fuller in this regard is as striking as that offered by Zenobia, as we shall see, Olive Chancellor has yet to be accorded her rightful place beside Zenobia in the literature inspired by Margaret's life. That this should be so is hardly surprising, for Hawthorne's Zenobia was first on the field by some thirty years, at a time when the memory of Fuller's death in 1850 was still fresh in the minds of those who had known her. Zenobia made her appearance to the American reading public in the summer of 1852, only a few months after the

garet fashioned by the editors of her posthumous *Memoirs* in the
ng of that year. The timing, for Hawthorne's purposes, was surely
ixed advantage, for while it helped to establish a decisive link between Hawthorne's fiction and the facts of Fuller's career, it also encouraged a narrow interpretation of this link, a reading of Hawthorne's
romance as a roman à clef rather than as the cultural commentary of
greater breadth and significance that appealed to Hawthorne and
James. Ignoring the preface in which Hawthorne urges a distinction
between the actual events and personages of the Brook Farm experiment and the "fictitious handling" (1) of these materials in his romance,
critics have proceeded to read the *Blithedale* narrative as a thinly
veiled autobiography in which among other things Hawthorne re-
created in Zenobia a full-scale portrait of Margaret Fuller. Consideration of Hawthorne's relationship with Margaret Fuller, based on the
unexamined assumption of a direct correspondence between fact and
fiction, has become embroiled in an endless controversy over the de-
tails of their private lives. As a result the moral preoccupations that
they shared have become obscured. Margaret Fuller was for Hawthorne, as much as she ever became for James, a representative type
of romantic individualism.

II

Hawthorne had every occasion to be familiar with the creed of self-
culture and the related problems of self-reliance, genius, and hero
worship preached by Margaret Fuller, Emerson, and others of the
transcendentalist circle with whom he was personally connected (especially during his residence at Brook Farm and Concord). In all
probability he read most of Fuller's writing, either in the *Dial* or in
book form, which would have been easily available to him through
the West Street bookshop of his sister-in-law, Elizabeth Peabody. The
Hawthornes corresponded with Fuller on the subject of her most influential work, *Woman in the Nineteenth Century*.[10] In its essence a
plea that women be granted an opportunity for self-development equal
to that enjoyed by men, this tract was the most extended single expression of her ideas published during her lifetime.

In addition to this exposure to major documents of transcendentalist
literature, Hawthorne possessed firsthand sources of information concerning the principal public display of Margaret Fuller's dedication to
self-culture, her "Conversations." These were held in Elizabeth's shop,

and both Elizabeth and Sophia Peabody took an active part in them. He had an extensive knowledge of Fuller's private pursuit of her ideal in her intense cultivation of friendships with many of his own acquaintances, including Emerson and the Peabody sisters. In his journal Hawthorne reported the following instance of the impact of Fuller's personality upon Emerson: "He seemed fullest of Margaret Fuller, who he says, has risen perceptibly into a higher state, since their last meeting. He apotheosized her as the greatest woman, I believe, of ancient or modern times, and the one figure in the world worth considering."[11] If Fuller was capable of eliciting such an extravagant response from the usually sober and reserved Emerson, her effect upon the more impressionable, enthusiastic Peabody sisters must have been considerable. Sophia apparently resented the fact that her generous, self-effacing sister, Elizabeth, whose "Reading Parties" had served perhaps as a prototype for Margaret's "Conversations," had allowed herself to be superseded by her more brilliant friend Margaret in the transcendentalist circle.[12] Sophia's own susceptibility to Margaret's spell is suggested by a letter she wrote to Margaret announcing her engagement to Hawthorne and enclosing a sonnet addressed "To a Priestess of the Temple not made with hands," which concludes: "Behold! I reverent stand before thy shrine/ In recognition of thy words divine."[13] For his part, Hawthorne expressed on one occasion considerable impatience with Sophia's involvement with Margaret and her "Conversations": "And what wilt thou do today, persecuted little Dove, when thy abiding place will be a Babel of talkers? Would that Miss Margaret Fuller might lose her tongue! or my Dove her ears, and so be left wholly to her husband's golden silence!"[14]

Hawthorne himself had made the trial of a friendship with Margaret Fuller; he had conversed with her about "matters of high and low philosophy"[15] in the solitude of the Concord woods. The continuing debate over his attitude toward Fuller and the contradictory nature of the evidence upon which it is based indicate that their friendship varied greatly in intensity and in satisfaction for both of them. An alternating impulse of attraction and repulsion seems to have governed Hawthorne's relations with Fuller, and to this extent his experience seems to have been typical, for Emerson commented in his *Journals* on "these strange, cold-warm, attractive-repelling conversations with Margaret" (MF, 108). If Hawthorne could observe with relief that he was able to avoid an encounter with her (December, 1839),[16] he was also capable of confessing a desire to impart to her his inmost thoughts. He had clearly experienced at one time (August, 1842) sufficient conviction of the value of her moral influence to write to her in the earnest vein that is so characteristic of the literature of self-culture: "There is nobody to whom I would more willingly speak my mind, because I can be certain of being thoroughly understood."[17] Fuller indicated that this sympathy was reciprocal when she wrote on another occasion: "I feel more like a sister to H., or rather more that he might be a brother to me, than ever with any man before. Yet with him it is, though sweet, not deep kindred; at least, not deep as yet."[18]

Hawthorne lived, however, to record in his Italian journal in 1859 a final estimate of Margaret Fuller as "a great humbug," absolutely reversing the tenor of his earlier relationship with her. In this passage, which caused considerable scandal at the time of its publication in 1884, he presented what is without doubt the most hostile version of Fuller's pursuit of self-culture to be found in the abundant literature about her which has survived:

> It was such an awful joke, that she should have resolved—in all sincerity, no doubt—to make herself the greatest, wisest, best woman of the age. And to that end she set to work on her strong, heavy, unpliable, and in many respects defective and evil nature, and adorned it with a mosaic of admirable qualities, such as she chose to possess, putting in here a splendid talent and there moral excellence, and polishing each separate piece, and the whole together, until it seemed to shine afar and dazzle all who saw it. She took credit to herself for having been her own Redeemer, if not her own Creator.

Significantly, Hawthorne attributed the failure of Fuller's egotistical, even blasphemous career to her intractable carnal nature. He concludes, with a certain unpleasant complacency:

> But she was not working on an inanimate substance like marble or clay; there was something within her that she could not possibly come at, to recreate or refine it; and, by and by, this rude, old potency bestirred itself, and undid all her labor in the twinkling of an eye. On the whole, I do not know but I like her the better for it; because she proved herself a very woman after all, and fell as the weakest of her sisters might.[19]

What is striking in this passage is not that Hawthorne's interpretation of Margaret Fuller has changed radically from his reading of her in

The Blithedale Romance, for he still sees in her sexuality the source of her drive toward self-culture, but rather that his attitude toward this sexuality has soured. He withholds from her here, as he did not from the dark heroines of his romances, any compassionate, attenuating, redeeming intimation of the agency of a Fortunate Fall.

In his journals and letters, then, Hawthorne freely expressed strong, ambivalent feelings toward Margaret Fuller *as a personality.* In the portrait of Zenobia in *The Blithedale Romance* he offered a more balanced, reasoned, coherent version of her *as a representative figure* of the transcendentalist movement. There is a marked strain of morbidity nevertheless in the point of view of Miles Coverdale, especially in his relationships with women: the mixed attitude of fascination and hostility which is so arresting in the private record still colors the perception that governs the romance. In the *Blithedale* preface Hawthorne may have claimed that the point of departure for his fiction had been the establishment of a theater of action "a little removed from the highway of ordinary travel, where the creatures of his brain may play their phantasmagorical antics, without exposing them to too close a comparison with the actual events of real lives" (1). It seems clear nevertheless that through a sympathetic identification with the character and the resources of such a woman as Margaret Fuller had been, tempered by an unsparing critical evaluation of the content of her aims and the nature of her commitment to them as revealed in the events of her dramatic career, Hawthorne sought an insight into the impulse that drove so many of his distinguished contemporaries to embrace the particular forms of self-expression to which they devoted their lives.

The parallels between the heroine of *The Blithedale Romance* and the historical Margaret Fuller must have seemed if anything still more striking in 1852 than they do today. Hawthorne might claim that his Zenobia, "the high-spirited Woman, bruising herself against the narrow limitations of her sex," was "entirely fictitious" (2); there was but one familiar prototype, however, of the mature, passionate woman prevented from achieving the development appropriate to her nature within the confines of New England, and that was Margaret Fuller. Fuller herself had helped to establish the inevitable association of Zenobia's plight with the drama of her own career when she described in *Woman in the Nineteenth Century* the common fate of women of genius in her time: "Such beings as these [Mary Wollstonecraft, George Sand], rich in genius, of most tender sympathies, capable of

high virtues and a chastened harmony, ought not to find themselves
by birth in a place so narrow that in breaking bonds they become out-
laws. Were there as much room in the world for such as in Spenser's
poem for Britomart, they would not run their heads so wildly against
the walls" (MF, 160–61).[20] Many a reader of Fuller's *Memoirs* must
have responded with a shock of recognition when Hawthorne sum-
marized the impact of Zenobia's personality, of her genius, her feminism, and her quest for self-development, upon her contemporaries:
"In fact, so great was her native power and influence, and such seemed
the careless purity of her nature, that whatever Zenobia did was generally acknowledged as right for her to do. . . . The sphere of ordinary
womanhood was felt to be narrower than her development required"
(22:189–90).[21] Further Zenobia's advocacy of women's rights can be
regarded as a dramatization of Fuller's creed of self-culture in *Woman
in the Nineteenth Century*, especially when she pleads for the emancipation of women to accommodate the indomitable impulse toward
self-development denied by the constraints of a conventional marriage,
a favorite Fuller theme. From Eliot's pulpit Zenobia preaches her belief in the intuitive genius of woman (that aspect of her nature which
Fuller associated with the Muse), to be fulfilled in the eloquence of
the spoken word.[22]

These correspondences between Zenobia and Margaret Fuller, while
suggestive, are comparatively superficial; it is when we observe the
revelation of Zenobia's character in her relationships first with Priscilla and then with Westervelt and Hollingsworth that we confront the
larger historical significance of Hawthorne's portrait. Hawthorne interpreted these relationships as manifestations of hero worship, which
his own relations with Margaret Fuller had disclosed as central to the
experience of self-culture. Let us consider the Zenobia-Priscilla axis
first, since the parallels it suggests with Fuller and her circle are more
immediately obvious. Coverdale's account of Priscilla's devotion to
Zenobia has been criticized by James and by Marius Bewley as an inadequate explanation of the psychological forces involved. Bewley
denounces the passage as "Hawthorne at his worst," attributing Hawthorne's failure here "to the Transcendental sweetness of Mrs. Hawthorne that was at last beginning 'to tell' on her husband."[23] The limitations, however, are Coverdale's, not Hawthorne's, and the passage is
a cultural document of considerable importance for any student of the
moral life as it was conceived by a typical New England intellectual of
Hawthorne's generation. It demonstrates the extent to which Cover-

dale had imbibed the gospel of self-culture that was the essence of
the writing and the career of Margaret Fuller. His interpretation of
Zenobia's influence closely resembles Fuller's reading of her own impact upon the numerous young women who were attracted to her. His
statement, with its reference to the agency of genius and spiritual love,
with its language of sentiment and its feminist bias, idealizes such a
friendship in the manner of Fuller's *Memoirs* and of her article on
Bettina Brentano. Any failure of perception then should be charged to
Coverdale alone, for the passage clearly authenticates Hawthorne's
claim as an initiated observer of the enthusiasms of self-culture:

> It was curious to observe how trustingly, and yet how timidly, our
> poor Priscilla betook herself into the shadow of Zenobia's protec-
> tion. She sat beside her on a stool, looking up, every now and then,
> with an expression of humble delight at her new friend's beauty.
> A brilliant woman is often an object of the devoted admiration—it
> might almost be termed worship, or idolatry—of some young girl,
> who perhaps beholds the cynosure only at an awful distance, and
> has as little hope of personal intercourse as of climbing among the
> stars of heaven. We men are too gross to comprehend it. Even a
> woman, of mature age, despises or laughs at such a passion. There
> occurred to me no mode of accounting for Priscilla's behavior, ex-
> cept by supposing that she had read some of Zenobia's stories, (as
> such literature goes everywhere,) or her tracts in defence of the
> sex, and had come hither with the one purpose of being her slave.
> There is nothing parallel to this, I believe—nothing so foolishly dis-
> interested, and hardly anything so beautiful—in the masculine
> nature, at whatever epoch of life; or, if there be, a fine and rare
> development of character might reasonably be looked for, from
> the youth who should prove himself capable of such self-forgetful
> affection. (5:32-33)

Indeed Coverdale eventually attributes to the ideal love that Priscilla
expressed in her ennobling "worship" of Zenobia the principle of the
girl's vitality, sustaining her amidst the adversity of her early years
(22:185-86).

It is interesting to observe in connection with this classic instance
of hero worship that Hawthorne presently contrives a curious encounter between Coverdale and Priscilla; the girl, who has come to deliver
him a letter from his friend Margaret Fuller, momentarily takes on to
his eye a striking if partial resemblance to the distinguished sender of

the letter which she bears. There is a suggestion that this "singular anomaly of likeness" to Fuller, whom Coverdale refers to as "one of the most gifted women of the age" (7:51–52), reflects Priscilla's susceptibility to the influence of genius. In any case, the incident serves to introduce Margaret Fuller by name into a series of reflections concerning the "involuntary affection," "the mysterious attraction" (7:49–50), which Priscilla "evinced" for Zenobia. Immediately following this episode the narrative proceeds with a discussion of Coverdale's reading in "Mr. Emerson's Essays, the Dial, Carlyle's works, George Sand's romances, (lent me by Zenobia,) and other books." Both Coverdale and Fuller, in the pursuit of a common ideal of "human progression" (7:52), turned for inspiration to the same body of contemporary literature. The presence of Margaret Fuller, by name and by association, pervades the entire chapter.

If Miles Coverdale seems all too ready to indulge in transcendentalist rhapsodies on the subject of Zenobia and Priscilla to suit Bewley (who apparently equates Coverdale's meditations here with Hawthorne's), he deserves to impress Bewley more favorably in his analysis of Zenobia's relationships with Westervelt and Hollingsworth. Presumably the "unintelligence," "the glaring deficiency," of Hawthorne's treatment of Priscilla for Bewley is his relative incapacity in dealing with complex psychological issues, more especially his failure to recognize the presence of sexual drives in his characters. Coverdale's repressed love for Priscilla would seem to offer a satisfactory explanation for his willingness to exempt her behavior from the ruthless scrutiny of motive he applies to all of the other characters. At any rate, even the infatuated Coverdale distinguishes between Zenobia's attraction to the shaggy blacksmith and Priscilla's pure aspiration—let us grant it—toward an ideal of spiritual love. From the outset Coverdale is preoccupied with "a certain warm and rich characteristic" (3:17) of Zenobia's personality. Fascinated by "her womanliness incarnated" (6:44), he concludes his feverish imaginings concerning her ripe physical presence and the history of her passionate nature—he pictures her "fine, perfectly developed figure" in "Eve's earliest garment" (3:17)—with this paraphrase of his obsession: "Pertinaciously the thought—'Zenobia is a wife! Zenobia has lived, and loved! There is no folded petal, no latent dew-drop, in this perfectly developed rose!'—irresistibly that thought drove out all other conclusions, as often as my mind reverted to the subject." Coverdale instinctively believes that the key to "the mystery" of Zenobia's life, of her very "consciousness" (6:47–48), lies in a complete knowledge of her sexual experience.

It is accordingly through conjectures about Zenobia's sexuality that Coverdale seeks to understand the vicissitudes of her career in the arena of reform. Why was it that of the two potential sources of growth in "the spacious plan of Zenobia's entire development" (3:15), her generous capacity for feeling strong emotion and her penetrating critical intelligence which probed unsparingly at quixotic forms of idealism, only the second was to be fulfilled, and only in part at that? Coverdale interprets the theatrical public version of her personality and her strident creed of feminism as a mask for the torment of her inner life. He emphasizes the irregularity, the incompleteness, of Zenobia's development, believing that the natural tendency of her genius lay elsewhere than in the world of periodical literature and reform in which her undisciplined sexual energies had sought release. Significantly, Coverdale traces the origin of the eccentric, ultimately tragic, unfolding of Zenobia's consciousness to a pivotal event of dislocation in her loveless alliance to Westervelt (a subject unexamined by Hawthorne). With the exception of its defiant conclusion, his imagined version of this disastrous union, a tale of self-deception, isolation, and suffering, resembles in its general outline the pattern of Isabel Archer's unfortunate marriage to Osmond:

> How many a woman's evil fate has yoked her with a man like this! Nature thrusts some of us into the world miserably incomplete, on the emotional side, with hardly any sensibilities except what pertain to us as animals. No passion, save of the senses; no holy tenderness, nor the delicacy that results from this. Externally they bear a close resemblance to other men, and have perhaps all save the finest grace; but when a woman wrecks herself on such a being, she ultimately finds that the real womanhood, within her, has no corresponding part in him. Her deepest voice lacks a response; the deeper her cry, the more dead his silence. The fault may be none of his; he cannot give her what never lived within his soul. But the wretchedness, on her side, and the moral deterioration attendant on a false and shallow life, without strength enough to keep itself sweet, are among the most pitiable wrongs that mortals suffer.

Now, as I looked down from my upper region at this man and woman—outwardly so fair a sight, and wandering like two lovers in the wood—I imagined that Zenobia, at an earlier period of

youth, might have fallen into the misfortune above indicated. And
when her passionate womanhood, as was inevitable, had discovered its mistake, there had ensued the character of eccentricity
and defiance, which distinguished the more public portion of her
life. (12:103)

Despite similarities in theme and tone between this passage and Fuller's *Woman in the Nineteenth Century,* the sequence of the argument here is different, and the difference is crucial: the point is not
that this particular marriage failed to accommodate Zenobia's pursuit
of self-development, but rather that this pursuit, expressed in her militant feminism, was the result of her unsuccessful marriage.

The validity of Coverdale's conjectures about Zenobia's reform impulses is presently confirmed in a clash between Zenobia and Hollingsworth at Eliot's pulpit in the Blithedale woods. Following a spirited
debate concerning the relation between the sexes, Hollingsworth opposed Zenobia's plea for the emancipation of women with an assertion of woman's role as the passive servant of the male. Coverdale's
expectation, however, that Zenobia will deliver a scathing feminist attack against Hollingsworth's intransigent position is sharply disappointed, and his own faith in the redemptive possibilities of womanhood badly shaken:

> Now, if ever, it surely behoved Zenobia to be the champion of
> her sex.
> But, to my surprise, and indignation too, she only looked hum-
> bled. Some tears sparkled in her eyes, but they were wholly of
> grief, not anger.
> "Well; be it so," was all she said. "I, at least, have deep cause to
> think you right. Let man be but manly and godlike, and woman is
> only too ready to become to him what you say!"

Coverdale does not need to seek far for the cause of Zenobia's submission, for at the conclusion of this scene he is watching her when she
impulsively grasps Hollingsworth's hand and presses it to her heart:
"Had Zenobia knelt before him, or flung herself upon his breast, and
gasped out—'I love you, Hollingsworth!'—I could not have been more
certain of what it meant" (14:123–25). "Had Zenobia knelt before
him"—this is the tell-tale posture of hero worship which we meet again
and again in the *Blithedale* narrative. Zenobia does not hesitate to

abandon her own intellectual commitment to the cause of reform when her attraction to Hollingsworth proves to be the stronger force.

Thus when Coverdale finally plumbs, as he believes, the depths of Zenobia's character in his encounter with her in the city, he discovers that her love for Hollingsworth is the very principle of her being, that it is the driving force behind the development of her genius, and that it is expressed in the psychology of hero worship in which she too, like Priscilla, inevitably becomes involved. It was precisely through his presentation of Zenobia's passionate sexuality that Hawthorne sought an insight into Margaret Fuller's ideals. The upshot of the Blithedale experiment as understood by Coverdale and by Hawthorne is this: that the life of the mind is contingent upon the reality of character and personality, that it reflects the peculiarities of the psychological, and especially the sexual, make-up of each individual. The striking and recurrent attitudes of dominance and submission assumed by the major characters at moments of moral crisis, the numerous scenes in which one character is seen kneeling at the feet of another, only serve to emphasize the dynamics of hero worship at play in their pursuit of social and spiritual ideals (such as feminism, communism, penal reform, self-culture, and the like). That is to say that the phenomenon of hero worship, which is constantly invoked in the literature of the period to describe the peculiar nature of the interpersonal relationships involved in the life of self-culture, functions for Hawthorne—and for Melville as well—as a metaphor to express a configuration of forces within the psyche, revealing a mind in the grips of an idea or passion. Even as they pursue their dreams of freedom, Hawthorne's seekers after self-culture enter into debilitating dependencies that seal their spiritual bondage.

For Hawthorne, the real tragedy of Zenobia lay in her failure to redeem the reformer Hollingsworth from an unnatural intellectual development that paralleled her own. Hawthorne's narrow, fanatical philanthropist is yet another type of the miscarriage of genius, much like Margaret Fuller's version of the later Goethe as a cold Olympian, in whom she beheld the death of the heart that threatened their shared ideal of self-culture. Far from preserving Hollingsworth from his selfish design and vindicating her reliance upon the redemptive power of her passionate womanhood, Zenobia's love is itself vulnerable and makes her own destruction inevitable. Hollingsworth, with a calculating materialism no less deadly than Gilbert Osmond's in *The Portrait of a Lady*, is determined to exploit her feelings in order to gratify his formidable ego by financing his scheme for penal reform with her private fortune. In succumbing to her mistaken hero worship of the blacksmith, Zenobia fails to free herself from the pattern of psychological and sexual tyranny she had experienced in her relations with Westervelt. Utterly defeated, first by Westervelt and then by Hollingsworth, she goes to her death with her potential unfulfilled, her development incomplete. For Coverdale, for Hawthorne, and surely for James, as we shall see, in the abrupt termination of Zenobia's career the realization of nature's highest purpose, "that of conscious intellectual life, and sensibility," had been "untimely baulked" (28:244).

Hawthorne's attitude towards this abortive development of consciousness in his heroine is clearly a complex one. In the exchange between Coverdale and Westervelt at the grave of Zenobia, which contains the most arresting statement of the opposing forces seeking control of her destiny, the balance of our sympathy rests with Coverdale's point of view, with his indignant repudiation of Westervelt's construction of her character. In the mouth of the materialistic mesmerist the pursuit of self-culture shows as a cynical, even sinister, will to power, the perversion of genius feared by Margaret Fuller and Emerson, antithetical to Zenobia's womanhood, which Coverdale believed to be the source of all her strength:

> "Her mind was active, and various in its powers," said he; "her heart had a manifold adaptation; her constitution an infinite buoyancy, which (had she possessed only a little patience to await the reflux of her troubles) would have borne her upward, triumphantly, for twenty years to come. Her beauty would not have waned —or scarcely so, and surely not beyond the reach of art to restore it—in all that time. . . . How forcibly she might have wrought upon the world, either directly in her own person, or by her influence upon some man, or a series of men, of controlling genius! Every prize that could be worth a woman's having—and many prizes which other women are too timid to desire—lay within Zenobia's reach."
>
> "In all this," I observed, "there would have been nothing to satisfy her heart."
>
> "Her heart!" answered Westervelt, contemptuously. "That troublesome organ." (28:240)

Yet it is Coverdale himself who undercuts the aura of tragedy surrounding Zenobia's suicide, for he detects an unsettling ambiguity of mo-

tive in her final gesture. Her act signifies to him at once the "immiti-
gable defiance" (27:235) of a rebel against a society too narrow to
accept her on her own terms and an impulse to appropriate in her
death the conventional image of an innocent girlhood betrayed:

> Zenobia, I have often thought, was not quite simple in her death.
> She had seen pictures, I suppose, of drowned persons, in lithe and
> graceful attitudes. And she deemed it well and decorous to die as
> so many village-maidens have, wronged in their first-love, and
> seeking peace in the bosom of the old, familiar stream—so famil-
> iar that they could not dread it—where, in childhood, they used
> to bathe their little feet, wading mid-leg deep, unmindful of wet
> skirts.

In allowing Zenobia's suicide to show in Coverdale's meditation as an
"Arcadian affectation" (27:236-37) of a lost idealism, as a studied per-
sonation of the wronged village maiden, Hawthorne encourages the
reader in these final pages to share in the ambivalent estimate of Zenobia that typifies Coverdale's response to her throughout, and Hawthorne's to Margaret Fuller, as we have seen. If Coverdale is irresistibly
drawn to Zenobia—her "whole character and history," he confesses toward the last, are the obsession of his "feverish" imagination (25:215)
—he feels threatened by her as well. Inadequate to cope with her ripe
sexuality, he seeks instead to submit to the influence of an idealized
virginal womanhood in his *unconfessed* love for Priscilla. The representative quality of Coverdale's mixed view of Hawthorne's heroine of
self-culture would seem to be confirmed by Emerson himself, who in
describing his response to Margaret Fuller in her *Memoirs* might have
been speaking for the narrator of *The Blithedale Romance*, ever the
helpless spectator of Zenobia's troubled fate: "When I found she lived
at a rate so much faster than mine, and which was violent compared
with mine, I foreboded rash and painful crises, and had a feeling as if
a voice cried, *Stand from under!*—as if, a little further on, this destiny
was threatened with jars and reverses, which no friendship could avert
or console" (Mem, I, 228).

In *The Blithedale Romance*, with Miles Coverdale as our guide, we
are forced into an oblique relationship with Zenobia; with him, as perhaps with Hawthorne, Emerson, and others in New England at the
time, we "stand from under." In *The Scarlet Letter* (1850) we view the
tragedy of self-culture with all its "painful crises," its "jars and re-

verses," from within, for Hawthorne gives us in Hester Prynne his most complete rendering of the lawless inner life implied by the striking events of Zenobia's history which Coverdale witnessed from without.

The development of Hester's intellect, like Zenobia's and like Miriam's in *The Marble Faun,* takes place at the expense of the life of the heart. Hawthorne traces the origins of this growth of consciousness in the commission of a sin, and he consistently locates the catalyst of this process in the circumstances of loveless marriage. He approaches his dark heroines, however, only after they have survived the dislocation of marital experience, while James was to make the institution itself the theater of his portrayal of Isabel Archer. Hester's emancipated intellect turns toward Europe. Hawthorne does not examine this shift very closely; he simply states that she somehow "imbibed" the progressive spirit of metaphysical inquiry which accompanied the social and political upheavals then taking place across the Atlantic. He does make it clear, however, that Hester's "freedom of speculation," the play of her consciousness as she "wandered without a clew in the dark labyrinth of mind," was leading her to conclusions that were potentially subversive to the established order of orthodox New England: "she might have come down to us in history, hand in hand with Anne Hutchinson, as the foundress of a religious sect. She might, in one of her phases, have been a prophetess. She might, and not improbably would, have suffered death from the stern tribunals of the period, for attempting to undermine the foundations of the Puritan establishment" (13:164–66). Given her revolutionary thoughts on the position of women, Hester might have become a figure of the world of reform, a Margaret Fuller, or a Zenobia, whom James described as "the passionate patroness of 'causes.' "[24] Her feminist views project the total reconstruction of society "as a first step," to be followed by a fundamental alteration of "the very nature of the opposite sex." Hawthorne perhaps expresses his own reservations concerning Hester's liberalism when he raises the doubt whether "the ethereal essence" (13:165) of womanhood might be destroyed by the very process that seeks its liberation.

Hawthorne concluded his portrait of Hester in *The Scarlet Letter* with an evocation of her dream of a new dispensation which would supersede the severity of Calvinist law, a gospel of woman's redemptive love. It may be that in composing Hester's plea Hawthorne recalled the conclusion of Margaret Fuller's *Woman in the Nineteenth Century* of five years before, for in the final pages of that tract Fuller had hailed the rise of a leader in a golden day soon to come, who would win for women their birthright. Even after the historical distance of Hester's story from Hawthorne's own time has been taken into account, one cannot help but feel that in projecting the realization of her hopes into a remote future, he cast a shadow of uncertainty upon Fuller's glowing prophecy, suggesting that its fulfillment was to be indefinitely deferred:

> She assured them, too, of her firm belief, that, at some brighter period, when the world should have grown ripe for it, in Heaven's own time, a new truth would be revealed, in order to establish the whole relation between man and woman on a surer ground of mutual happiness. Earlier in life, Hester had vainly imagined that she herself might be the destined prophetess, but had long since recognized the impossibility that any mission of divine and mysterious truth should be confided to a woman stained with sin, bowed down with shame, or even burdened with a life-long sorrow. The angel and apostle of the coming revelation must be a woman, indeed, but lofty, pure, and beautiful; and wise, moreover, not through dusky grief, but the ethereal medium of joy; and showing how sacred love should make us happy, by the truest test of a life successful to such an end! (24:263)

If the import of Hester's vision points clearly toward the thought of Margaret Fuller and Harriet Beecher Stowe, Hawthorne's own attitude toward his heroine and her ideals is definitely ambivalent, for his picture of Hester is darkened by his sense of the dangerous consequences attendant on the development of her consciousness. The course of Hester's passionate womanhood runs contrary to the received moral order of society. The punishment imposed by the law leads not to a reconciliation of the individual with his community but instead to a further alienation. The secret passages of Hester's inner life, born of the suppression of her essential nature as a woman, reveal a barren moral landscape. Her evolving self-awareness not only uncovers killing doubt of the orthodox scheme of salvation embraced by Dimmesdale at his death (to his final triumphant question, "Is not this better . . . than what we dreamed of in the forest?" she hauntingly replies, "I know not! I know not!" [23:254]), but it destroys her womanhood as well and the alternative possibility of redemption offered by the mystery of love.

Clearly the moral values of Mrs. Stowe's New England no longer had any meaning for Hawthorne's Hester Prynne. Yet Hawthorne's indubitable fascination with the unfolding consciousness of his dark heroines is always accompanied by the expression of the orthodox moral position that such knowledge might be purchased only by the death of the soul. This double view of the inner life perhaps accounts for his approach to his numerous studies of the figure of the romantic seeker through the medium of the Faust legend and the drama of salvation usually connected with it. In dealing with his ambivalent evaluation of consciousness in his romances, Hawthorne's expedient was to exploit the convention of paired heroines which Scott, Cooper, and their followers had made an essential feature of the conceptual framework of romantic fiction.[25] By contrasting the heretical consciousness of a defiant dark heroine with the redemptive innocence of a submissive blonde, Hawthorne attempted to explore an uncharted realm of experience and at the same time remain within the pale of the accepted order of society. His series of portraits of the New England girl, however, in the three romances that were to follow *The Scarlet Letter*, records the decline of her efficacy as a redemptive figure,[26] a decline which we shall see repeated in the history of the heroines of Howells and James.

In Phoebe Pyncheon of *The House of the Seven Gables* (1851) Hawthorne presented an ideal of domestic womanhood which closely resembles that portrayed by Mrs. Stowe in her New England girls, principally Mary Scudder of *The Minister's Wooing*.[27] Only this once did Hawthorne match with any conviction the traditional moral power that is the hallmark of the Stowe heroine; significantly, fair Phoebe makes her show of strength in the absence of any competition from Hawthorne's dark alternative, the doubting, even unbelieving woman. The girl is repeatedly associated with a commonplace reality, with "the well-worn track of ordinary life." Like Mary Scudder, Phoebe is distinctly a household presence ("a verse of household poetry" [9: 142]) likened to the fire at the hearth or under the teakettle. She possesses "activity" (what Mrs. Stowe would call "faculty"), which Hawthorne describes as "one of the most valuable traits of the true New England woman" (5:73–74), a primary virtue of village life. She proves a wonder in the home with her baking, brewing, and arranging, and a wonder in Hepzibah's shop as well. Like Mrs. Stowe, Hawthorne attributes to this "activity" a "spiritual quality" (5:82) which ennobles the humblest household chore.

Hawthorne underlines the essentially religious nature of the ideal that Phoebe expresses in a description of the girl on her way to church:

> She was like a prayer, offered up in the homeliest beauty of one's
> mother-tongue. Fresh was Phoebe, moreover, and airy and sweet
> in her apparel; as if nothing that she wore—neither her gown, nor
> her small straw bonnet, nor her little kerchief, any more than her
> snowy stockings—had ever been put on, before; or, if worn, were
> all the fresher for it, and with a fragrance as if they had lain
> among the rosebuds.[28]

Although Phoebe is, like Mary Scudder, "a Religion in herself" (11:
168), standing to the other characters as a representative of the received moral order of society, her ideal girlhood remains virtually untested. She instinctively recoils from the presence of evil in her encounter with Judge Pyncheon, and her unspeculative nature, "in order
to keep the universe in its old place" (8:131), represses the potentially
disturbing significance of this experience. In the scheme of the narrative, simply to radiate New England goodness provides an adequate
demonstration of her value. Despite her own sense of the limited redemptive power of her love, the "sweet and order-loving" (20:303)
Phoebe is able to restore the wayward, freethinking artist Holgrave
to a conformity to the laws and "the peaceful practice of society" (20:
307).[29]

In *The Blithedale Romance* of the following year, Hawthorne attributes to Priscilla a capacity like Phoebe's for an elevated love of a distinctly religious quality. In contrast to the easy resolution provided by
Phoebe's marriage to Holgrave, however, the moral equilibrium which
Priscilla is called upon to reestablish has been much more violently
challenged by the turbulent events of the summer at Blithedale. The
stabilizing force which the orthodox piety of conservative girlhood ex-
erts upon the anarchical tendencies of the masculine radical is strained
to the breaking point. Hollingsworth is much more fanatical and self
destructive than Holgrave; a blasted figure at the time of his marriage
to Priscilla, he is not saved by her from ruin but only comforted in his
desolation. In this role the frail, insubstantial girl proves much more
vulnerable than the healthy and joyous Phoebe. Given the desperate
circumstances, Zenobia's pessimistic view of the outcome of the drama
of salvation in the relationship of Hollingsworth and Priscilla is surely
the only possible conclusion. While she charges Hollingsworth with a
willingness to sacrifice Priscilla, chosen by Providence to work his

redemption, to his insatiable egotism, she is at the same time scornful of the resources of the girl's womanhood: "Pity that she must fade so soon! These delicate and puny maidens always do" (26:226).

Indeed Priscilla's sterling moral qualities provide but an uncertain guarantee for her own spiritual welfare. Her selfless love makes her liable to the dangers of hero worship in all of her relationships, with Hollingsworth, with Zenobia, with Westervelt.[30] It is the overbearing Hollingsworth who rescues the girl from a passive enslavement to the demonic egotism of Westervelt. In his description of this incident Miles Coverdale makes a solemn declaration of his belief in her inviolable innocence which preserved her from the contamination of evil:

> She threw off the veil, and stood before that multitude of people, pale, tremulous, shrinking, as if only then had she discovered that a thousand eyes were gazing at her. Poor maiden! How strangely had she been betrayed! Blazoned abroad as a wonder of the world, and performing what were adjudged as miracles—in the faith of many, a seeress and a prophetess—in the harsher judgment of others, a mountebank—she had kept, as I religiously believe, her virgin reserve and sanctity of soul, throughout it all. Within that encircling veil, though an evil hand had flung it over her, there was as deep a seclusion as if this forsaken girl had, all the while, been sitting under the shadow of Eliot's pulpit, in the Blithedale woods, at the feet of him who now summoned her to the shelter of his arms. And the true heart-throb of a woman's affection was too powerful for the jugglery that had hitherto environed her. She uttered a shriek and fled to Hollingsworth, like one escaping from her deadliest enemy, and was safe forever! (23:203)

A hint of the latent ambiguity of Priscilla's situation, which both Howells, in *The Undiscovered Country* (1880), and particularly James, in *The Bostonians*, were to explore, is contained in the image of pastoral security, clearly intended here as reassuring, that Coverdale associates with the girl's love for Hollingsworth. In fact in an earlier scene at Eliot's pulpit, when Coverdale observed the girl at the feet of Hollingsworth, he was disturbed by his impression of her trusting weakness ("the gentle parasite") at the mercy of the reformer's "masculine egotism" which "centred everything in itself, and deprived woman of her very soul" (14:123). Priscilla's incapacity for action severely limits the potential value of her redemptive love for others; her lack of volition makes even her own survival seem at best precarious.

In his final portrait of the New England girl, the one that James was to single out for special notice, Hawthorne most thoroughly tested the tradition of moral idealism that he consistently associated with his ethereal young women. In Hilda of *The Marble Faun* (1860) Hawthorne is directly concerned with the value of the religious belief that she represents, rather than with any of its related manifestations, whether the ordinary village domesticity of a Phoebe or the eccentric gift of clairvoyance of a Priscilla. He takes as his point of departure Hilda's rejection of the guilt-stricken Miriam's plea for compassion and guidance. Shaken by her discovery of the existence of evil in the world, the girl is reluctant to become involved in the drama of Miriam's salvation for fear of endangering her own spiritual well-being. The Stowe heroine of course would leap at such a chance. In the several chapters devoted to Hilda's moral crisis (36–42), his only extensive picture of the inner life of the New England girl, Hawthorne describes the anguish of her puritan conscience, so familiar to the readers of Mrs. Stowe: she is torn between her love for Miriam and her allegiance to an absolute morality which Miriam has transgressed through her participation in Donatello's crime. In her confusion the girl is led to doubt the perfection of her Protestant faith, which provides no resolution for her torment. Driven at last to confess her trouble to a Catholic priest at St. Peter's, Hilda surrenders to an alien religion and feels herself restored to her original purity. This "daughter of the Puritans" (39:362) is able to experience this renewal, however, only by the momentary suppression of her intractable, useless conscience which Hawthorne presents as central to her New England belief.

In Hilda, Hawthorne presents the drama that James described as "the loss of perfect innocence,"[31] yet in his critical revaluation of the girl's Protestant heritage he stops short of the conclusion implied by her inadequate response to the dark knowledge of evil. Kenyon, who had observed Hilda at the confessional, fears that the girl's restless imagination has led to a betrayal of the moral idealism of her New England girlhood: "You were a creature of imagination, and yet as truly a New England girl as any with whom you grew up in your native village. If there were one person in the world, whose native rectitude of thought, and something deeper, more reliable than thought, I would have trusted against all the arts of a priesthood—whose taste, alone, so exquisite and sincere that it rose to be a moral virtue, I would have rested upon as a sufficient safeguard—it was yourself!" In her reply to Kenyon's challenge, Hilda refuses to acknowledge that her anguish and her confession have carried her beyond the boundaries of New England orthodoxy marked by village, mother, and conscience, the moral world of Harriet Beecher Stowe: " 'I am conscious of no such high and delicate qualities as you allow me,' answered Hilda. 'But what have I done that a girl of New England birth and culture, with the right sense that her mother taught her, and the conscience that she developed in her, should not do?' " (40:367). Although Hawthorne suggests that Hilda's character had developed "a sturdier quality, which made her less pliable to the influence of other minds" (41:375), the course of her development is in fact regressive. Unlike Isabel Archer with her fine gift of consciousness, Hilda has no resources to deal with the experience of evil excepting the defensive strategy of repression: "Hilda (as is sometimes the case with persons whose delicate organization requires a peculiar safeguard) had an elastic faculty of throwing off such recollections as would be too painful for endurance" (42:382). She does not move forward toward a deeper understanding, an enlarged moral wisdom; she returns instead to the narrow sanctuary of her earlier innocence. Once Hilda's moral isolation has been shown to be vulnerable, it is no longer possible to accept Hawthorne's continued affirmations of the security of this New England girl's self-reliant innocence, such as this one:

> In all her wanderings about Rome, Hilda had gone and returned as securely as she had been accustomed to tread the familiar street of her New England village, where every face wore a look of recognition. With respect to whatever was evil, foul, and ugly, in this populous and corrupt city, she had trodden as if invisible, and not only so, but blind. . . . Thus it is, that, bad as the world is said to have grown, Innocence continues to make a Paradise around itself, and keep it still unfallen. (42:387)[32]

Hilda's knowledge has not humanized her intransigent Protestantism. She strenuously rejects Kenyon's speculation (an echo of Miriam's) concerning the possibility of a Fortunate Fall, which would provide a favorable construction for the growth of consciousness of Hawthorne's dark heroines. Hawthorne presents a conventional alternative to such dangerous experience in Kenyon's redemptive courtship of Hilda's ideal womanhood, but this formula seems a singularly hollow conclusion to the portrait of her weakness. Kenyon marries Hilda, and, upon their return to America, she is "to be herself enshrined and worshipped as a household Saint" (50:461) in the fashion of Mrs. Stowe's

New England heroines. Yet Hilda is clearly closer to James's vision of precarious innocence than she is to Mary Scudder.

In *The Marble Faun* Hawthorne seems to be struggling to transcend the barriers separating the respective spheres of action of his light and dark heroines. Not only does he expose the innocent Hilda to a knowledge of evil but he involves the sinful Miriam, for all her speculations which proceed beyond the bounds of received moral law, in the orthodox drama of Donatello's salvation. In so doing, he has given to the dark heroine, with her superior capacity for action, the redemptive role usually assigned to the passive innocence of the fair heroine, in whom he had uncovered fatal signs of weakness and exhaustion. In *The Marble Faun* Hawthorne has pushed his use of the romantic convention of paired heroines to the limit. The varieties of spiritual experience in New England finally eluded the discipline that his fictions might bring to bear on them. The orthodox values of the New England village enshrined in the novels of Harriet Beecher Stowe failed to offer a refuge from the dangerous pursuit of the Emersonian ideal of self-culture in Hawthorne's romances. The conscience, morbid and inflexible, spending its reserves of redemptive energy in sterile and selfish exercises, was powerless to arrest the heretical, potentially self-destructive, growth of the emancipated consciousness.

Part Two

*The New England Girls of
William Dean Howells
& Henry James*

Chapter 4

THE HOWELLS HEROINE: FROM *THE LADY OF THE AROOSTOOK* TO *APRIL HOPES*

I

IN JANUARY, 1875, while the aging Harriet Beecher Stowe continued to bend her unflagging energy to the restoration—if only in fiction—of an earlier ideal of womanhood in her final, loving portraits of sober, old-fashioned New England girls, the young standard-bearers of the coming literary generation, William Dean Howells and Henry James, were becoming engaged in the celebration of the contemporary American girl, the felicitous and peculiarly national incarnation, so it struck them, of the moral life of the country. In Florida Vervain of *A Foregone Conclusion* (1875) James praised what, he affirmed, admirers of Kitty Ellison in Howells's earlier novel, *A Chance Acquaintance* (1873) had already discovered, the freshness, the "singularly original conception" of the Howells heroine. In his two reviews of Howells's second novel of consequence, James envisioned a glorious future for the young woman who had captured Howells's imagination and his own. Speaking of Kitty and Florida, he confidently announced that Howells's career was fairly launched:

> In these two figures Mr. Howells has bravely notched the opposite ends of his measure, and there is pleasure in reflecting on the succession of charming girls arrayed, potentially, along the intermediate line. He has outlined his field; we hope he will fill it up. His women are always most sensibly women; their motions, their accents, their ideas, savor essentially of the sex; he is one of the few writers who hold a key to feminine logic and detect a method in feminine madness.[1]

James's verdict has since become an established fact of our literary history, and Howells is generally credited with the invention of the American girl who was destined through the combined efforts of both novelists and their followers not only to achieve the distinction of a literary type but finally to win enduring popular recognition as a telling representation of the national character.

James's reviews have made it easy and even convenient to use the early novels of Howells as a port of entry to the exploration of James's American heroines, his Daisy Millers and his Isabel Archers. Read in this way Howells becomes, perhaps unfairly, a foil for James, a literary John the Baptist preparing the way for the work of the Master, *il miglior fabbro*. James himself lends encouragement to such a reading of the relationship between the two men in his now famous early letter to Norton at the outset of their careers: "Looking about for myself, I conclude that the face of nature and civilization in this our country is to a certain point a very sufficient literary field. But it will yield its secrets only to a really *grasping* imagination. This I think Howells lacks. (Of course *I* don't!) To write well and worthily of American things one need even more than elsewhere to be a *master*. But unfortunately one is less!"[2] In any case, the incontrovertible fact remains that James warmly acknowledged his confrere as the father of the American girl, no mean accomplishment, considering the decisive role she was to play in the unfolding of James's own genius and her flowering—if so it may be called—in the subsequent literature that she inspired. Reserving for later the history of her progress in the fiction of James, I wish to record in this chapter what fortune she found in the novels of Howells, beginning with *The Lady of the Aroostook* (1879), the first novel published after *A Foregone Conclusion*, and concluding with *April Hopes* (1888), which marks something of a turning point, if not a terminus, in her long career.[3] In choosing Howells's heroines as the focus for my consideration of his development as a novelist during these years, I follow James's sense of the central position they occupy in Howells's art. James wrote:

> Not the least charm of the charming heroines he has already offered us has been their delicately native quality. They have been American women in the scientific sense of the term, and the author, intensely American in the character of his talent, is probably never so spontaneous, so much himself, as when he represents the delicate, nervous, emancipated young woman begotten of our institutions and our climate, and equipped with a lovely face and an irritable moral consciousness.[4]

In this memorable definition of the character of the American girl, one to which Howells himself would surely have subscribed, James trains a novelist's angle of vision upon the possibilities of this "emancipated" heroine, endowed not only with a capacity for action but with a direction for it as well, "equipped" as she is with "an irritable moral consciousness."

Turning from James's sanguine projection of the bright future awaiting the American girl in 1875 to read through the sequence of Howells's novels—nearly a dozen in all—of the next fifteen years, one is struck by the decline in value of the moral authority which the Howells heroine could be said to possess by 1888. In particular, while the "irritable moral consciousness" that James perceived as the vital principle of Howells's American girl continued to determine her personality, it did so no longer as a source of strength. Indeed that it should have figured as an asset to the heroine of *A Foregone Conclusion* had made that early novel something of a tour de force for James. In the character of Florida Vervain he was persuaded that Howells had succeeded in a bold attempt to enlist the reader's imagination "on behalf of a young girl who is positively unsympathetic"; for all her "appearance of chilling rigidity and even of almost sinister reserve," this heroine somehow ripened into an exemplary if fiercely zealous wife and mother at the last. In Alice Pasmer of *April Hopes* (1888) and Olive Chancellor of *The Bostonians* (1886), however, Howells and James respectively offered a darker reading of the "positively unsympathetic" heroine: no happy ending awaited the "irritable moral consciousness" that made Alice cold and stiff and Olive truly "sinister"; in maturity it hardened beyond even what Howells called the "power and need of loving" to save.[5]

Surveying Howells's work of the years that lie between *A Foregone Conclusion* and *April Hopes*, a second major and complementary development presents itself: the increasing prominence of the matter of New England in Howells's art, not simply as a place, a source of setting and local color, but as a period in time, a passage in the history of manners and morals, a state of mind. It was to the decadence of the moral tradition of New England, more than to any other single cause, that the searching, realistic appraisal of Howells's mature novels of the 1880s attributes the spiritual limitations of the heroine whose redemptive possibilities, romantically idealized, had inspired his bright, brief fictions of the 1870s.[6] It is then the connection between Howells's conception of the future of the American girl and his identification of her with a New England past that I wish to consider in this phase of his career, a connection which first appears in *The Lady of the Aroostook*.

For if he presents as usual in the foreground of this narrative the radiant figure of the American girl familiar to readers of *A Chance Acquaintance* and *A Foregone Conclusion,* he nevertheless allows the decay of puritanism to begin to cast the shadow that, lengthening in subsequent novels, eventually throws the promise of so many of his heroines into eclipse. To read the book for shadow, however, is to read it deliberately against the grain in the light of the fiction that was to follow, and any faithful account of the moral atmosphere of the narrative must properly begin with a recognition of the prevailing sunshine in these pages.

Howells's reading of the story of the American girl, always a fable of courtship, was never more optimistic than in *The Lady of the Aroostook.* Here he gives his first extensive rendering of what the wooing of this heroine by a deserving young man of appropriate ideals and nationality might be expected to accomplish. The romance of *A Chance Acquaintance* had come to nothing. The brief encounter between Kitty Ellison and Miles Arbuton had only served to demonstrate the incompatibility of the country girl from Eriecreek, New York, and the priggish proper Bostonian. The primary love story of *A Foregone Conclusion* had proved equally abortive, for this time the hero was by very definition unacceptable: "A Venetian priest in love with an American girl,—there's richness, as Mr. Squeers said!"[7] Hitherto thwarted or long delayed, love's young dream—to borrow a characteristic formula from one of the chapter titles of *A Chance Acquaintance*—was fulfilled at last in *The Lady of the Aroostook.* In this charming marine pastoral a handsome, worldly Bostonian, James Staniford, a dilettante artist at a loss what to do with himself, postpones the responsibility of a career by taking a trip to Europe instead; on board the *Aroostook,* bound for Italy, he meets and falls in love with Lydia Blood, village maiden from South Bradfield, Massachusetts; in the high-minded fashion of the decorous hero from the pages of Mrs. Stowe, Staniford's declaration takes the form of a confession to the New England girl that she has become his "outer conscience";[8] they are married in Venice and presently settle on a ranch in California. Just as the Stowe heroine could bring salvation to her unregenerate lover, the Howells heroine could work a fundamental if more secular conversion in her suitor, providing the irresolute, careerless, expatriate American hero with a direction for the future, an occupation, a place in the national life of his country.

During the long sea voyage Staniford's imagination gives itself up to an endless analysis of Lydia's character. Her beauty inspires the young man with as lively a sense of her manifold possibilities as James entertained of her predecessors, Kitty Ellison and Florida Vervain: her unstudied grace reminds Staniford at once of the perfection of art and the spontaneity of nature; her dark hair, of a puritan; her pallor, of a southerner. While Staniford admits that "anything is predicable of a girl who says so little and looks so much" (9:109), Howells sets the keynote of his hero's fancies in his own initial description of his heroine as the American girl of the village stamp: "She showed, now that she stood upright, the slim and elegant shape which is the divine right of American girlhood, clothed with the stylishness that instinctive taste may evoke, even in a hill town, from study of paper patterns, Harper's Bazar, and the costume of summer boarders" (1:7). Lydia figures accordingly as the village "Lurella" of Staniford's daydreams; the young man is inspired in his choice of this name by the charm of the girl's lack of sophistication and the colloquial savor of her country speech. Expanding his conception of the name Lurella, he would have it bear witness to the latter-day aberrations of the New England mind which Howells was to explore in *The Undiscovered Country* of the following year: "Where the Puritanism has gone out of the people in spots, there's the rankest growth of all sorts of crazy heresies, and the old scriptural nomenclature has given place to something compounded of the fancifulness of story-paper romance and the gibberish of spiritualism" (6:59).[9] In his favorite image the New England girl resembles not a little the Isabel Archer of James, "the ordinary, futureless young girl, voyaging under the chaperonage of her own innocence" (10:114–15).

It is this extraordinary innocence of Lydia Blood that engages Staniford's imagination. So great is the disparity between the mores of the provinces and those of the capital of New England that it is possible for Lydia, still trusting in 1874 to the strength of her native tradition of self-reliance, to be completely unaware that her unchaperoned voyage on board the *Aroostook*, whose other passengers number three young men, places her in a "delicate" position in the eyes of a cultivated Bostonian.

The quality of her innocence, however, is most fully expressed in the purity of her voice, the primary emblem of her distinction in her village world and the occasion for her career abroad: "It was this voice which, when Lydia rose to join in the terrible hymning of the congregation at South Bradfield, took the thoughts of people off her style and beauty; and it was this which enchanted her father's sister when, the summer before the date of which we write, that lady had come to America on a brief visit, and heard Lydia sing at her parlor organ in the old homestead" (3:33). In Lydia's voice resides not only the promise of her future but the legacy of her past. It is most of all in her singing during religious services—in her New England meeting-house, on shipboard, in the English chapel in Venice—that Howells captures the essence of his heroine. Her moral elevation is further displayed in the leadings of her "pitiless Puritan conscience" (18:214) and in the seriousness of her observation of the Sabbath. "Lyddy," early an orphan, apparently derives her strength of character largely from her upbringing in the home of her grandfather, Deacon Latham, and her Aunt Maria. Howells's fine sketch of the rock-bound tender-ness of this country woman, with her skill at her needle and her thoughts of Mirandy Holcomb's "fune'l" sermon, captures the arche-typal spinster who in the work of Sarah Orne Jewett and Mrs. Stowe became the tutelary genius of the New England spirit. The sweet sing-er of South Bradfield is the flower of a village culture, a worthy de-scendant of Mary Scudder, and it is his reverence for this unspoiled native ideal of womanhood that moves Staniford to regret the impact of "that depraved Old World" (18:216) upon Lydia Blood: "With a suddenly depressing sense of loss, Staniford had a prevision of splen-dor in her, when she should have wholly blossomed out in that fervid air of art and beauty; he would fain have kept her still a wilding rose-bud of the New England wayside" (18:207).

Howells's belief that the village world that had created Lydia Blood was dying must have contributed a sense of urgency to his desire to idealize its survival in his New England heroine, for Staniford was well aware, whatever his wishful visions, that the wayside itself had not been spared by the inexorable forces of change. The young man contemplates the moral distance stretching between Lydia's South Bradfield and the Newport, say, of Mary Scudder when he observes of his "Lurella": "If she were of an earlier generation, one would expect to find something biblical in her; but you can't count upon a Puritanic culture now among our country folks" (8:83). The passage of time has brought "a decay of the religious sentiment" (7:70), and the villagers have withered—"they don't seem to live; they are just staying." For a young woman in such a place life can only be dull and lonely, and Staniford imagines with dismay his "wilding rosebud" blighted alto-gether in her impoverished native soil: "He was thinking what sort of an old maid she would have become if she had remained in that village. He fancied elements of hardness and sharpness in her which would have asserted themselves as the joyless years went on, like the bony structure of her face as the softness of youth left it." The origin of Staniford's mixed feelings as he beholds the lady of the *Aroostook* on the threshold of her "prodigious transition" (9:106–7) from South Bradfield to Venice lies in Howells's double evaluation of his heroine's country heritage, comprising as it does the traditional church-going strength of the Latham household and the spiritual drift of the community that surrounds it. Staniford can only conclude that for Lydia to remain in the village is to place her in greater jeopardy than to leave it, and the girl herself confesses that she has, in her progress from the village to the world, passed the point of no return: "I could n't go back there and be what I was. I could have stayed there, but I could n't go back" (18:211).

Howells seems to prefer the relative security of the limited theater of action on board the *Aroostook* in mid-Atlantic for his leisurely contemplation of the destiny of his American heroine. Here, midway between America and Europe, in a charmed suspension of time and space, the novel lingers, allowing Lydia Blood to stand free of the past and unencumbered as yet by the future. Seeking an indefinite prolongation of this idyl, Howells manages wonderfully to locate his young lovers on a ranch in California remote from the difficulties of the South Bradfield–Boston axis: the rosebud from New England, transplanted by the Bostonian artist-farmer, is to bloom in the garden of the West. This is the fairy-tale resolution which *The Lady of the Aroostook* supplies to the problems arising in the transition from country to city life, the major fact of social change in America in the years following the Civil War, the archetypal plot of all of Howells's fiction. Howells permits Staniford's class-conscious sense of the very real differences of breeding and background which separate him from Lydia, clouding their relationship in the early chapters, simply to disappear. The hero's adjustment is assisted by the rather special makeup that Howells attributes to the character of his heroine: if Lydia possesses the simple goodness of the village past with none of its present narrowness, Staniford is persuaded that she is endowed as well with an innate social genius for an urban elegance and style: "Give that girl a winter among nice people in Boston, and you would never know that she was not born on Beacon Hill" (7:72). With the happy ending of his comedy of courtship safely in hand, Howells can turn at the last to rejoice with Staniford in Lydia's liberation from the "savage desolation" (27:321) of

South Bradfield in winter, the spiritual season, now and to come, of a diminished New England: "Oh, my darling, . . . when I think that it's my privilege to take you away from all this, I begin to feel not so very unworthy, after all" (27:323).

II

Not long after the appearance of *The Lady of the Aroostook*, Hawthorne's New England provided the text for a debate between Howells and James on the future of the American novel. James published his *Hawthorne* in 1879 and Howells reviewed it for the *Atlantic* in February of the following year. In his highly favorable notice Howells did not hesitate to point out the shortcomings of James's critical judgment, keen though it was. His friend had unaccountably blurred Hawthorne's crucial distinction between the novel and the romance and had set too low a value upon the achievement of *The Blithedale Romance*. Howells took particular exception to James's insistence—"not once, but a dozen times"—upon the "provincial" character of American society in the age of Hawthorne. Howells was willing to acknowledge "the value and delightfulness of those chapters on Salem and Brook Farm and Concord" which constituted the heart of James's biography, and he even pronounced "exquisite" "the treatment of the culture foible and of the colorless aesthetic joys" which were their theme. He took James to task for his failure "sufficiently" to recognize "the essential large-mindedness of Concord, as expressed in literature," in the writing of Thoreau ("parochial" for James), in the poems of Channing (James: "more esteemed by the few than by the many"), in Emerson's "grand poem" on the Concord Fight (James: "little hymn").[10] James had called even Hawthorne, the artist whom both revered as the greatest writer America had yet produced, "exquisitely provincial."

Provincial Hawthorne might be, if by *provincial* one understood "a thing of the experiences" rather than "a thing of the mind or the soul."[11] But presently Howells so qualified the substance of this concession as virtually to take it back. From the evidence of the notebooks James had incorrectly inferred that Hawthorne "sets down slight and little aspects of nature because his world is small and vacant." He had enlarged his mistake when he made Hawthorne's case representative of the dilemma of the American writer confronting a country totally wanting in the materials of civilization, the traditions and institutions of a class society (Howells: "that dreary and worn-out paraphernalia")

that alone supply the form and substance of the novel. Rejecting
James's indictment of the poverty of the American scene, his misread-
ing of the lesson of Hawthorne, Howells bravely replied, "We have the
whole of human life remaining, and a social structure presenting the
only fresh and novel opportunities left to fiction, opportunities manifold and inexhaustible."[12] Although James was not persuaded of the
truth of this assertion, he admired its courage, and he dared his friend
to meet the challenge of the peculiarly American problem it presented,
to become without the assistance of the "paraphernalia" indispensable
to the novelist, "the American Balzac."[13]

While the brother novelists might draw from Hawthorne's career
antithetical conclusions about the future of the American novel, probably neither foresaw in 1880 the extent to which in the rest of that
decade the solution for both to the vexed issue of native resources for
fiction would lie in the exploitation of the provincial character and
consciousness of New England. Following Hawthorne and Harriet
Beecher Stowe, moving in the company of James, Howells had already
begun to use the story of his heroine as an opportunity to explore the
latter-day vicissitudes of puritanism in *The Undiscovered Country*
(1880). In this novel, Howells's first extended scrutiny of an American
setting since his early, experimental pieces collected in *Suburban
Sketches* (1871), a sense of the past, of the forces of social, religious,
and literary history, informs his vision of the American girl.

Opening the novel with an invocation of an age of transition, "when
the rapid growth of the city was changing the character of many lo-
calities" (1:1), Howells presents the American girl in surroundings altogether different from any he had hitherto suggested as appropriate
to her character. He introduces Egeria, the heroine inevitably pretty
and pure, a tall, blonde, blue-eyed young woman, a village maiden
dressed in white, as the featured attraction of a spiritualist gathering
in Boston sponsored by her father, the mesmerist Dr. Boynton, and a
professional medium named Mrs. Le Roy. What was once a private
family sanctum, a temple of genteel culture perhaps in its better days,
serves now as the theater for the public display of Egeria's "gift." In
this sorry parlor in "a haggard old house, that's once been a home"
(1:2), lost somewhere in the back reaches of the city on a run-down
street haunted by fortune-tellers, the curious and the credulous assem-
ble to participate in Dr. Boynton's search for a new dispensation to be
revealed through the extraordinary powers of his daughter. Once the
little congregation has linked hands and begun to sing, Egeria appears:

"A draught of cold air struck across the room, and through the door at the head of the table, which unclosed mysteriously, as if blown open by the wind, a figure in white was seen in the passage without. It drifted nearer, and with a pale green scarf over her shoulders Egeria softly and waveringly entered the room. Her face was white, and her eyes had the still, sightless look of those who walk in their sleep" (1: 22). Hypnotized by her father and heralded by favoring whispers and raps, the girl is to enact her role as the messenger of salvation, a spiritualist savior who will redeem the hope of a life beyond the grave through communion with the spirits of the dead.

Never before had higher hopes been entertained of the spiritual capacity of the American girl. In Howells's comedies of courtship, his heroine had always been admired by her suitors not only for her undisputed physical beauty but for her moral qualities as well. Now in *The Undiscovered Country* he dramatized the story of an attempt to invite a more general worship of her redemptive possibilities, to make them the foundation of a new religion. Never before, however, had the character of the American girl seemed less equipped to sustain such a bold program for her future. Involved in proceedings far other than any church service ennobled by the singing of Lydia Blood, the passive subject of the mesmerist's will betrays little family resemblance to the self-reliant young women of the earlier novels. If the portrait of Egeria Boynton creates a new and strange effect in the gallery of Howells's heroines, it conveys a sense of the old and familar to one discerning spectator in the audience, who beheld in the picture of the innocence and freedom of the American girl in jeopardy a spectacle "worthy of Hawthorne" (7:110):

> The girl is such a deliciously abnormal creature. It is girlhood at odds with itself. If she has been her father's "subject" ever since childhood, of course none of the ordinary young girl interests have entered into her life. She has n't known the delight of dress and of dancing; she has n't had "attentions;" upon my word, that's very suggestive! It means that she's kept a child-like simplicity, and that she could go on and help out her father's purposes, no matter how tricky they were, with no more sense of guilt than a child who makes believe talk with imaginary visitors. Yes, the Pythoness could be innocent in the midst of fraud. (7:109)

Howells was surely thinking here of pale Priscilla, the representative of a traditional idealism enslaved to the materialism of the godless

Westervelt, the mesmerist villain of *The Blithedale Romance*. Through a clever double exposure—a technique which James was to employ to even greater advantage in *The Bostonians* under similar circumstances and with a like reference to Hawthorne—in which the image of a well-known victim from the past is superimposed on the image of the girl as savior of the future, Howells set a definite boundary to the hitherto potentially limitless sphere of the moral agency of the American girl.

The strain which the moral ambiguity of the situation has brought to bear upon Egeria's spirit manifests itself physically in the best Hawthornian fashion when the pathetic ritual of the girl's "dark séance" (1:13), by turns sentimental and grotesque, reaches its melodramatic climax. A shriek shatters the darkness, the gas is lighted, and the upshot of the spiritualist endeavor is discovered in a lurid image of violation: "Egeria lay stretched along the floor in a swoon, the masses of her yellow hair disordered and tossed about her pale face. Her arms were flung outward and the hand on which she wore her ring showed a stain of blood, oozing from a cut in a finger next the ring; the hand must have been caught in a savage clutch, and the sharp point of the setting crushed into the tender flesh" (1:32). It is Ford, one of the young men present and the hero of the narrative into the bargain, who, detecting the presence of fraud in the manipulations of Mrs. Le Roy and revolted by the degrading use to which the girl's simplicity had been subjected, interrupts Egeria's performance, not without injury to the girl herself whom he presently carries swooning in his arms to the safety of her room. His gallant gesture repeats Hollingsworth's rescue of Priscilla from the platform of the Lyceum and prefigures Basil Ransom's abduction of Verena Tarrant from the stage of the Music Hall in *The Bostonians*. Only Howells was willing to suggest that in the marriage to the hero with which all three narratives conclude lay a cure for the heroine's exposure to the forces of moral disorder in New England, forces which made of her in turn a mesmerist's "Veiled Lady," a "Pythoness" of spiritualism, and a feminist "*improvvisatrice*," the plaything of jaded Bostonians.

Any identity and consciousness that could properly be said to be Egeria's own have been sacrificed to her role as her father's medium; in her self-eclipse she functions as an extension of his will, an expression of his character. Pursuing the logic of this conception, Howells studies her "girlhood at odds with itself" in the disequilibrium of her father's personality. Through Dr. Boynton the weight of the past is brought to bear on Egeria; the father's career becomes a metaphor for a larger passage of spiritual history in New England which has made the daughter what she is.[14] Howells knew as well as Mrs. Stowe the swing of the pendulum that set the soul-searching of the introspective descendant of the puritans in motion; thus Dr. Boynton observes, "I had been bred in the strictest sect of the Calvinists, from which I had revolted to the opposite extreme of infidelity" (12:178).[15] Cut loose from traditional Calvinist moorings and moving with the current of the moment from shoal to shoal, from materialism to mesmerism and then to spiritualism, Dr. Boynton could find no further harbor in the little town in Maine—"that hole where I have stifled all my life" (4:62)—where his practice dwindled, deserted by those still anchored in the belief he had rejected. Withdrawing from the village, he is forced to support the life of wandering and poverty to which he and Egeria have been reduced by making a public exhibition of the girl's "gift." The Boyntons drift along the highways and byways of Massachusetts, swelling the ranks of the tramps to whom Howells refers so often in these pages as a sign of the times, landing now with the spiritually dispossessed in Boston, now with the Shakers in their enclave at Vardley. The itinerant healer and his hapless daughter are only the most striking of the company of displaced persons in this novel whom the decline of Calvinism, the underpinning of the New England community, has freed to blow about the countryside.

It is fitting that Howells should have been so largely inspired by Hawthorne in his first novel of the crisis of belief in the nineteenth-century New England mind, for the earlier writer had made it the theme of his romances. Howells's account of the ideas and events of Dr. Boynton's career recalls at numerous points the fable of Hawthorne's romantic seekers after truth. Like Ethan Brand's unfortunate Esther, Egeria becomes for her father a "subject for psychological experiment" (12:179); through the instrumentality of her "gift" the mesmerist is determined to restore his shaken faith in the immortality of the soul. Accordingly he transforms the girl, as Rappaccini had his daughter and Aylmer his Georgiana, to suit the requirements of his misguided vision: "I have seen her change from a creature of robust, terrestrial tendencies to a being of moods almost as ethereal as those of the spirits with which it has been my struggle to associate her" (12:180). Exploiting her love for him, Dr. Boynton has brought about Egeria's compliance with his scheme; his control is total: "You have seen, heard, touched, tasted, spoken, whatever I willed. . . . You have no manner of responsibility, moral or otherwise, in the affair" (4:70–

71). Boynton's fondness for the rhetoric of pseudo-science and his conception of his séances as contests of the will—especially against the malign and hostile force of the unbelieving hero, Ford—complete his resemblance to Hawthorne's moral monomaniacs. It is his destiny, as it was theirs, to perceive in his dying hours the magnitude of his delusion: in his "whole system of belief," "a heap of rubbish" (24:363); in Egeria's "gift," "the perishable efflorescence of a nervous morbidity" (21:317). One hears in the words of his confession, uttered in an agony of contrition and bitter self-knowledge, a voice from the world of Hawthorne: "I seized upon a simple, loving nature, good and sweet in its earthliness, and sacred in it, and alienated it from all its possible happiness to the uses of my ambition. I have played the vampire!" (21:318–19).

For all these points of likeness,[16] it would be mistaken to conclude that Howells's story is nothing more than a reworking of Hawthorne— one looks in vain for Byronic fire and steel in bumbling Dr. Boynton. That Hawthorne's *Blithedale Romance*, for example, should have continued to speak with authority some thirty years later to Howells and to James, supplying their work with a source of plot, character, and theme, is not merely a tribute to the creative power of Hawthorne's imagination but an indication of the extent to which he had grasped the reality of the moral life in New England with which they were concerned. That Egeria Boynton and Verena Tarrant should be condemned to replay in their queer performances a worn-out drama from Hawthorne's romances, reflects not the poverty of their authors' powers of invention but rather the enduring nature of the obsessions of the New England consciousness, doomed to contemplate the present and the future with the eyes of the past. Henry Adams offers the classic diagnosis of this inveterate infirmity of puritan vision in his self-portrait of a nineteenth-century New Englander whose ruling ambition to comprehend the twentieth-century was thwarted by the limitations of an eighteenth-century mind.

In the later chapters of *The Undiscovered Country*, Egeria Boynton moves from Hawthornian shadows into the sunshine of a Howellsian courtship, her proper sphere and calling. After the "dark séance" in Boston the girl had fallen gravely ill and the Boyntons had eventually sought shelter with the Shakers at Vardley. Her convalescence here, like Priscilla's at Blithedale, reverses the transformation wrought by her mesmerist days. No longer a drooping medium performing in darkness, Egeria emerges as a buoyant nature-maiden once more, a

"Young Ceres" (14:213) gathering huckleberries from New England hillsides. The significance of her new identity lies in Howells's conception of his hero Ford. If Egeria is a "sylvan creature" in "exquisite harmony with the great natural frame of things" (13:191), Ford is the alienated young man betwixt and between: "I dare say," he observes, "I should have been uncomfortable anywhere" (20:301). In Ford, Howells offers a new version of the *déraciné,* a man of greater drive and masculinity, closer to home than the indecisive, Europeanized expatriate who figures so often in his work. Fleeing "the narrow and importunate conditions" (16:249) of his native village, the kind of place a hard-headed, energetic young man would associate with "not getting on" (20:301), Ford had made his way in Boston as a professional journalist, preferring as a man of "simple social traditions" to hold himself "aloof" from the life of the "complex society" of the city (16:250). If he had cast off the frustrations of the country, however, he had left behind the faith of his fathers as well. In his unbelief he anticipated "the last breath of consciousness" before death as a dreadful passage into an absolute annihilation (18:276). In his providential wooing of Egeria Boynton, which unfolds significantly against the charming backdrop of the Shakers' anachronistic attempt to establish a pastoral ideal in their communal living at Vardley, Ford discovers the pristine promise of country life missing in the fallen village world of his embittered childhood: "He saw her in this old garden by the riverside, before any blight had fallen upon her life. He imagined her a very happy young girl, there; not romantic, but simple and good, and even gay" (20:300). The reigning presence of this vision, moreover, quickens the skeptical spirit of her lover with a new hope of faith: "I find it hard not to imagine something better than this life when I think of Miss Boynton!" (24:363). Ford himself, now the impassioned convert, articulates the cardinal doctrine of the nineteenth-century religion of woman's redemptive love, that marriage to an exemplary girl is virtually equivalent to salvation: "Can you dream of anything nearer the bliss of heaven than union with such tenderness and mercy as hers?" (23:352). In the unabashedly happy ending—Howells, perhaps defensively, allows one of his characters to laugh at it as "the vulgarest commonplace" (28:417)—the Fords settle neither in the country nor in the city but in the convenient, compromise middle ground of suburbia where they live on in joy and presently in affluence.

It would be tempting to say that the ease, the simplicity of this dénouement is somehow out of phase with the seemingly insoluble complexity of the events that precede it. Howells, however, went out of his way to suggest precisely the reverse, insisting that the pressures of social displacement and religious uncertainty which Egeria Boynton has long endured have left no permanent mark upon her. The young knight has only to awaken the sleeping princess from the spell of the evil enchanter. Not content simply to restore his heroine to the customary health and freedom of American girlhood, Howells implies that the decadent moral tradition that had victimized the girl for a time was totally alien to any consciousness of her own; thus Dr. Boynton's remorse can be softened by the thought, "She *is* unharmed by all that she has suffered" (24:362). Yet it is difficult to dismiss the Boyntons' quest for a new ground of belief, which ended only with the sickness of the one and the death of the other, as merely a bad dream out of Hawthorne. The power of *The Undiscovered Country* lies in its understanding of the condition of the uprooted, a power which remains undiminished by last-act reversals of fortune. The changes that removed Ford and the Boyntons from the village world did leave their mark, hardening the young man, weakening the girl, deranging the father. Howells would not continue indefinitely to protect his heroine from the consequences of her identification with a region which increasingly commanded the allegiance of his imagination. In *Dr. Breen's Practice* (1881) he would attribute to her a New England consciousness of her own; in *A Modern Instance* (1882) he would leave her to work out her destiny without the assistance of the worthy young man who had been hitherto her unfailing resource.

III

With *Dr. Breen's Practice* Howells began a new chapter in the life of the American girl. In his earlier novels he had conducted his inquiry into the ideal possibilities of this figure largely from the point of view of her admirers, for whom she became the focus of speculation, the spring of ambition, the inspiration of dreams. Now in his narrative of young Grace Breen at the threshold of her career in medicine, he made the story of his heroine what she would make of it herself, and accordingly he rendered the drama of her inner life in considerable detail for the first time, casting her more nearly as the dominant center of consciousness, no longer the mirror but the lamp. To supply the

material for this new interior dimension of her character he attributed
to her a pattern of thought and behavior which he wished to be recognized as distinctively New England in nature.

Howells brings this regional identity into play from the outset of the
novel in his account of Grace Breen's decision to become a doctor,
"what was thought a strange eccentricity in a girl such as she had
been" (1:12). Believing herself to have failed where "other women's
hopes are" (2:43) following an early "disappointment" in love, Grace
had determined in turning to medicine to locate a new, alternative role
in which she might vindicate herself as a woman. Her intimates
thought that their serious-faced, grey-eyed friend had embraced her
profession "in the spirit in which other women enter convents" (1:12),
and indeed Grace herself had been tempted to symbolize somehow in
her dress her nunlike renunciation of the world of love and courtship
which had always been the Howells heroine's native sphere of action.
Yet Dr. Breen is quite devoid of any feminist affectations, and the
deliberateness with which Howells relegates the opportunity to investigate the woman question to a position of secondary importance only
serves to underline his primary conception of the girl.[17] With her
oversimplified, almost Manichean version of the moral life as a theater
of conflict and pain, in which the militant pursuit of good works is
somehow inseparably linked with aggressive suffering, Grace Breen's
motivation for her calling marks her not as a new woman but as a
daughter of the puritans:

> In tutoring her soul to bear what it had to bear, [she] mistook her
> tense effort for spiritual repose, and scarcely realized through her
> tingling nerves the strain she was undergoing. In spite of the bitter
> experience of her life, she was still very ardent in her hopes of
> usefulness, very scornful of distress or discomfort to herself, and a
> little inclined to exact the heroism she was ready to show. She had
> a child's severe morality, and she had hardly learned to under-
> stand that there is much evil in the world that does not charac-
> terize the perpetrators: she held herself as strictly to account for
> every word and deed as she held others, and she had an almost
> passionate desire to meet the consequence of her errors; till that
> was felt, an intolerable doom hung over her. (1:14)

Dr. Breen's mother, all conscience herself, has encouraged this rather
grim flowering of the girl's righteous nature, educating her daughter
to make conscience her ruling passion by "fretting a New England

girl's naturally morbid sense of duty in her daughter, and keeping it in the irritation of perpetual self-question" (1:13).

In Grace Breen, Howells returned to his study of the "irritable moral consciousness" which he had inaugurated with Florida Vervain, capturing the attention of James in his reviews of *A Foregone Conclusion*.[18] With considerable irony he introduces the motivation that informs her career as a doctor in the context of the world of courtship which the girl has sought to renounce. Just graduated from the homeopathic school of medicine in New York, Grace finds herself vacationing at a seaside resort on the New England coast with her mother and her old schoolmate and patient, Louise Maynard, sick and separated from her husband. Trouble begins when young Mr. Libby, handsome and single, the close friend of the absent Mr. Maynard, asks Grace to accompany Mrs. Maynard and himself on a morning sail. Oblivious to Libby's obvious attraction to herself, the girl refuses to go because she will not condone with her presence what she considers the young man's unseemly attentions to a married woman, and because she is accustomed to denying herself pleasures of any kind. When she communicates her disapproval indirectly, observing that the sea air won't do Mrs. Maynard any good, Libby, eager to please her, presently invents the approach of bad weather as an excuse for calling off the excursion. Proudly refusing to countenance this fabrication, "in that helpless subjection to the truth in which so many New England women pass their lives" (2:30), Dr. Breen now insists that Louise go sailing with Libby after all, in spite of the professional and moral scruples which she had previously urged to them both. Frustrated in her attempt to exact from Libby an open and absolute compliance with her own sense of the impropriety of the outing, she perversely sabotages her strenuous efforts after virtue, at the same time assuming the burden of the irresponsibility of the others in order to redress the balance required by her conception of the inexorable moral law. Grace Breen's stubborn, narrow vision of the good ends in disaster. Chance—or Providence, as the girl would have it—intervenes, bringing a storm suddenly out of the east and with it an altered view of the situation she had presumed to judge: "She remained staring at the dark wall across the sea, and spiritually confronting her own responsibility, no atom of which she rejected. . . . She condemned herself to perpetual remorse" (3:54). Her "passionate desire to meet the consequence of her errors" is amply rewarded when Libby's boat capsizes and her friends are nearly drowned. Yet while blaming "her own wilfulness and self-righteousness" for the sorry outcome of the affair, the girl continues to cling to the vanity of her moral ambitions: "The degradation of the affair, its grotesqueness, its spiritual squalor, its utter gracelessness, its entire want of dignity, were bitter as death in her proud soul. It was not in this shameful guise that she had foreseen the good she was to do" (3:60).

When Mrs. Maynard comes down with pneumonia in the aftermath of the storm, Grace Breen's morbid desire for self-punishment will be satisfied with nothing less than a reenactment of the original drama of transgression in which she substitutes herself for the hapless Mrs. Maynard. With "a sudden impulse, unreasoned and unreasonable, in which there seemed hope of some such atonement, or expiation, as the same ascetic nature would once have found in fasting or the scourge" (7:128), she proposes to go out with Libby in his boat in the hope that a storm will arise in which she can risk her own life as she had once risked that of her innocent friend. The wished-for storm fails of course to materialize. Worse still, Libby usurps the stage reserved for tribulation to declare his love for Dr. Breen. She sternly rejects such joy as undeserved, unsought, and absolutely inappropriate to her scheme of unhappiness, but her fidelity to her ideal of retribution and the bitter heroics it entails momentarily collapses when Libby presently undermines the ground of her responsibility in the sailboat affair, informing her that neither he nor Mrs. Maynard had taken seriously the threat of the storm: "She turned her head away. Her tragedy had fallen to nothing; or rather it had never been. All her remorse, all her suffering, was mere farce now" (7:157).

The New England girl seems to be powerless, however, to interrupt the self-destructive cycle of guilt and punishment on which her conscience feeds, even after Libby's revelation of the mistaken ground of its agency. Following her interview with him, at the very moment when in a posture of recognition before her glass she seems most to question her moral sense, its failings and its dangerous presumption, she resigns herself to its authority once more: she must bear the responsibility for her senseless sense of responsibility:

"Once," she went on, "I thought I had everything clear before me; but now I seem only to have made confusion of my life. Yes," she added drearily, "it was foolish and wicked, and it was perfectly useless, too. I can't escape from the consequences of what I did. It makes no difference what he believed or any one believed.

I drove them on to risk their lives because I thought myself so much better than they; because I was self-righteous and suspicious and stubborn. Well, I must bear the penalty: and oh, if I could only bear it alone!" With a long sigh she took back the burden which she had been struggling to cast off, and from which for a time she had actually seemed to escape. She put away her hat and shawl, and stood before the glass, smoothing her hair. "When will it ever end?" she moaned to the reflection there, rather than to her mother, who did not interrupt this spiritual ordeal. In another age, such a New England girl would have tortured herself with inquisition as to some neglected duty to God; in ours, when religion is so largely humanified, this Puritan soul could only wreak itself in a sense of irreparable wrong to her fellow-creature. (8:170)

In Dr. Breen's endless introspection Howells observes a representative, hereditary pattern of the New England mind at work; having survived the Calvinist theology which once supplied its motivation, this compulsive habit of consciousness has been driven in a secular age to spend its unflagging energy for moral litigation on such meager issues as the sailboat episode affords.

It is only when Dr. Mulbridge seeks to win Grace Breen by wooing her "irritable moral consciousness" that the girl achieves full knowledge of the wasteful expense of spirit it has cost her. Mulbridge, a local physician to whom she has appealed for help in the difficult Maynard case, is a cynical older man who finds himself attracted to the strength of the New England girl despite his profane laughter at her moral ambitions and anxieties. When the young woman, overwhelmed by her sense of failure in her treatment of Mrs. Maynard, contemplates abandoning her profession altogether, Mulbridge sees his opening. Like Gilbert Osmond in his conquest of Isabel Archer, he adopts Grace Breen's moral rhetoric as a screen for his design to bend her puritan spirit to his will. Mulbridge frames his declaration of love in the customary language of her do-good discourse, speaking of her obligation to persevere in her calling, and offering to help her carry out her "plan of life" (10:225) as his wife and colleague: "I won't urge you from any personal motive to accept my offer. But I know that if you do you can realize all your hopes of usefulness" (10:224). When Grace rejects him because she does not love him, he presses his suit to the court of last resort, confidently invoking the authority of her conscience to recognize the justice of his cause. With this last stroke, however, Mulbridge overreaches himself, precipitating to his own disadvantage a decisive crisis in the girl's spiritual history:

> "You will do what seems your duty."
>
> "You must n't trust to my conscience. I fling it away! I won't have anything to do with it. I've been tortured enough by it. There is no sense or justice in it!"
>
> He laughed easily at her vehemence. "I'll trust your conscience. . . ."
>
> . . . After he was out of sight, she followed, scared and trembling at herself, as if she had blasphemed. (10:230)

After this reckless moment of abandon, when the girl expresses her determination not to repeat the misguided suffering of her mistaken part in the sailboat affair, her faith in the religion of duty never recovers its original force.

From the sharpened vantage point of her apostasy she can view Mulbridge's "great, and unselfish, and magnanimous reasons" (11:231) with irony: "I won't keep up the delusion that because I was very unhappy I was useful, and that it was doing good to be miserable." She has had her fill of being the kind of good New England girl Mary Scudder had been when she resigned herself to marry Dr. Hopkins with the words, "Well, mother, I will do whatever is my duty." Like Gertrude Wentworth in *The Europeans* (1878), she proclaims in an outburst of defiant euphoria the end of the oppressive reign of conscience that had ruled Dr. Breen and the restoration of the freedom of girlhood, the Grace she had formerly renounced: "I am sick of duty! . . . I like pleasure and I like dress; I like pretty things. There is no harm in them. Why should n't I have them? . . . I believe I should like to do wrong for a while" (11:234–35). She realigns her destiny with that of the pretty American girl, boldly offering herself to Libby. The hitherto indecisive, rather bland young man is delighted to unite himself to the highly-motivated girl who has given direction to his aimless days, inspiring him to accept his father's offer to set him up in the textile business. After enacting the Howells heroine's required course of travel abroad, however, Grace Libby is glad to exchange the "sweetest irresponsibilities" (11:238) and "aesthetic dissipations" (12:270) of an emancipated American girlhood for a way of life more congenial to her sober New England temper. Settling in a milltown in southern New Hampshire, she assumes the double role of her ideal marriage as wife of the American businessman and doctor to the children of the operatives. Of Dr. Breen's short-lived attempt to remake herself in the image of the American girl Howells sagely observes, "At the end of the ends she was a Puritan; belated, misdated, if the reader will, and cast upon good works for the consolation which the Puritans formerly found in a creed" (12:270).

Howells's consideration of an alternative to the traditional role of the nineteenth-century heroine in *The Undiscovered Country* and *Dr. Breen's Practice* follows in its general outline a pattern of characterization to be observed in the work of Mrs. Stowe, Hawthorne, and James. The conventional domestic comedy in which the heroine fulfills herself by saving the hero through the redemptive power of her love is supplanted by an essentially tragic drama in which she is wedded to a flawed ideal of womanhood, becoming priestess, sister of mercy, or nun, abandoning herself to morbid martyrdoms and strange renunciations. In the novels of these writers the native setting and the psychological conditioning of this celibate existence are usually those of New England—it is a puritan conscience, for example, rather than any feminist impulse, that drives Grace Breen into medicine—and are usually developed as an opportunity to investigate the perversions of the moral life to which the New England character is predisposed. Sometimes, like Dr. Breen and Olive Chancellor, the heroine elects of her own free will to dwell in the lonely Calvinist country of the soul which is the theater of her suffering; sometimes she is passively drawn into it, like Egeria Boynton and Mary Scudder. In either case her entry there is invariably the result of some scarring dislocation in love, an ill-starred courtship or an incompatible marriage, and the dangerous consequences of the repression, the violation of her primary nature as a woman, which attends her sojourn there are registered in the deterioration of her physical and spiritual health, her tortured introspection, her sickness, and even her wish for death. While safe return from this moral wasteland which stretches beyond the pale of hearth and home is more readily available to the heroines of Howells and Mrs. Stowe than it is to those of Hawthorne and James, none of these writers would ultimately deny, however reluctantly, the vulnerability of marriage and family life, none would maintain indefinitely the convenient fiction that excluded tragic experience from the stage of domestic tranquility in some of their work. In 1882 Howells and James would add to *The Scarlet Letter* their own contemporary versions of domestic tragedy in *A Modern Instance* and *The Portrait of a Lady.* Howells had concluded *Dr. Breen's Practice* with this light-hearted assertion of the limits of the knowledge he chose to assume at that time: "It is well, perhaps, not to be too explicitly in the confidence of one's heroine. After her marriage perhaps it is not even decorous" (12:272). In *A Modern Instance,* however, he would no longer abide by these restrictions. Following his trial of alternative roles for his New England girls—Egeria Boynton as medium, Grace Breen as doctor—he returned to reexamine the traditional conception of woman's place in the home, previously his heroine's haven of security in the happy endings he had so liberally bestowed, only to find this bulwark of help in ages past disastrously eroded.

IV

At the beginning of *A Modern Instance,* in the most powerful opening chapter he was ever to write, Howells returned to the snow-bound New England village, which the lady of the *Aroostook* had been so grateful to escape, to present for the first time an extended study of his heroine in her native setting. Marcia Gaylord and Bartley Hubbard, dashing in a cutter "under the naked elms" (1:2) of the main street in town, offer the only sign of life in Equity, Maine, on Saturday night, two figures of easy youth and high spirits against a difficult, unaccommodating winterscape of "arctic quiet" (1:1) and "desolation" (1:2). Presently the lamp lifted high in Marcia's hand as she admits Bartley to the Gaylord mansion accentuates the sexuality of Howells's latest avatar of the pretty American girl: "The action brought her figure in relief, and revealed the outline of her bust and shoulders, while the lamp flooded with light the face she turned to him." If the "peculiar charm" of Marcia's mouth, suggesting "a certain demure innocence that qualified the Roman pride of her profile," serves as a kind of naturalistic signature for her character, similarly Bartley's chin, which "failed to come strenuously forward" in a face which "had otherwise the regularity common to Americans" (1:3), stamps him as the handsome but weak young man. As they sit alone before a midnight fire in the parlor with its mezzotints and family photographs, Howells shows that Marcia and Bartley are no better than they should be and no worse, that their behavior offers a representative picture of the custom of courtship in any New England village still loyal to its traditions:

It was midnight, as the sharp strokes of a wooden clock declared from the kitchen, and they were alone together, and all the other inmates of the house were asleep. The situation, scarcely conceivable to another civilization, is so common in ours, where youth commands its fate and trusts solely to itself, that it may be said to be characteristic of the New England civilization wherever it keeps its simplicity. It was not stolen or clandestine; it would have interested every one, but would have shocked no one in the village if the whole village had known it; all that a girl's parents ordinarily exacted was that they should not be waked up. (1:4)

When Bartley seeks to give his playful attentions to Marcia the ring of orthodoxy in a carefully-modulated crescendo of uplift, he speaks in words that might seem to link Howells's scene with many another in the pages of Harriet Beecher Stowe, who attempted in such an idyl as *The Pearl of Orr's Island* (1862) to chronicle her own idealized vision of the simplicity of the New England civilization: "But of all the women I have known, Marcia, . . . I believe you have had the strongest influence upon me. I believe you could make me do any thing; but you have always influenced me for good; your influence upon me has been ennobling and elevating." Here the resemblance between the worlds of Mrs. Stowe and Howells ends, for if Bartley's strain is pious, it is also secondhand, echoing a lecture "which they had lately heard . . . on the formation of character" (1:10). The lover's confession of faith, set as it is in the context of Bartley's more usual vein of sarcastic banter and flirtatious innuendo, punctuated by laughter, blushes, and the clearly visible marks of sexual violence ("he released her wrists on whose whiteness his clasp left red circles" [1.0]), shows not as the gracious stirring of an unregenerate heart but rather as the easy flattery of a salesman's pitch. This lip-service to the worship of an ideal woman, sealed in a first kiss, inflames the lips of a real woman to a passionate worship of her own in a second kiss:

At the door he bent down his head and kissed her. "Good night, dear—friend."

"Good night," she panted; and after the door had closed upon him, she stooped and kissed the knob on which his hand had rested. (1:10)

Rising from this outspoken gesture of abandon, Marcia turns to behold her father, the old man fully dressed in the manner of an old-fashioned country lawyer, descending the stairs, candle in hand:

> "Marcia," he asked, grimly, "are you engaged to Bartley Hubbard?"
>
> The blood flashed up from her heart into her face like fire, and then, as suddenly, fell back again, and left her white. She let her head droop and turn, till her eyes were wholly averted from him, and she did not speak. He closed the door behind him, and she went upstairs to her room; in her shame, she seemed to herself to crawl thither, with her father's glance burning upon her. (1:11)

Squire Gaylord's blunt challenge and warning make it plain that this stern, unbending figure of authority has witnessed in the parting of Marcia and Bartley not the promise of a young man's salvation but the threat of a young woman's undoing. With this stroke Howells completes his initial picture of the simplicity of the New England civilization, not as it might be but as it is.

. When Marcia and Bartley become engaged the next day on the spur of the moment, the event signifies something well less than the consummation of an ideal love. Women in nineteenth-century American fiction are predisposed to hero worship, and the heroine of this modern instance, stooping to kiss the knob her lover's hand had touched, proves no exception. The very posture of such an act, at once reverent and vulnerable, invariably symbolized the ambiguity of a morality founded upon a psychology of hero worship, as Hawthorne's Coverdale, haunted by images of Priscilla and even proud Zenobia, kneeling before the unscrupulous Hollingsworth, knew well. Mary Scudder might worship in James Marvyn the Christian hero he might become, while Marcia Gaylord might worship Bartley Hubbard such as he is and fail to see the difference. At the heart of her engagement to Bartley, Marcia enshrines her confusion between body and soul, the confusion expressed in the two parting kisses of the night before:

> "Do you know," she went on, . . . "what pleased me more than anything else you ever said to me?"
>
> "No," answered Bartley. "Something you got out of me when you were trying to make me tell you the difference between you and the other Equity girls?" . . .
>
> "When you told me that my influence had—had—made you better, you know—"

"Oh!" said Bartley. "That! Well," he added, carelessly, "it's every word true. Didn't you believe it?"

"I was just as glad as if I did; and it made me resolve never to do or say a thing that could lower your opinion of me; and then, you know, there at the door—it all seemed part of our trying to make each other better. . . . And you *do* think I shall always *try* to make you good and happy, don't you?" (4:35–36)

If in her infatuation Marcia willingly deceives herself, mistaking the throbs of her passion for an ennobling spiritual love, Bartley parallels her self-deception, working up to a fitting degree of intensity the desire for sympathy and adulation he calls his love for Marcia: "I don't think you can make me much happier than I am at present, and I don't believe anybody could make me feel better." Bartley's construction of the girl's enthusiastic vision of the moral improvement to flower from their engagement is light, to be better and to feel better are one and the same, and even Marcia herself, in a moment of calm following her effusion on the goodness of their love, clearly perceives the nature of the impulse that led Bartley to her house the day of his proposal: "And you came up here for a little petting from me, didn't you?" (4:36). In fact, he has no special reverence for Marcia Gaylord, no edifying conception of her love for him. She is, quite simply, as "the prettiest girl in the place" with "more style than any other girl began to have" (2:14), the natural right of the successful young man on the make, an adjunct to his own self-image: how much does a young man who has made good need a young woman to make him good? How relevant is the fable of the selfless heroine's redemptive love to the fable of the self-made hero's rise to success? Marcia is valued not for herself but for the extent to which she might conveniently be worked into Bartley Hubbard's ambitious program for the advancement of Bartley Hubbard. Howells writes:

Her adoration flattered his self-love to the same passionate intensity, and to something like the generous complexion of her worship.

"Marcia," he answered, "I am going to try to be all you expect of me. And I hope I shall never do anything unworthy of your ideal."

She could only press his arm again in speechless joy, but she said to herself that she should always remember these words. (5:43–44)

So much for Bartley's less than ideal worship of Marcia's less than ideal love.

The spiritual devaluation of the fable of courtship had been long in progress, running in the blood, before Bartley's weak chin met Marcia's vulnerable mouth in self-deceiving kisses. If Bartley, an orphan with no demonstrable antecedents, is the self-made man with a self-made morality or lack of it, Marcia is the daughter of Squire Gaylord, the last of the puritans, resembling her father feature for feature in that "consanguinity" (1:11) Howells makes so much of in this novel. In "the rude and bold infidelity" of lawyer Gaylord the original energy of Calvinism has survived any belief in its theology, and the intellect of this embattled latter-day incarnation of the New England mind is reduced in the moral vacuum of Equity, where "religion . . . had largely ceased to be a fact of spiritual experience" (3:18), to spend its powers in sterile legalistic exercises: "He maintained the superiority of the old Puritanic discipline against them [church sociables] with a fervor which nothing but its re-establishment could have abated" (4:25). In the case of Squire Gaylord the traditional paradigm of woman's redemptive love which Bartley and Marcia invoke to bless their future has already proved a failure, for if Marcia's mother, in her marriage to "an unbeliever," "had some such hopes of converting him as women cherish who give themselves to men confirmed in drunkenness," she lived to find that "in this great matter of his unbelief, her love was powerless" (4:26). Ironically Mrs. Gaylord is herself corrupted by woman's supreme act of self-sacrifice: "She gave up for him, as she believed, her soul's salvation, but she held him to account for the uttermost farthing of the price" (8:71). Her aspiration checked, the unbeliever's defeated wife offers a disquieting picture of the pretty American girl frozen in spiritual death, foreshadowing her daughter's ruin:

> She had grown an elderly woman, without losing the color of her yellow hair; and the bloom of girlhood had been stayed in her cheeks as if by the young habit of blushing, which she had kept. She was still what her neighbors called very pretty-appearing, and she must have been a beautiful girl. The silence of her inward life subdued her manner, till now she seemed always to have come from some place on which a deep hush had newly fallen. (4:26)

The cycle of self-deception drawing Bartley and Marcia together,

though briefly interrupted, proceeds on its course: what they are willing to believe is determined by the feelings they wish to indulge, and
so the moral ideal of their relationship becomes a plaything of the
emotions. Thus Marcia, aching over the engagement which she has
broken off in her jealousy over Bartley's attentions to another girl, can
decide that it is she herself who is at fault and that Bartley is "good,"
resolving to grovel at his feet, begging forgiveness and mercy, in order
to get him back. Thus Bartley, leaving Equity under a cloud, having
lost his job and his position in the community in the aftermath of a
scrape, can give way to an access of self-pity in which he blames
Marcia for the reversal in his fortunes. Sitting at low ebb in the depot,
waiting for the night train to Boston, the success-story hero makes of
the love-story heroine's lapse in her role of redemptive love the sancti-
monious rationale for his untimely defeat, confessing a dependence
which the self-made man has hitherto dismissed as secondary to the
drama of his rise· "He owned even then that he had committed some
follies; but in his sense of Marcia's all-giving love he had risen for
once in his life to a conception of self-devotion, and in taking herself
from him as she did, she had taken from him the highest incentive
he had ever known, and had checked him in his first feeble impulse
to do and be all in all for another. It was she who had ruined him"
(12:102–3). When Marcia unexpectedly appears at the Junction and
humbles herself before her god, his ego merely rolls over for petting
on the other flank:

> "I wanted to tell you that I was wrong, and not let you go away
> feeling that—that—you were all to blame. I thought when I had
> done that you might drive me away,—or laugh at me, or anything
> you pleased, if only you would let me take back—"
> "Yes," he answered *dreamily*. All that wicked hardness was
> breaking up within him; he felt it melting drop by drop in his
> heart. This poor love-tossed soul, this frantic, unguided, reckless
> girl, was an angel of mercy to him, and in her folly and error a
> messenger of heavenly peace and hope. "I am a bad fellow, Mar-
> cia," he faltered. "You ought to know that. You did right to give
> me up." (12:105; italics mine)

Marcia, the agent of his fall only moments before, becomes Marcia
"the angel of mercy"—it is all the same to Bartley as long as his satisfaction is guaranteed. *Dreamily* gives the clue: for grace, read gratification; for the process of regeneration, the chemistry of indulgence.

The perversion of a woman's love, that greatest of all misfortunes for Harriet Beecher Stowe which she treated at one remove in such secondary figures as Emily Rossiter in *Oldtown Folks* and Madame de Frontignac in *The Minister's Wooing*, becomes in *A Modern Instance* the destiny of the heroine herself. When the fitful courtship of Bartley Hubbard and Marcia Gaylord reaches a hasty conclusion at the Junction—they are married the same night by a minister near the station and elope to Boston—Howells has brought the Stowe tradition to the crossroads: with a pastoral idyl that never was behind her and the divorce courts waiting for her ahead, the pretty American girl sacrifices her pride, her love, her all to an unworthy young man who is capable of seeing in her not his fair savior but the cause of his ruin. With their departure from the village world which is no longer strong enough to hold them, the first section of the novel comes to an end.[19]

Unlike the earlier novels, *A Modern Instance* does not end with the heroine's marriage. "The future of any heroic action," Howells wrote, "is difficult to manage; and the sublime sacrifice of her pride and all the conventional proprieties which Marcia had made in giving herself to Bartley was inevitably tried by the same sordid tests that every married life is put to" (17:145). Marcia's departure from the village leads not to a new life of freedom and purpose as it had for the lady of *Aroostook* but to one of dislocation and loss. Her dependence on Bartley grows inversely to his indifference to her: while he is increasingly content with empty shows of togetherness—he likes to be seen with his wife and baby in a conventional image of conjugal prosperity—she remains "the young wife who devotedly loves her husband, who lives in and for him" (19:167). Marcia's one-sided love fails to provide either herself or her husband with the center of moral strength which marriage invariably conferred on the happy couples of Mrs. Stowe and Howells heretofore; in the uncertainty of her life with Bartley she presently finds herself groping for some alternative source of direction to guide her in bringing up her daughter Flavia. Uprooted from the blighted soil of Equity, the New England girl, lost in Boston, seeks shelter in the home of the Hallecks. Here an earlier ideal of country life, vanished in Equity, has somehow managed to survive in Boston, a precious enclave—like the Shaker community in *The Undiscovered Country*—in the midst of urban change: "[The Hallecks] had come to the city simple and good young village people, and simple and good they had remained. . . . They were of faithful stock, and they had been true to their traditions in every way. One of these was constancy to the orthodox religious belief in which their young hearts had united, and which had blessed all their life" (19:163). When Mrs. Halleck tells Marcia the story of her son Ben's lameness, the occasion marks a turning-point in Mrs. Bartley Hubbard's quest for faith. Inspired by her sentimental vision of a cripple's heroic acceptance of his misfortune, Marcia seeks to possess his goodness for herself and for her child in the most literal way: "I made up my mind that I wanted Flavia to belong to Ben Halleck's church,—or the church he did belong to; he doesn't belong to any now!" (27:234). Never baptised herself and ignorant of the orthodox view of conversion, the girl's conception of religious experience is rudimentary in the extreme. When Ben Halleck remarks, "I suppose you would want to believe in the creed of the church, whichever it was," Marcia replies, "I don't know that I should be particular" (23:198). Of Marcia's stunted moral development Mrs. Halleck observes, "I couldn't have believed that there was any person in a Christian land, except among the very lowest, that seemed to understand so little about the Christian religion, or any scheme of salvation" (23:203). The spiritual world of Mary Scudder is dead to Marcia Gaylord; in Howells's modern instance the New England girl is "a pagan," unfamiliar with Calvinism. With Marcia Gaylord the moral history of the Howells heroine passes into its declension.

In her search for roots Marcia has turned to one of the uprooted, for in Ben Halleck, who enters the novel uttering the familiar refrain, "I belong nowhere; I'm at odds" (20:170), Howells unites the two types of the *déraciné* that figure previously in his work. Ben is a kind of combination of Staniford and Ford, a Europeanized Bostonian whose expatriation symbolizes the exhaustion of his New England village background, a rather tired angry-young-man, with his limp and his ironies a Ralph Touchett gone sour.[20] Halleck had known Hubbard when they were classmates at a small Down East denominational college, and the comparison between the two men suggested by this connection, by their failure to enter the ministry, and by their consideration of the law as an alternative career, and underlined by the similarity of their names (which Howells exploits later on in the working out of the plot), is heightened when Ben falls in love with Bartley's wife. The irony of Marcia's location of a model of goodness in a man who rightly thinks of himself as "an orthodox ruin" (20:170) given over to a "somewhat melancholy indifferentism" (21:174) is compounded by Ben's equally unjustified, equally sentimental elevation of Marcia to an ideal stature. Convinced after his first meeting with Mrs. Bartley Hubbard that he has rediscovered the original of a photograph he inscribed "My Lost Love," the cherished souvenir of a pretty schoolgirl he saw once "in the street of a little Down East town" (19:166), he soon exchanges his conventional fidelity to his village dreamgirl for a no less conventional devotion to a long-suffering wife, not however, without a certain strain: "When she came so proudly to show her baby to them all, it seemed to him like a mockery of his pity for her captivity to the love that profaned her. . . . He exacted of his ideal of her that she should not fall beneath the tragic dignity of her fate through any levity of her own" (23:196–97). Halleck's discomfort in adjusting his romantic image of an unspoiled country innocence to meet the prosaic conditions of his heroine's marriage and motherhood is representative of the painful response of many of the characters in *A Modern Instance* to the disparity between traditional ideals and an intractable contemporary reality.

As Bartley makes his way in Boston as an unscrupulous journalist of considerable talent, his rise to success crowds out his at best perfunctory commitment to the domestic drama of his supposedly uplifting relationship with Marcia, and the Hubbards move at an accelerating pace in a downward spiral, marked by the growing frequency, intensity, and duration of their quarrels. Bartley's first spree offers a characteristic example of the decadence of the moral tradition to which he and Marcia and Ben variously appeal in an attempt to cast the weakness of the Hubbard marriage in an edifying light. Halleck finds Hubbard collapsed on his doorstep, and escorts him home to his shocked and self-accusing wife. Ben, "as miserable as if the disgrace were his own" (25:220), is shaken when he observes in his next encounter with the Hubbards that Marcia "looked as if nothing unusual had happened at our last meeting." Has he spent his "melodramatic compassion" on a "magnanimous" woman or is she "obtuse"? Is she truly the picture of innocence abused as he would have it or only "playing a part"? Agonizing over his inability to reconcile Marcia's seeming unconcern with the image of her that haunts him, a "pathetic figure, with its sidelong, drooping head" "when she opened the door for her blackguard . . . that morning" (26:226–27), Ben is compelled one night to revisit the site of the Hubbards' troubled home:

> He lingered for a moment before the door where this vision [of pathetic beauty] had claimed his pity for anguish that no after serenity could repudiate. The silence in which the house was

wrapped was like another fold of the mystery which involved him. The night wind rose in a sudden gust, and made the neighboring lamp flare, and his shadow wavered across the pavement like the figure of a drunken man. This, and not that other, was the image which he saw. (26:230)

In the finely modulated conclusion of this passage, self-knowledge penetrates the defenses of Halleck's self-deception, the attractively high-minded construction of his love for another man's wife: "the figure of a drunken man," the image for Ben of the squalid, the sordid in the affair, is at once Bartley's and his own.

Like Halleck, Hubbard seeks to bolster his self-respect by cutting out figures from temperance-novel cardboard, pasting them over the unflattering reality of his conduct. In his specious moralizing his surrender to temptation becomes a vindication of his purity, his loss of control exemplory:

"And there's this consolation about it, if there isn't any other: that it wouldn't have happened now, if it had ever happened before." . . .

She had been listening intensely, exculpating him at every point, and now his innocence all flashed upon her. "I see! I see!" (26: 222–23)

As for Marcia, the ease with which she indulges the inverted morality of these trite histrionics, mistaking this premonition of disaster for a reassurance of Bartley's goodness, accounts for the complacent serenity which puzzled Halleck in her response to the episode.

The Hubbard marriage comes to an end only a year and a half after the drunken escapade when Bartley, in yet another quarrel with Marcia, simply refuses to make the effort to defend himself one more time against the jealous accusations of his wife. When Marcia, furious, walks out of the house for an hour, Bartley walks out for good. Unsustained by an allegiance to any code of conduct, Hubbard is the first to tire of the moral heroics which Marcia and Halleck, closer to puritanism even in drift and revolt, continue for a time to stage. The night of the break Marcia and her child take shelter at the Hallecks'; when Ben escorts her back home through the rain, as he had her husband on another memorable occasion, Marcia, weakening, throws herself upon his protection: "I left him— . . . Oh, come in with me! You are good, —and then I shall not be afraid!" Halleck, recoiling from the very abandon to

which he would all too willingly surrender, makes the response required by the code in which he no longer believes: "You must go in
alone! No man can be your refuge from your husband!" Howells suggests the hollowness and desperation of this painful gesture of self-
sacrifice in his account of Ben's flight from the scene of his temptation:
"He turned, and ran crookedly down the street, wavering from side to
side in his lameness, and flinging up his arms to save himself from falling as he ran, with a gesture that was like a wild and hopeless appeal"
(33:295).

Although it may well be that the loss of control which is Howells's
subject in the final section of *A Modern Instance* extends in part to his
presentation, as it does, for example, in Faulkner's *Intruder in the
Dust,* there is considerable justification for the shrill sound of raised
voices, the plethora of rhetoric, and the posturing which characterize
this section of the novel—frequently criticized as a falling-off from the
power of the earlier pages—in his theme of a failed spiritual tradition.
Howells, like Mrs. Stowe, was fully alive to the ironies of self-sacrifice,
and as his story moves toward its ending, he focuses on the morbid desire—so characteristic of the literature of New England tragedy—of
Ben, of Marcia, of Squire Gaylord, to immolate themselves on the
blunted ends of moribund ideals. Thus Marcia in the confusion following the wreck of her marriage turns feverishly to a cult of domestic
love in order to disguise the defeat of her womanhood from the world
and from herself. In her frantic pose as defender of the faith in hearth
and home, she seeks to conceal her fate as the deserted wife not so
much to save her pride but to protect her belief in Bartley's goodness:
"He must find me here, in our own house. . . . I can starve there and
freeze, and if he finds me dead in the house, none of them shall have
the right to blame him,—to say that he left me,—that he deserted his
little child! Oh! oh! oh! oh! What shall I do?" (34:304). Adopting the
fiction that Bartley has merely wandered off somewhere in a temporary
lapse of sanity, Marcia dwells for a time in a never-never land in which
her broken home becomes a temple of domestic fidelity and the husband who left her its patron saint, a fragile web of illusions raised to
the status of a religion, a precarious stay against hysteria and thoughts
of suicide: "She was beginning to canonize him" (35:312).

Two years after Bartley's desertion, Ben Halleck returns from a self-
imposed exile abroad, admitting the defeat of his conscience and ready
to declare his love to Mrs. Hubbard; Marcia, having given up all hope
of her husband's return, is ready to break off her lonely vigil in the

house the Hubbards failed to make a home and retreat to Equity. It is
precisely at this point, when Ben and Marcia have lost their appetite
for the moral sublime, that the hunger which nearly starved their capacity for feeling passes to Marcia's father. When the news arrives in
Boston that Hubbard has filed for divorce in Tecumseh, Indiana, on
the ground of "abandonment and gross neglect of duty" (37:322), it is
only Squire Gaylord's appeal to the very jealousy he knew too well had
been Marcia's undoing that prevails upon her to go west to fight the
suit lest Bartley win by default. Despite the lesson of his own marriage
to Mrs. Gaylord, the spiritual blank of all those years, the fanatical old
lawyer is determined not merely to vindicate his daughter's innocence
but to prove the existence of a moral design in the universe which
Bartley's crime, his failure to be suitably moved by Marcia's self-
sacrificing love, would deny: "I think I shall be able to convince Bartley Hubbard that there is a God in Israel yet!" (38:336). To rest such
a case on the goodness of Marcia Gaylord, this is puritanism in extre-
mis, a crisis of belief as pathetic and desperate as Dr. Boynton's attempt to found his hopes of the immortality of the soul on Egeria's
"gift."

The realities of Tecumseh belie the Squire's exalted conception of
his role at the trial as an angel of retribution appointed by Providence
to bring an arch-villain to the bar of divine judgment. The Indiana
town, "very much . . . like a New England village" but "more careless
and unscrupulous" (40:348), shows as in a glass what Equity has become. The stern messenger of a justice not impartial but possessed proclaims in an outburst of hate to an audience of tobacco-chewing loafers
the purity of a woman's love. When the Squire, following his grandilo-
quent defense of the innocent wife forsaken ("a woman waiting in
hunger and cold for his return" [40:354]), damns the wicked husband,
Bartley the perjurer, to "a felon's cell in a felon's garb" (40:355) be-
fitting the hell he is bound for, Marcia intervenes. Bartley Hubbard is,
after all, for better or for worse, only himself, for there had never been
enough soul in him to fit him for the parts in the drama of salvation—
saint or sinner—that Marcia and her father variously proposed. The
inner tendency of the handsome young man shows in Tecumseh as all
flesh: "It was not the fat on Bartley's ribs only that had increased; his
broad cheeks stood out and hung down with it, and his chin descended
by the three successive steps to his breast" (40:350). Marcia had never
quite understood the impulse that had brought her to Indiana ("Now
tell me again . . . why are we going" [39:343]), and when she with-

draws her support from her father's holy war, the last of the puritans, God's lonely advocate in Israel, suffers a stroke and collapses.

Reversing the well-established pattern of Howells's fables of courtship—and Mrs. Stowe's as well—the ending of *A Modern Instance* offers no optimistic prospect for the future; the mood is equally distant from, say, *The Lady of the Aroostook* and *The Minister's Wooing*. The movement of the final chapter leads the battered survivors of the action back into a past without youth, love, or faith, Marcia Gaylord to her mother's house, Ben Halleck to his father's church. The twin flames, domestic and religious, on the altars of New England have burned out. While Bartley follows the course of empire westward to a violent end in a shooting at Whited Sepulchre, Arizona (as a novelist's luck would have it), his wife retraces her steps to Equity, leading her broken father home to die. The "rich nature" of the Howells heroine has been "wasted, and turned back upon itself" (36:321), and when the townspeople decide that "Marcia was as queer as her mother" (41: 358), Howells reminds us that the redemptive possibilities of woman's love were played out already in Mrs. Gaylord's day. The link between the daughter and her mother encourages a larger view of the breakdown of the traditional nineteenth-century ideal of domestic womanhood in Marcia Gaylord, namely, that the origins of the tragedy of "the New Medea" (vii) lie not so much in her betrayal by a small-time Jason but in the flawed formation of her own character, in the spiritual exhaustion of her father and of the village culture which he represents.

In the symbolic conversion of Dr. Hopkins by Mary Scudder, Harriet Beecher Stowe had celebrated the redirection of Calvinist energy in a new dispensation of love; when that dispensation failed—as in *A Modern Instance*—it was perhaps a sign that the original energy itself had waned. This Howells suggests when Ben Halleck, closing his eyes, returns to Calvinism as "a city of refuge" from doubt and unbelief, becoming the minister of "a backwoods church down in Aroostook County" (41:359). A year later Halleck writes to Atherton, a voice from the wilderness appealing for advice on the morality of asking Bartley Hubbard's widow to be his wife: "There are times when I rebel against these tortures; when I feel a sanction for my love of her, an assurance from somewhere that it is right and good to love her; but then I sink again, for if I ask whence this assurance comes—I beseech you to tell me what you think. Has my offence been so great that nothing can atone for it?" (41:361). This tortured letter raises a ghost from the world of Stowe, the vision of a minister's wooing which shows here as the obsession of a classic case of morbid conscience of the sort Howells studied in Dr. Breen. Here, on this note of sickness, the novel ends. The love triangle of *The Minister's Wooing* reappears in *A Modern Instance* strangely altered, Marcia the less-than-saintly saintly girl, Bartley the incurably unregenerate boy next door, and Ben the unbelieving Calvinist divine. The changes in the casting are decisive, marking the greater distance of Howells from the New England ideals which both he and Mrs. Stowe admired in spite of so many damaging reservations, a distance grown at last too great to bridge with wishful fiction.[21]

V

If Marcia Gaylord is one of Howells's most interesting and fully realized heroines, Helen Harkness, the genteel girl whose story he told in *A Woman's Reason* the following year, is one of the least. He had been slow to finish this novel which he had begun as early as 1878, and the wornout contrivances introduced to accomplish a happy ending for this conventional story of romantic love are only the most obvious of the many signs of flagging inspiration in the narrative. By the end of *A Modern Instance* his study of the New England girl and of the village culture that had formed her was largely complete; her distinction as the repository of New England values was played out. The Howells heroine would never again occupy so large a place on her creator's stage as she had in the past. Already in *A Modern Instance* the story of the hero's success had challenged the supremacy of the fable of the heroine's love, and Howells, perhaps instinctively recognizing this shift, abandoned the original title, *The New Medea,* shortly before publication.[22] In any case, *The Rise of Silas Lapham* (1885) and *The Minister's Charge; or, The Apprenticeship of Lemuel Barker* (1887) would testify to the increasing dominance of the male figure in Howells's imagination. There were to be memorable heroines in the later novels of the decade, Imogene Graham, for example, of *Indian Summer* (1886), or Penelope Lapham, but it is fair to say that after *A Modern Instance* Howells never reverted to the early conception of his heroine as an ideal figure offering to the hero and to a changing community a source of strength, purpose, and permanence in a period of social upheaval. His young woman, he discovered, had too many problems of her own; she was too busy glorifying herself as a savior to devote much time to saving the hero.[23] Indeed in *April Hopes* (1888) Howells completely reversed the redemptive pattern of *The Lady of the Aroostook:* here the principal impediment to the hero's moral development resides in the heroine and her ideals.

Only ten years separate the publication of these two novels but in fact more than thirty years have elapsed in Howells's imagination. It is this heightened sense of the passage of time that accounts for the diminished stature of his heroines. When in 1885 Howells re-enters the world of "love's young dream," the world of *A Chance Acquaintance, A Foregone Conclusion,* and *The Lady of the Aroostook,* taking up once more the adventures of the American girl abroad, the season is *Indian Summer.* Imogene Graham is very much as young as Kitty Ellison, Florida Vervain, and Lydia Blood, but we behold her this time chiefly from the point of view of an older man, the middle-aged bachelor, Theodore Colville, who is himself the focal center of consciousness in the novel.

No exception to the earlier heroes who invariably regard the heroine as the incarnation of the ideal, Colville romanticizes Imogene as the epitome of youth. It is his consciousness of the lapse of years, however, that is to prove decisive in his relationship with the girl: Imogene's youth must by its very nature elude the aging Colville, for his own lies in some lost realm before the Civil War. His retrospective stance in the opening scene informs his thoughts and actions throughout the novel: revisiting Florence, the setting of his first love affair some twenty years before, he stands appropriately on the Ponte Vecchio, gazing into the Arno which becomes in his meditation a mirror of his past. His revery is presently interrupted by a chance encounter with an old acquaintance, charming Mrs. Bowen, the lovely Lina Ridgely of the earlier time. Observing her well-trained daughter, Effie, Colville conjures up a vision of a pre–Civil War model of girlhood, now vanished from the national scene:

> It amused him to see the child referring even this point of propriety to her mother, and his thoughts idled off to what Mrs. Bowen's own untrammelled girlhood must have been in her Western city. For her daughter there were to be no buggy rides or concerts or dances at the invitation of young men; no picnics, free and unchaperoned as the casing air; no sitting on the steps at dusk with callers who never dreamed of asking for her mother; no lingering at the gate with her youthful escort home from the ball—nothing of that wild, sweet liberty which once made American girlhood a long rapture. But would she be any the better for her privations,

for referring not only every point of conduct, but every thought and feeling, to her mother? He suppressed a sigh for the inevitable change, but rejoiced that his own youth had fallen in the earlier time. (2:15–16)

As he looks wistfully through little Effie Bowen, the jeune fille, Colville's longing for an innocence and freedom untamed by the hothouse conventions of the Continent and the convent evokes the Emersonian lustre of Kitty Ellison and Lydia Blood.

Given the marked shift in the nature of his heroines that had occurred since the salad days of the 1870s, it seems more than likely that the older Howells shared this nostalgia. Furthermore the affinity between Colville's dream and the Howells heroine of the previous decade suggests that a large share of the inspiration for the figure of the American girl who had seemed so new to James and other admirers was in fact derived from native sources reaching back to Emerson. The progress of his heroine from novel to novel, which had seemed to lead her backward in space and time from the openness of the West to the confinement of New England, from the freshness of the present to some bondage to the stale values of the past, had paralleled Howells's own movement from a pastoral vision of New England in the golden age —transplanted intact in Eriecreek and points west—to a sober study of that region in the age of iron. James had believed that the future of the Howells heroine lay in her "irritable moral consciousness," but Howells came to abandon his conviction that his remarkable girls, rescued in time by obliging young men, could escape into the freedom of a new setting, somehow miraculously endowed with all the strength of their village culture and none of its weakness. Accordingly when Colville would turn back the clock, making Imogene the medium of an impossible attempt to relive the past, Howells criticizes in the bachelor's idealization of the girl and his ridiculous posturing as a "Lost Youth" (9:107) the immaturity of a man old enough to know better, a criticism from which the characteristically youthful heroes of his earlier fiction—Staniford of *The Lady of the Aroostook* or Ford of *The Undiscovered Country*—were exempt. At the close of the novel, upon his recovery from his illness and his infatuation with Imogene, the only alternative left for Colville, determined as he is to maintain his loyalty to "the old national ideal of girlish liberty as wide as the continent, as fast as the Mississippi" (4:37), is to marry its survivor, Mrs. Bowen. Howells expresses the wisdom of this choice in his initial

description of the woman Lina Ridgely had become: "She was herself
in that moment of life when, to the middle-aged observer, at least, a
woman's looks have a charm which is wanting to her earlier bloom. By
that time her character has wrought itself more clearly out in her face,
and her heart and mind confront you more directly there. It is the
youth of her spirit which has come to the surface" (2:12).

One of the delicious ironies of the world of *Indian Summer* is that
Imogene Graham appears there out of season. Remembering as she
does only the end of the war, she is too young for Colville, while for
Howells she is not old enough to be, like Mrs. Bowen, truly young.
That is to say that Howells's criticism of the hero's idealization of the
heroine extends to the heroine's ideals as well. Kitty Ellison's self-
reliance was rooted in Howells's own idyllic conception of Eriecreek
in which the best of the moral tradition of New England was preserved, indeed rejuvenated. Kitty's Western home was a picture of domestic happiness presided over by her Uncle Jack in whom the spirit
of the Boston of Whittier, Lowell, and Garrison bravely burned. Imogene's Buffalo, on the other hand, is simply a blank, a city without a
moral history. She has ideals of course, for who ever heard of a Howells heroine without any, but they are secondhand, inspired by her
reading, as her diary reveals in its account of her would-be sublime
offering of her own youth to Colville in restitution for a disappointment in love he had suffered long ago:

> "*You*, Di, will understand how I was first fascinated with the idea
> of trying to atone to him here for all the wrong he had suffered.
> At first it was only the vaguest suggestion—something like what
> I had read in a poem or a novel—that had nothing to do with me
> personally, but it grew upon me more and more the more I saw
> of him, and felt the witchery of his light, indifferent manner,
> which I learned to see was tense with the anguish he had suffered.
> . . . It came upon me like a great flash of light at last, and as soon
> as this thought took possession of me, I felt my whole being ele-
> vated and purified by it, and I was enabled to put aside with con-
> tempt the selfish considerations that had occurred to me at first."
> (15:186–87)

Imogene's sentimentalization of suffering and self-sacrifice leads her as
it does many another young woman in the novels that follow, to be-
have not with the spontaneity that had contributed so much to the

grace of Kitty and Lydia but with unnatural constraint, inhibited by some flawed conception of her role, of her duty as a heroine. As Howells studies the dynamics of self-sacrifice his emphasis changes from fiction to fiction: in the case of Penelope Lapham, the notion of self-sacrifice is borrowed from literature; in the case of Alice Pasmer, it expresses her morbid temperament. But whatever the emphasis, the heroine and her conduct have lost much of their representative quality. The world-travelling American girl and especially her stay-at-home country cousin, the New England girl, continue then as standard performers in Howells's comedies of manners, joining the permanent repertory. Their perennial concern with a misguided ideal of self-sacrifice, however, no longer serves as the medium for the revaluation of the New England mind as it had in *Dr. Breen's Practice* and *A Modern Instance*; it has become once more the stuff for the contretemps of the conventional boy-girl romance.

Accompanying Howells's sense that the girl who embodies the national, or at least the regional, character is only a memory of the past if she ever existed at all is his conviction that the fable of her courtship has come to occupy too large a place in American fiction. Speaking of the typical sentimental masterpiece, *Tears, Idle Tears*—the title tells all—the Reverend Mr. Sewell observes in *The Rise of Silas Lapham:* "The whole business of love, and love-making and marrying, is painted by the novelists in a monstrous disproportion to the other relations of life. Love is very sweet, very pretty. . . . But it's the affair, commonly, of very young people, who have not yet character and experience enough to make them interesting" (14:198). Now Howells's own novels through *A Modern Instance* were built largely, some entirely, around the very fable of courtship that Sewell attacks. After *A Modern Instance* he would write two major novels in the remaining years of the decade, *Indian Summer* and *April Hopes*, in which courtship holds the center of the stage, as well as a third, *The Rise of Silas Lapham*, in which it figures as an extensively developed subplot. But his interests in the 1880s, in *The Rise of Silas Lapham*, *The Minister's Charge*, and *Annie Kilburn*, were to move away from a preoccupation with the spiritual code of New England in particular toward a more generalized concern with the obsolescence of the individual's traditional moral responsibility to his community in the complex society of the Gilded Age.

Never before *The Rise of Silas Lapham* is there so sharp a sense in Howells of the conventional aspects of courtship, satirized for exam-

ple in the justly celebrated episode in which Tom Corey, quite without "intentions," gallantly offers Irene Lapham not a flower but a
wood-shaving, or again in the scene that follows, in Penelope Lapham's
teasing comments on "the language of shavings" (9:122). It is one
thing when a pretty, giddy girl with a "vegetable" (2:27) innocence
like Irene loses her head over a handsome young man who means only
to be agreeable to her; it is another when a plain, shrewd young
woman like Penelope, gifted with the comic spirit of a realist, determines to model herself after the heroine of such a novel as *Tears, Idle
Tears*. What is it that compels a sensible girl, hitherto remarkable for
her satiric cast of mind which thrives on the exposure of affectation in
others, in herself, in the characters of the novels she reads, suddenly to
reject the handsome hero's declaration of love in favor of some melodramatic renunciation of her own on the ground that her sister and
her parents have assumed mistakenly that Corey was in love with
Irene? To the surprise of readers of Stowe and the early Howells it must
be said first of all that she behaves as she does not because she is a
New England girl, the sort of young woman in nineteenth-century fiction to whom self-sacrifice is second nature. Her conduct might be interpreted as a manifestation of the psychology of the plain girl that
she is. It is true that Howells has attributed to Penelope in the earlier
chapters a painful consciousness of her plainness in contrast to the
prettiness of Irene whom the family accordingly regards as its heroine,
casting her quite on its own initiative as the object of Corey's suit.
Building on this groundwork of her characterization and pursuing the
reading it suggests well beyond any further encouragement from Howells, Penelope's indulgence in sentimental novels would reflect her desire to become through identification with the heroines of fiction, the
pretty girl she isn't in real life. Such a girl would naturally leap at the
chance to act out the "pretty girl" role, self-sacrifice and all. This explanation, surely the most interesting one latent in the material, is not,
unfortunately, explored in any depth by Howells.

The only answer that Howells fully develops to account for Penelope's renunciation is, quite simply, that she has read too many sentimental novels. Why, given his growing impatience with the conventional in literature, should he revert to the infancy of the novel, raising
in his portrait of Penelope the eighteenth-century spectre of the innocent young woman undone by the reading of fiction? Searching for a
remedy for her case, the girl herself seems to grasp the fact that she is
suffering from a literary disease: "I've read of cases where a girl gives

up the man that loves her so as to make some other girl happy that the man doesn't love. That might be done" (17:230). In fact, so caught up is she in the sentimental sublime that she can approach the sensible resolution of her dilemma at the end of the novel, acceptance of the lover she loves, only by performing her renunciation a second time. In the light of the Reverend Mr. Sewell's remarks on the exaggerated significance given to "the whole business of love, and love-making and marrying" in contemporary fiction, the importance of Penelope's self-fabricated crisis for the minister and surely for Howells is her false sense of its importance. Yet Sewell and Howells proceed to treat her problem with the highest seriousness. Sewell condemns the sentimental gospel of self-sacrifice preached by *Tears, Idle Tears* and practiced by Penelope Lapham as "nothing but psychical suicide, . . . as wholly immoral as the spectacle of a man falling upon his sword" (14:198). As for Howells, that he should have the Laphams in their trouble turn instinctively to Sewell for counsel and should present their interview with the minister in a solemn tone charged with pulpit piety, calling them "these poor outcasts of sorrow" (18:240), reveals the extent to which the fable of courtship, secularized and hence emasculated though it is, has continued to operate in a moral context with disastrous consequences. Curiously then the fable of courtship in the novel that Penelope Lapham proposes to reenact in real life is at once trivial and of the gravest significance. An examination of this double view provides the clue to the puzzling contradictions of Howells's characterization of his heroine.

Sewell makes two points about courtship in fiction: first, novelists paint courtship in "monstrous disproportion to the other relations of life," and second, they inculcate a pernicious ideal of self-sacrifice. His first charge states that the matter of such novels is not important in life and is to be discredited for its failure to reflect reality accurately, while his second charge is based on the assumption that novels, whatever their subject matter, have the power to shape reality, that they can make the unimportant important in life as well as in literature. In other words, when speaking of the relationship between literature and life, Howells is distinguishing implicitly between reality and fiction as he would like them to be, and as they are. Given these views, when Howells takes a young woman like Penelope who is at once a keen observer of the life around her and an avid reader of fiction, especially of the sentimental variety, he is faced with a problem in characterization of considerable difficulty. Grant the truth of Sewell's position. Then

Penelope, who shares the realistic thrust of her creator's temperament, will be fully aware that the renunciation in *Tears, Idle Tears* is "rather forced" (16:217), yet, if novels exert the influence Sewell and Howells attribute to them, she will be vulnerable to such a story, crying over a "silly" and even "wicked" tale which she proceeds presently to adopt as her own. So exclusively in fact does Howells trace the springs of his heroine's conduct to a literary source that the two phases of her character, the comic and the sentimental, are easily identified with the kinds of literature then in conflict in the contemporary scene, the insurgent realism that Howells himself championed against the residual romanticism surviving from the pre–Civil War generation.

In any case, Penelope's renunciation has nothing to do with any legacy of Calvinism. She is a New England girl but she is not endowed with the characteristic consciousness Howells associates heretofore with the region. Moving from a conviction of the importance of New England values in such heroines as Lydia Blood and Dr. Breen to a study of the dangers attending their decline in Marcia Gaylord, he considers here an ordinary young woman for whom these values, or their lack, have ceased to matter. Her mistaken self-sacrifice is purely extraneous to the world in which she moves, a generation removed from the village origins of Howells's earlier New England girls. It shows as a gratuitous imposition on an otherwise normal and healthy personality: "When I want to do what I oughtn't so much that it seems as if doing what I didn't want to do *must* be doing what I ought!" (24:304–5). When finally in *April Hopes* Howells returns once more to a New England girl with a puritan temperament, the first since Dr. Breen, he regards her not as a representative but as an idiosyncratic figure, an exception, a sport. Alice Pasmer is only Alice Pasmer; she is never made to enter that larger realm of significance in which the Howells heroine of an earlier time might become the Westward Star of Empire or the New Medea.

A curious amalgam of the beautiful Europeanized American girl educated by an ambitious mother to make a brilliant match abroad and the "serious," "pensive" New England girl she is through heredity, Alice Pasmer would seem to offer her creator an opportunity of special significance, uniting as she does the two principal varieties of young women that had been his study for fifteen years. To the hero, Dan Mavering, she is every inch the heroine, glowing with the requisite spiritual credentials, as he points out to his good-natured, skeptical confidant in the following effusion:

She's so *good*, Boardman! Well, *I* give it up! She's religious. . . .
And she's all the more intoxicating when she's serious. . . . There's
a kind of look comes into her eyes—kind of absence, rapture, don't
you know—when she's serious, that brings your heart right into
your mouth. . . . She has a soul full of—of—you know what,
Boardman. (22:143)

When Alice, her head turned with visions of renunciation, reviews
with Dan the catechism of their approaching union on the day after
their engagement, she elicits in the unregenerate young man a confession of faith in which he dedicates himself to the worship of her redemptive love in the best nineteenth-century fashion:

[Alice]: "I wish our life to begin with others, and not with ourselves. If we're intrusted with so much happiness, doesn't it mean
that we're to do good with it—to give it to others as if it were
money?"
   The nobleness of this thought stirred Dan greatly; his eyes wandered back to the silken rope [the belt of her dress]; but now it
seemed to him an emblem of voluntary suffering and self-sacrifice,
like a devotee's hempen girdle. He perceived that the love of this
angelic girl would elevate him and hallow his whole life if he
would let it. (27:183)

Given the correctness with which the lovers chant the familiar responses, chapter and verse, of the conventional gospel of courtship and
its litany of self-sacrifice, it is all the more remarkable that the heroine's
ideals and the hero's worship of them do not command respect in this
novel, that Alice Pasmer should prove to be the least attractive of all
of Howells's young women to date. Further, Howells attributes the
girl's failings to the very "irritable moral consciousness" that James, in
his review of *A Foregone Conclusion* years before, had posited as the
peculiar distinction of the Howells heroine. In the midst of his praise
of Florida Vervain as "a singularly original conception," James had
warned that she "just escapes being disagreeable, to be fascinating."
No longer disposed to save his heroine from herself, Howells allows
Alice Pasmer to remain "positively unsympathetic."
   Once the superficial nature of the resemblance between Alice and
her predecessors is recognized, however, Howells's harsh treatment of
her seems hardly surprising. Unlike her sisters of the 1870s, she is frustrated by the pointlessness of her existence. She has, to be sure, vague

thoughts of becoming a nun, that Catholic role always coveted by Protestant women whose religion failed to provide them with a similar emblem of woman's highest calling. No one need wonder then that a sentimental fiction, preaching the gospel of woman's self-sacrificing love, continued to find an audience in America for more than a hundred years, transferring as it did the aura of the nun to the Christian matron, canonizing its tearful saints with wedding bells as wives and mothers in the Protestant home. (See for example the conclusion of *The Minister's Wooing*, 42:410.) When Alice Pasmer embraces courtship and marriage with the fervor of a convert, she would seem to align herself with many another heroine in this great tradition. Yet, taking nothing for granted, she feels compelled to supply her adopted religion of heart and hearth with a moral content which it would not apparently otherwise possess. Here for example in one of the lulls of Dan's infatuation, he observes Alice with amused incredulity as she pants for the sublime, straining to breathe new life into the old formulas; determined to transform their courtship into an edifying spectacle for the world, Alice becomes incoherent and Dan responds with a "sputtering laugh":

> "How in the world does it concern others whether we are devoted or not, whether we're harmonious and two-souls-with-but-a-single-thought, and all that?" He could not help being light about it.
>
> "*How?*" Alice repeated. "Won't it give them an idea of what—what—of how much—how truly—if we care for each other—how people *ought* to care? We don't do it for ourselves. That would be selfish and disgusting. We do it because it's something that we owe to the idea of being engaged—of having devoted our lives to each other, and would show—would teach—" (40:262)

Nowhere are the absurdities of nineteenth-century conventions of courtship, the rhetorical excesses, the spiritual pretensions, more fully satirized than in these pages.

Intoxicated with the nobility of self-sacrifice, especially the sacrifice of happiness in love as the ultimate virtue, Alice finds that she cannot feed her appetite for heroics on rhetoric alone, and so she proceeds first to reject her lover before she accepts him, then to break her engagement and to make it again, then to unmake it and make it once more before she is through. To be engaged to Dan, or not to be, the question is largely academic for Alice, since the yield in the self-flattering pangs of renunciation is the same. The girl tastes her highest moral pleasure in pain and suffering, and even the young man learns to glory in her morbid if not masochistic plans for his, for their mutual, "perfectiona- tion" (49:330): "She said that they ought each to find out what was the most distasteful thing which they could mutually require, and then do it; she asked him to try to think what she most hated, and let her do that for him; as for her, she only asked to ask nothing of him. Maver- ing could not worship enough this nobility of soul in her" (39:256). The wages of such virtue is unhappiness for Dan, and as for the neur- asthenic Alice, such promptings make her sick. Towards the end of her self-made ordeal she takes on, with her "thin cheeks and lack-lustre eyes" (52:349), the familiar attributes of the victim of renunciation in the annals of New England literature. Unlike the more fortunate lov- ers in *The Lady of the Aroostook* and *The Undiscovered Country*, Alice and Dan play upon each other's weaknesses. From the point of view of Indian summer, the forecast of their April hopes as they marry at the last is not the consummation of "love's young dream" that a younger Howells dreamed. The final sentences read: "If he had been different she would not have asked him to be frank and open; if she had been different, he might have been frank and open. This was the beginning of their married life" (52:354). There was no need to say any more.

What causes Alice Pasmer to pervert the very sacrament of court- ship and marriage that Harriet Beecher Stowe had celebrated in the heroine of *The Minister's Wooing* some thirty years before? Isn't she every bit as much the New England girl as Mary Scudder, say, or Grace Breen? Curiously Howells encourages an identification of her moral consciousness as distinctly New England in character through- out the novel, yet he offers nothing of his heroine's family or her re- gional background to support it. In Alice's debased ideals there is no trace of the residual Calvinism that lent a certain dignity to the strenu- ous exercises of Dr. Breen's sterile conscience. Insofar as her second- hand ideals can be traced to any specific origin, her inspiration proves to be literary rather than religious: she borrows the phrasing for one of her renunciations from George Eliot's *Romola* (43:275). Howells does not subject her motivation for her renunciations to any detailed scrutiny. Were such reasons lacking, or was he determined to height- en the impression of the arbitrary, the perverse, in the girl's conduct?

Howells constantly reminds his reader that something in any case is clearly the matter with Alice Pasmer. Even the admiration of her staunchest supporters, the "Aliceolaters" (13:87), is scarcely a healthy

phenomenon. These "ladies of her cult" (13:74), a group of "elderly
and middle-aged Boston women" (11:67) who lavish all the gush at
their command upon the truth, beauty, and goodness of the young
woman's selfless soul, resemble the febrile feminists who worshiped
Grace Breen in *Dr. Breen's Practice* and Verena Tarrant in James's
The Bostonians. Theirs is the collective voice of the Feminine Oversoul that sought to extend its parlor tyranny upon the literary expression of the age of James and Howells; theirs is the collective heart,
surely, that thrilled to the trash of *Tears, Idle Tears*. Having treated
his heroine to a generous dose of such compromising adulation, Howells proceeds to approach her from increasingly hostile points of view,
notably that of Mrs. Brinkley. Her observation of Alice and her renunciations persuades her that "the ascetic impulse is the most purely
selfish impulse in human nature . . . though it might have had for the
girl the last sublimity of self-sacrifice" (51:342).

Whether they read her distinction as ennobling superiority or debilitating eccentricity, Alice Pasmer's friends and critics agree that she is
not like other girls. With what justification then can Howells, midway-
on, offer the following account for one of Alice's sacrifices? "Girlhood
is often a turmoil of wild impulses, ignorant exaltations, mistaken
ideals, which really represent no intelligent purpose, and come from
disordered nerves, ill-advised reading, and the erroneous perspective
of inexperience" (38:246). This wise summation of the limitations of
girlhood helps to explain the novelist's mature decision to remove such
girls in the future from the center of his stage, yet Howells has not prepared for an acceptance of his heroine as a young woman like any
other. Quite the contrary, in fact: she is not; and the reader has been
liberally primed to concur in the verdict of Miss Julia Anderson—
whom Howells tags as "the ordinary slender make of American girlhood" (11:67)—when she speaks in her incredible New York accent of
the peculiarity of her friend, the Boston Alice: "I think she was very
moybid. She was like ever so many New England giyls that I've met.
They seem to want some excuse for suffering, and they must suffer
even if it's through somebody else. I don't know; they're romantic,
New England giyls are; they have too many ideals" (49:330). What
is the force of this identification of Alice as a New England girl? It
is finally not a major part of Howells's conception of his heroine, and
his treatment of it is indecisive.[24] If he is content to appraise Alice's
New England malady as some hereditary queerness, an oddity running

in the blood, he is at the same time willing to suggest that it is highly contagious, easily transferred from the native to the outsider. Thus Miss Anderson is fully capable of a morbid renunciation of her own in the chapter immediately following her criticism of such behavior in Alice. Stripped of her larger significance, her spiritual history, the New England girl has entered a new phase of her literary existence, becoming a comic stereotype, a moral fashion to dress up the self-importance of an otherwise ordinary American girl from Gotham.

Annie Kilburn (1889), a story of homecoming, represents a departure for Howells. To begin with, he relegates to the background the fable of courtship that provided the resolution of the destiny of the single woman in his fiction heretofore, for he takes up Annie Kilburn at the age of thirty-one, "when the flattering promises of youth have grown vague and few" (5:36). She is his first full-length portrait of the older woman as central character. Although he gives in this last major novel of the decade the fullest rendering of a heroine's point of view and the most complete anatomy of a New England village setting since the days of *Dr. Breen's Practice* and *A Modern Instance*, his approach to the matter of New England has changed fundamentally: no longer his primary subject, it serves instead as an illustration of his own troubled sense of the breakdown of any comprehensible moral relationship between the individual and society.

Returning home to Hatboro', Massachusetts, after eleven years of residence abroad, Annie Kilburn confidently expects that her ancestral New England village will provide her with the opportunity for moral action that she is seeking: "I feel that I must try to be of some use in the world—try to do some good—and in Hatboro' I think I shall know how" (1:4). She is to learn, however, and painfully, that her unexamined notion of dispensing "good works, as it were, in a basket" (5: 47) has little to do with the economic, let alone spiritual, reality of Hatboro', and she swiftly exhausts the tired possibilities of genteel moral experience, the complacency of the Lady Bountiful and the sentimentality of the Sister of Mercy. Hers is the dispiriting knowledge that the impulse to do good might be and often was easily confused with the desire to feel better. "To set up for a saint" (18:202) in a New England village—as Ralph Putney, voice and type of Yankee failure in the novel, terms Annie's dream of success—proves to be no easy undertaking when that village has become "a sprawling American town" (11:117). Unhaunted by Calvinist ghosts, Hatboro' is filled instead with the hum of the mills. In Annie Kilburn's enlarged version of life's complex design at the end of the novel there could be no place for the simple village order memorialized by Mrs. Stowe:

> A perception of the unity of all things under the sun flashed and faded upon her, as such glimpses do. Of her high intentions, nothing had resulted. An inexorable centrifugality had thrown her off at every point where she tried to cling. Nothing of what was established and regulated had desired her intervention; a few accidents and irregularities had alone accepted it. But now she felt that nothing withal had been lost; a magnitude, a serenity, a tolerance, intimated itself in the universal frame of things, where her failure, her recreancy, her folly, seemed for the moment to come into true perspective, and to show venial and unimportant, to be limited to itself, and to be even good in its effect of humbling her to patience with all imperfection and shortcoming, even her own. She was aware of the cessation of a struggle that has never since renewed itself with the old intensity; her wishes, her propensities, ceased in that degree to represent evil in conflict with the portion of good in her; they seemed so mixed and interwoven with the good that they could no longer be antagonised; for the moment they seemed in their way even wiser and better, and ever after to be the nature out of which good as well as evil might come. (30:320)

In such a mixed, more nearly modern universe the purely ideal figure, the heroic moral agent, was not merely obsolescent but by definition irrelevant. The day of the Howells heroine was over.

Chapter 5

HENRY JAMES AND THE
NEW ENGLAND CONSCIOUSNESS:
RODERICK HUDSON,
THE EUROPEANS, HAWTHORNE

HENRY JAMES joined Stowe, Hawthorne, and Howells in recognizing
in the heroines of his fiction in the 1870s and 1880s the presence of a
moral consciousness that he came to identify with New England, and
like them he adopted a fable of courtship as the medium for his study
of his heroine and her ideals. All four of these nineteenth-century
American writers explicitly acknowledged the Calvinism of the seventeenth and eighteenth centuries as the foundation of New England
spiritual life, and it is not surprising that the differences among their
respective versions of the New England character should be in large
part a direct function of the distance between each writer and the
moral tradition which was their common concern. Mrs. Stowe's novels
proposed—what those of Howells and James could not—that the
nineteenth-century wanderer could find a home in the surviving puritan ethos of an earlier time through the wooing of a village heroine.
Hawthorne's New England girls, on the other hand, presented at best
only a momentary stay against confusion. Howells traced the decline
and fall of Mrs. Stowe's puritan heritage. Only for a brief moment did
anything like the pristine glory of her vision of New England life shed
its radiance upon his heroine, and then indeed only to illuminate the
girl's definitive departure from the village world which had formed her.
Dry rot had set into the country, and only her removal could preserve
her pastoral virtues intact. Following the precarious tribute of *The
Lady of the Aroostook,* Howells proceeded to anatomize the break-up
of the village culture in a trio of novels—*The Undiscovered Country,
Dr. Breen's Practice,* and *A Modern Instance*—in which the heroine as
savior was supplanted by the heroine as victim. The theology of Dr.
Hopkins which instilled the sublimity of self-sacrifice in Mary Scudder's
soul ossified in Grace Breen's brittle and anachronistic conscience. In
his more truly modern instance of the daughter of the puritans, Howells
rendered Marcia Gaylord's soul as an empty, churchless shell, still
stubbornly echoing with the rhetoric of a recently vanished faith. In the

later novels of the 80s—in *The Rise of Silas Lapham*, for example, or
April Hopes—he extended his inquiry into the moral tradition of New
England beyond the point of its extinction as religious belief into its
dubious afterlife in the contemporary literature of sentimentalism,
which continued to decorate the irrelevant corpse of Calvinism with its
wreaths of artificial flowers.

Turning now to James, bearing in mind the ostensible similarity of
his literary ambitions to Howells's, their almost simultaneous discovery of the same American material, one might expect an analogous unfolding of his preoccupation with New England in his fiction. Yet this
is not the case. Howells, once launched in his New England trio,
pushed his scrutiny of his young women's capacity for significant moral
action rapidly to the end, so rapidly indeed that in the later novels of
the 80s a new urban or urbanized cast of characters and locales pre-
empted his stage, throwing into eclipse the village which had been
the precinct of his heroines' power. How is it then that the latter-day
history of the New England mind proved so much richer á vein for
James to work than it had for Howells? Merely to say that James saw
more, probed deeper than Howells, just as Isabel Archer is fundamentally, absolutely more interesting than Marcia Gaylord, is to speak
perhaps the truth, and also to beg the question.

To begin with, Howells's picture of the extinction of the puritan
strain in the New England character refers almost exclusively to its
origin, omitting any detailed consideration of the intermediate passages of its history with which he was, nevertheless, authoritatively
familiar. The principal omission in his reckoning, and one that was to
make for so much of the difference between him and James in their
conception of the matter of New England, is the account outstanding
of the age of Emerson and Hawthorne. What it comes to finally is this:
although he praised James for his "exquisite" treatment of "the culture foible" in his *Hawthorne*, Howells himself never entered into the
problem of self-culture, the pivotal issue in James's inquiry into the
puritan spirit in *The Portrait of a Lady* and *The Bostonians*, the primary manifestation of the New England mind before the Civil War,
indeed the basis of the literature of the American Renaissance. To
measure the diminished drama of the inner life in New England, the
drastic shrinkage of the moral sublime, Howells set the idle tears of
Penelope Lapham against Edwards on the will, passing over as it were
the Sturm und Drang of Margaret Fuller's *Memoirs*, as fitting a symbol as any of the missing link between them.

Further, Howells's conception of the way in which puritanism survived within the New England character is narrowly defined, highly
localized: its agency is invariably the morbid conscience, a malignant
tumor poisoning an otherwise healthy spirit. For James it is the imagination that is the source of the ancestral disease. This shift in the
diagnosis is decisive, extending as it does the consideration of this
moral heritage into a distinctly aesthetic sphere and focusing upon a
faculty so capacious in his view that it becomes virtually inseparable
from the totality of consciousness. Embracing a more radical because
more inclusive version of the dynamics of intellectual history, James
entertained the possibility that the spiritual life of the puritans might
endure in their descendants not simply as a set of familiar ideas, the
abstract distillation of a once living mental reality, but more immediately as a series of characteristic states of mind. The distinction between Howells and James on the moral drives of the New England
character is the distinction between conscience and consciousness. The
New Englandness of the Howells heroine resides above all in her conscience, the repository of orthodox values, a kind of doctrinal morgue
in which some ideal version of the act of moral choice, once felt experience, now reduced to statement, to precept, is stored away to instruct
her in the immutable laws of duty, that single word which speaks to
the daughter of the puritans as the iron voice of hereditary moral
claims. For the James heroine it is her imagination that confers upon
her a New England identity; it is a way of seeing, an inherited mode
of vision preceding moral choice, upon which moral choice is founded,
that makes her what she is.

It may be that the quantitative difference between James's and Howells's inquiry into the New England past—that for James there was
more to the moral history of the region, or more at any rate that survived for his heroines to reckon with than Howells believed—reflects a
qualitative difference in their perceptions as well. It may be that James,
the arch expatriate, somehow managed to acquire a depth of experience of the New England character never achieved by Howells, the
Ohioan transplanted to Boston soil. Take James at his word nevertheless, that the Howells heroine broke new ground for American literature; grant even that James took her in some part as the prototype for
his own young women; we may still wonder how he arrived at the creation of a heroine who moves in *The Portrait of a Lady* and *The Bostonians* in a complex, richly ambiguous, moral and aesthetic realm for
which there is no parallel in the career of her counterpart in Howells.

Study of James's production in the late 1870s, of his tales of courtship and his biography of Hawthorne, suggests a double answer: that his heroine evolved in part from his conception of the hero in these stories, an expatriate observer of the national scene, often an artist who resembles to a degree James himself, and in part from his vision of the representative genius of the age of Emerson and Hawthorne. His young woman became to this extent an amalgam of pre–Civil War and post–Civil War types of the American artist, a projection at once of personal and national intellectual history, Roderick Hudson and Rowland Mallet fused in a single personality. I have dealt with the first of these answers in my commentary on "Daisy Miller" and "An International Episode." In this chapter I should like to treat the second, tracing in *Roderick Hudson, The Europeans*, and *Hawthorne* James's growing interest in Hawthorne's world, in the heroines of his romances and the consciousness and moral vision he associated with them.[1]

It will become clear that I take the Americanness of the fiction of Henry James, perennially a subject of dispute, to reside in certain qualities of moral consciousness, especially evident in his portraits of young women. Following F. O. Matthiessen, who collected the leading examples of James's fiction that feature America as their locale,[2] Peter Buitenhuis concentrates on "the fiction that is set entirely in the United States" for his recent study of *The Grasping Imagination: The American Writings of Henry James.* In limiting in this way the boundaries of his account of James's search for artistic "schemata" adequate to render the burden of his experience of American life, Buitenhuis emphasizes setting at the expense of consciousness. Thus he finds *The Portrait of a Lady* a "non-American" fiction, "not germane" to the theme of his undertaking. He accords to *The Bostonians,* on the other hand, a central place in his discussion of James's American canon, for here James applied a "technique of literary impressionism" that enabled him to write about American life "more realistically than he had ever been able to do before."[3] James himself provides a salutary corrective to distinctions of this sort when he writes to Thomas Sargeant Perry from Cambridge, Massachusetts, on September 20, 1867: "We [American writers] must of course have something of our own—something distinctive and homogenous—and I take it that we shall find it in our moral consciousness, our unprecedented spiritual lightness and vigour."[4] Arguing that James's view of the American consciousness was derived from his father's idiosyncratic version of Swedenborgianism, Quentin Anderson proceeds in *The American Henry James* to divide

James's work into those narratives which are "strongly colored by the American moral passion" and those which "show hardly a trace of it."[5] Defined in this way, *The Bostonians* stands on the periphery of James's American preoccupations for Anderson, while *The Portrait of a Lady* is central to them. Anderson's provocative thesis, however, has never been widely accepted, probably beause Henry James himself said virtually nothing to encourage the kind of elaborate allegorical readings that Anderson proposes.

James did, however, write deliberately, openly, and extensively in his fiction and in his criticism about "the American moral passion," its ideals, its limitations, its principal incarnations, most notably in his *Hawthorne* (curiously neglected by Buitenhuis) and in both *The Portrait of a Lady* and *The Bostonians*. James traced this moral passion to its antecedents in the emancipated puritan consciousness of New England in the age of Hawthorne, Emerson, and Margaret Fuller. Alfred Kazin's view of the distinctively American quality of James comes closest to my own. In a fine essay, entitled "The First and the Last: New England in the Novelist's Imagination," placing James in the company of Hawthorne, Stowe, Jewett, Howells, and others, Kazin writes that "it is important to remember that for Henry James, the American landscape was usually a New England landscape, and the American character in its virtuousness a New England character."[6] That is to say that in writing a novel about New England, as he did in *The Bostonians*, James could pursue by symbolic extension of his chosen material an inquiry into the American character at large; at the same time, even when dealing with so archetypally American a figure as the heroine of *The Portrait of a Lady*, he could and did refer to a strain of moral idealism specifically New England in derivation. The sureness of James's use of an American spiritual geography is confirmed in his choice of the point of departure for Isabel Archer's moral pilgrimage. "The Emersonian philosophy," as James called it in his *Hawthorne*, might still survive in all its Adamic freshness in the imagination of a lonely young woman in an old house in Albany after the Civil War; the Arcadian glory and the dream, however, were gone from Boston, where transcendentalism had descended to decadent exercises in Olive Chancellor's "strenuous" Charles Street parlor. I should emphasize that in placing Isabel Archer in the context of a discussion of New England heroines in nineteenth-century American fiction I do not mean to confuse her with the likes of Hawthorne's Hilda, Stowe's Mary Scudder, Howells's Grace Breen, or James's own Olive Chancellor. If she is not to be recognized as a regional type like those I have mentioned, she is nevertheless endowed with a moral consciousness and set of values that are distinctly New England in character. James himself, after all, as we shall see, identified so exotic and seemingly foreign a heroine as Zenobia with Hawthorne's insight into the hidden inner life of New England.

I

In *Roderick Hudson* (1875), later referred to by James as his "first attempt at a novel,"[7] he made a considerable experiment with the romantic convention of paired heroines which Hawthorne had exploited in his longer fictions. In his characterization of Mary Garland and Christina Light he indicated at once both the limitations and the possibilities of Hawthorne's example as a precedent for the forms in which the play of his own imagination was to seek expression. Mary Garland is James's earliest and his only extensive portrait of the New England girl of the Stowe-Hawthorne construction. Always seated in a chair sewing, Mary, like Phoebe Pyncheon, is consistently associated with the village virtues of hearth and home. In her domestic activity this daughter of a family of clergymen from West Nazareth, Massachusetts, expresses her ardent belief in a gospel of works. Mary's inconclusive performance as a redemptive agent, however, in her relationships with Roderick Hudson and with Rowland Mallet, clearly separates her from the heroines of *The Minister's Wooing* and *The House of the Seven Gables*.

As a type of the romantic artist, the mercurial Roderick Hudson looks to Mary Garland as a source of stability and moral purpose for his career as a sculptor. Like Holgrave and Kenyon, his counterparts in Hawthorne's romances, he associates the New England girl with the law and order of village life, and he loves her because she is "a stern moralist," "with rigid virtue in her person."[8] When Hudson separates from his mentor Rowland Mallet in Switzerland to pursue for the first time a wholly independent course of action, even the conservative Rowland endorses Mary's love as an emblem of the health of nature protecting his manic friend from the corruption of civilization: "He [Roderick] was among forests and glaciers, leaning on the pure bosom of nature. And then—and then—was it not in itself a guarantee against folly to be engaged to Mary Garland?" (3:117). Later, however, when Mary is summoned to Europe as a last resort to check the downward spiral of Roderick's flagging inspiration, she remains an almost wholly passive witness of his self-destruction. As for Mary's influence on Hudson's friend Mallet, the possibilities of this relationship are never actualized, for Rowland's love remains largely unconfessed. Although his early meeting with her in the New England woods evokes the pastoral hopes of courtship that were the staple of Howells's fiction in these years, the promise of the sober and dedicated young woman as a solution to the future of the rootless dilettante is never fulfilled.

In his portrait of Mary Garland, James gave a definitive revaluation of the type of the New England girl established by Hawthorne and Mrs. Stowe. Mary's character does not lend itself to either the romantic convention of courtship or that evolved by the rising generation of realists, for she is clearly unsuccessful in the role of a nature-maiden who disciplines the lawless genius (Roderick), and the possibility that the love of this native girl might achieve the repatriation of the fugitive aesthete (Rowland) never materializes. All of the major characters in *Roderick Hudson*, Rowland, Roderick, and Christina Light, look to Mary Garland as a source of moral inspiration, but her spiritual resources prove somehow inadequate to meet the urgency of their demands. Even Mallet concedes, "She was evidently a girl of great personal force, but she lacked pliancy" (2:50). James himself remarks an "oddity" in the fact that Mallet could continue to find Mary "intolerably interesting" (2:65), "that so deep an impression should have been made by so lightly-pressed an instrument" (8:284).

Mary Garland is in fact a stiff and rather inexpressive figure, and there is nothing to confirm Rowland Mallet's assertion that she is "a person of great capacity" (3:79). James virtually acknowledges the weakness of his heroine and even makes a half-hearted attempt to rehabilitate this obsolescent model of puritan morality by putting her through a crash course in self-culture midway on. His brief but suggestive account of the impact of Europe upon her in one of the rare passages in which he treats her extensively (chapter 9, entitled "Mary Garland") is analogous in intention to Hawthorne's exposure of the inflexible Hilda to a knowledge of evil: if her cloistered virtue were only humanized, the New England girl might be transformed into an effective moral agent.

Mary Garland has the seriousness, the distinctly intellectual cast of mind, that is so typical of James's New England heroines as a group, without at the same time possessing that restless imagination which is their most distinguishing characteristic. Like Bessie Alden of "An International Episode," she is rather bookish, and she shares with Gertrude Wentworth of *The Europeans* what James thought of as a distinctly puritan conflict between moral duty and aesthetic pleasure in her approach to living. Most of all, in her self-conscious introspection, of which James shows almost nothing, she resembles Isabel Archer: "She wished to know just where she was going—what she would gain or lose" (9:312). Mary lacks, however, the adventurous, expansive consciousness of these later heroines, and she hesitates, as they do not, before the spectacle of the "old and complex civilization" (9:305) that she encounters on the Continent. She has a sense of the change, the break with the past, that the experience of Europe requires of her, and she confesses to Mallet, "It seems to me very frightful to develop" (9: 304). Convinced that she is destined to remain "a young woman from the country" (9:306), she believes that the strenuous pursuit of "culture" upon which Mallet has encouraged her to embark will involve a fundamental shift away from her belief in "'nature' and nature's innocent laws" (9:312), the vital principle of her New World idealism. Mallet's view of the probable impact upon Mary of a program of self-culture is distinctly ambivalent. At one moment he champions this formative process, holding that an expansive, aesthetic experience of Europe will transform the girl, the "stubborn" product of a narrow village world, into a model of superior womanhood; at another he admits that he would like to send Mary straight back to the United States: "America has made you thus far; let America finish you!" (9:316). Mallet's shifting attitude toward the growth of Mary's character, which resembles Staniford's mixed view of the lady of the *Aroostook*, indicates that James may well have shared Howells's reservations concerning the future of the New England country girl in the cosmopolitan world which lay beyond her village home. The growth of Mary's consciousness might lead to a greater capacity for moral action, but it would necessarily challenge the very moral tradition that had conferred upon the girl her value as a symbol of order in an uncertain world.

In *Roderick Hudson* Christina Light represents the alternative to Mary Garland, and here again James is exploring a moral terrain with Hawthorne as his guide: if his conception of Mary seems largely derived from the New England girls of Hawthorne's romances, in his creation of Christina, a character of remarkable vitality, he drew substantial inspiration from Hawthorne's dark heroines, especially Zenobia. Rowland Mallet's impression of Christina Light, which suggests the nature of her difference from Mary Garland, might be applied with equal justice to Zenobia to distinguish her from Priscilla: "It is altogether a very singular type of young lady. . . . It may be a charm, but it is certainly not the orthodox charm of marriageable maidenhood, the charm of shrinking innocence and soft docility. Our American girls are accused of being more knowing than any others, and Miss Light is nominally an American. But it has taken twenty years of Europe to make her what she is" (5:170). Christina resembles Zenobia not only in her sensuous beauty, with her mixed blood and her abundance of dark hair, but in her lively intelligence as well, her wit, her satirical bent, and her impatience with conventions. For all her generous capacities, she is unable to locate a source of moral purpose either in herself or in her surroundings. Her moral isolation is not illuminated by a belief such as Miriam's in a Fortunate Fall or by a vision such as Hester's of the redemptive power of a woman's love. She speaks candidly of her spiritual discontent: "I am tired to death of myself; I would give all I possess to get out of myself; but somehow, at the end, I find myself so vastly more interesting than nine tenths of the people I meet" (5: 187). Like Zenobia and Margaret Fuller, Christina dreams of transcending her egotism through recognition in another of a great self, a genius who would possess an Olympian creativity, and she believes in the redemptive value that such a recognition would contain: "I should know a great character when I saw it, and I should delight in it with a generosity which would do something toward the remission of my sins" (7:235). In Mary Garland James chronicled the failure of New England goodness to save others; his complementary heroine, Christina, is clearly in need of salvation herself. Christina's disappointment in Hudson, when he fails to measure up to her expectations of heroic grandeur, repeats Zenobia's disillusionment with Hollingsworth.

If James envisaged a strenuous pursuit of self-culture as the prerequisite for the development—never in fact completed—of innocent Mary Garland, he presents as the drama of sophisticated Christina Light her abortive attempt to acquire a moral education, to school herself in the Stowe ideal of a New England renunciation. Again *The Marble Faun*, where Miriam, the sinner, is made an instrument of Donatello's regeneration, provides the model. Christina initially appreciates moral action only for its value as theatrical gesture. When Rowland Mallet appeals to her to break with Roderick Hudson, she wants to know if in so doing, she will have accomplished "something magnanimous, heroic, sublime—something with a fine name like that?" (7:

262). Of her subsequent performance Mallet remarks, "She's an actress, she couldn't forego doing the thing dramatically, and it was the dramatic touch that made it fatal" (8:270). Christina herself observes, with not a little cynicism, that she had experienced none of the "ineffable joys" (8:280) of a Saint Theresa as a result of her conduct. She does nevertheless perform what the fastidious Mallet comes to accept as a genuinely disinterested moral action, repudiating in her rupture with the Prince not only the worldly opportunities offered by his wealth but the corruption of her mother's materialistic influence as well. Significantly, Christina claims as the source of her inspiration the moral example that she discovers in the "beautiful character" (10:346) of Mary Garland; she has sought to appropriate the idealism of the New England girl and make it her own. Mallet, moved by his sense of the "painful effort and tension of wing" required by Christina's "ethereal flight" (10:373), yields her at last the precious tribute of his belief in the sincerity of her conduct. The courageous young woman is no match for her tyrannical mother, however, and she is coerced into accepting the hand of the Prince. In his final meeting with Christina shortly after her marriage, Mallet views her as an almost tragic figure, darkened by the experience of her "sacrificed ideal" (12:449). Her aspirations have been utterly defeated after her single brief flight.

Christina Light can no more remake herself in the image of Mary Garland than Mary can acquire the force of Christina; ethics and energy remain disjoined in *Roderick Hudson*. Christina's renunciations first and last betray a theatrical approach to moral action which recalls the "Arcadian affectation" that qualified the significance of Zenobia's defiant suicide. The conception of her act, however, originates in a play of consciousness which James was to establish as the vital principle of his distinguished series of New England heroines, including Gertrude Wentworth, Bessie Alden, Olive Chancellor, and especially Isabel Archer. Rowland Mallet traces the ambiguity of Christina's conduct, the confusion between aesthetic gesture and the moral intention which it reflects, to the primacy of her imagination:

> She herself was evidently the foremost dupe of her inventions. She had a fictitious history in which she believed much more fondly than in her real one, and an infinite capacity for extemporized reminiscence adapted to the mood of the hour. She liked to idealize herself, to take interesting and picturesque attitudes to her own imagination; and the vivacity and spontaneity of her charac-

ter gave her, really, a starting-point in experience; so that the many-colored flowers of fiction which blossomed in her talk were not so much perversions, as sympathetic exaggerations, of fact. And Rowland felt that whatever she said of herself might have been, under the imagined circumstances; impulse was there, audacity, the restless, questioning temperament. (7:251–52)

In her admiration for the act of renunciation, in the restless activity of her imagination with its dreams of heroic action and its capacity for self-deception, Christina Light, destined to the imprisonment of a loveless marriage, anticipates the heroine of *The Portrait of a Lady*. Here the resemblance ends, however, for Isabel Archer still honors in defeat her betrayed ideals, to which she pays tribute in her final renunciation, while Christina, her scruples abandoned, tells Mallet that she means to cultivate pleasure: "You remember I told you that I was, in part, the world's and the devil's. Now they have taken me all" (12:450).

By the end of *Roderick Hudson* (1875) James had reached something of an impasse in his experimentation with Hawthorne's convention of paired heroines, much as Hawthorne himself had at the conclusion of *The Marble Faun*.[9] His Mary Garland, for all her goodness, lacked a capacity for action; in Christina Light he portrayed a personality of great energy yet unprovided with an ideal of moral conduct. James, like Hawthorne and Howells, was concerned with the failure of the New England girl as an agent of redemption. His innovation in approaching this figure in the years following *Roderick Hudson* was to relocate within her character the consciousness necessary to achieve self-knowledge that Hawthorne had attributed exclusively to his dark heroines. The movement of Isabel Archer's career in *The Portrait of a Lady* (1881) from a world of innocence to a world of experience and mature womanhood presents the most appropriate symbol of James's salutary transformation of Hawthorne's played-out convention. Contributing an added, a complicating, dimension to James's investigation of the moral problems of his young women were the unmistakable misgivings, even anxiety, that their presence seems to have generated in his imagination. His study of his heroines in this early novel revealed that they were not merely ineffectual as moral agents, but that they were perhaps even harmful in their impact upon the men who fell in love with them. In his preface to *Roderick Hudson* James was to criticize his casting of Christina Light in "the character of well-nigh sole agent" of Roderick's catastrophe as a violation of his "sense of truth and proportion."[10] She is presented in fact as a kind of *belle dame sans merci* who lures the young sculptor to his destruction. The presence of danger in a woman's love seems to extend to the beneficent Mary Garland as well. In his confession to Hudson of his love for Mary, Rowland Mallet makes his first positive assertion of himself as a strong personality with a capacity for action. Mallet's declaration of independence from his alter ego is immediately followed by Hudson's death. This sequence of events suggests the presence of a defensive strategy adopted by James's imagination in evaluating the redemptive mission of his heroines. An artist preoccupied with his sense of himself as "other" felt compelled to present involvement with women as somehow potentially dangerous, even fatal in its consequences.

II

By the time of *The Europeans* James was ready to work more boldly with the legacy of Hawthorne's romances, his heroines, and the New England values associated with them than he had in *Roderick Hudson*. This time, in his analysis of his pair of heroines, Gertrude Wentworth and the Baroness Eugenia Münster, he explored the possibilities for self-expression offered by the venerable moral tradition of New England to representative models of native and foreign womanhood. Arriving at a double rejection of New England as a favorable climate for the life of the imagination, he forced both the woman of Continental sophistication and the innocent New England girl to withdraw in search of greater freedom in Europe. Eugenia returns alone to take up her past, while Gertrude sets out with her lover to discover her future. This exile of his heroines in this preliminary study of the matter of New England is then both an ending and a beginning: if Eugenia's defeat marks James's failure once and for all to root the dark heroine in American soil, in Gertrude he invented a viable American alternative to the ineffectual morality of Mary Garland and the aimless energy of Christina Light. Gertrude is James's first extensive portrait of an American heroine in her native setting. A young woman with precedents, with the promise of a novelistic substance that was to be fulfilled in *The Portrait of a Lady* and *The Bostonians*, she is James's first attempt at an answer to the "flatness" of Daisy Miller and her sisters, the "unprecedented creatures" of his cycle of international fables.

In Eugenia's story James tested the power of an imported model of womanhood to adapt itself to a distinctly native, even intensely local theater of action—to win, in short, a permanent place in American fiction. Facing the potential dissolution of her morganatic marriage to a German prince, she returns to America with her brother, Felix Young, to try her fortune in the New World through a visit to her relatives, the Wentworths, in the environs of Boston. In this milieu, where Continental manners are unknown, the Baroness intends precisely to exploit her superiority as a woman to achieve a position of financial security and social eminence. Her sardonic intelligence, her restless imagination, and her generous sexuality, her abundance of dark hair and her exotic ornaments—these attributes recall the dark heroine of romantic fiction and her familiar points of strength, and Eugenia regards her success in America accordingly as a foregone conclusion. Graciously received by the Wentworths, she swiftly scans the field and singles out Robert Acton, the Wentworths' cousin, as her target. Training her shrewd appraiser's eye on the character of this wealthy, travelled, not quite worldly though altogether eligible bachelor, she reads his simplicity as tractable by and large to her purposes. Although he is easily captured by the spell of the Baroness, the Bostonian is troubled by the anomaly of her position, "this being known as a repudiated wife."[11] The cavalier allowance that Eugenia makes for Acton's scruples, however, epitomizes her unexamined belief that she is in full command of her situation in New England: "One's impression of his honesty was almost like carrying a bunch of flowers; the perfume was most agreeable, but they were occasionally an inconvenience" (6:133).

Eugenia has in fact grossly miscalculated the place of the moral life in New England and the power of the women in which it is incarnated. She learns to her surprise and displeasure that moral authority in the Acton household, as in many another in the pages of Harriet Beecher Stowe, resides in the figures of sister and mother. In an early meeting with Acton's sister, the Baroness recognizes little Lizzie as the type of the American girl; to her Continental sense of social forms, Lizzie, however pretty and self-possessed, is discredited by her general lack of manners. The girl, however, a kind of cross between Daisy Miller and Phoebe Pyncheon, impresses Eugenia as a kind of "household fairy" (6:131) with a power of her own, who proves to be a formidable adversary not to be dismissed with the scorn of a Zenobia for her want of mature womanhood: "It was a source of irritation to the Baroness that in this country it should seem to matter whether a little girl were a tri-

fle less or a trifle more of a nonentity; for Eugenia had hitherto been
conscious of no moral pressure as regards the appreciation of diminu-
tive virgins" (6:132).

Eugenia's perception of the latent tension between opposing conceptions of womanhood in her unsatisfactory encounter with Lizzie Acton
is presently confirmed when she is ushered by Robert Acton into the
moral center of his family to meet his mother, a gentle, dying invalid
with a taste for Emerson's essays and "a voice that had never expressed
any human passions" (11:231). Entering this desiccated realm of the
New England spirit, the fashionable intruder receives the first important check to her "European" strategy of manner as she delivers a well-
turned compliment to Mrs. Acton: "Your son . . . has talked to me immensely of you. Oh, he talks of you as you would like . . . as such a
son *must* talk of such a mother!" Robert Acton's response to her gesture is quite the reverse of what Eugenia had intended: "He never
talked of this still maternal presence. . . . The Baroness turned her
smile toward him, and she instantly felt that she had been observed to
be fibbing. She had struck a false note. But who were these people to
whom such fibbing was not pleasing?" (6:134–35). Suddenly on the
defensive, Eugenia breaks off her performance and brings her visit to
a close.

This character, designed for the European novel of manners, has
strayed in this symbolic encounter into the wholly unfamiliar and in-
hospitable ground of the moral life, the world of Hawthorne, Emerson,
and Mrs. Stowe. Deceived by the material richness of the setting, Eugenia is not prepared to deal with the unworldly Mrs. Acton and the
stubborn strain of transcendental idealism radiated by her muted presence. She begins to realize that Robert Acton's honesty counts for something more than a disposable stage property, that his New England
conscience is not to be lightly manipulated by her art. Eugenia's
unfortunate experience in this scene clearly foreshadows her final judgment, and James's, concerning the possibility of transplanting an imported model of womanhood and manners in American life and literature: "The conditions of action on this provincial continent were not
favorable to really superior women. The elder world was, after all,
their natural field" (12:279). The only alternative available to the Baroness is to return once more to Europe. Excluded from a position in
the New World, Hawthorne's Zenobia had drowned herself, and Eugenia, too, finds herself sinking in the striking image which James
chooses to express her sense of failure: "Now she felt the annoyance

of a rather wearied swimmer who, on nearing shore, to land, finds a smooth straight wall of rock when he had counted upon a clean firm beach. Her power, in the American air, seemed to have lost its prehensile attributes; the smooth wall of rock was insurmountable" (10:207–8). Behind the apparent blankness of the American scene stood a monolithic moral consciousness that resisted domination from abroad. Latent in the volume of Emerson's essays on Mrs. Acton's chair is Eugenia's wall of rock, and in his *Hawthorne* of the following year Henry James would detail all that a reading of Emerson might signify for a descendant of the puritans.

As Eugenia's star is sinking, Gertrude Wentworth's is rising. In Gertrude, breaking free of the Hawthornian mold, James ushered in a distinctly fresh avatar of the New England girl in American fiction, a young woman with both the moral seriousness of the fair heroine and the vitality of the dark heroine together with the indomitable independence of a Daisy Miller. Imagine a rebellious Phoebe Pyncheon, a churchless Mary Scudder, an imaginative Mary Garland, and it is immediately clear that there is no single prototype for Gertrude Wentworth in the pages of Hawthorne, Stowe, or James himself. James's description of Howells's Florida Vervain as a "delicate, nervous, emancipated young woman . . . equipped with a lovely face and an irritable moral consciousness,"[12] comes closest to defining the novelty of Gertrude Wentworth. In *A Foregone Conclusion* (1875), however, Howells had been content to allow the heroine's moral consciousness to stand as a given, while James began to trace its antecedents in *The Europeans* to the puritan heritage of the New England mind.

Gertrude, who shares with Eugenia the center of the stage in *The Europeans*, would seem to be the natural flower of the American soil, possessing as her birthright that fortune which the older woman sought in vain to achieve. The New England girl first appears as a solitary figure strolling in an idyllic pastoral setting redolent of purity and prosperity. Alice C. Crozier has enlarged my sense of the resonance of this scene, suggesting to me that James has captured in it truly archetypal qualities of the New England character, just as Mrs. Stowe did in her evocation of the world of Mary Scudder. Quoting Emerson's tribute to "that old religion which, in the childhood of most of us, still dwelt like a sabbath morning in the country of New England, teaching privation, self-denial and sorrow," Crozier writes, "Here not only the religion of self-denial but also the lovely metaphor of the sabbath morning seems to reproduce, with Emerson's brilliant brevity, the whole

impression of *The Minister's Wooing*."[13] James presents his heroine as
the simple, conventional type predicated by such a landscape, "a young
lady of some two or three and twenty years of age . . . walking bare-
headed in a garden, of a Sunday morning in spring-time," only to reach
beyond this proposition immediately for a characterization of greater
depth. He announces that his "innocent Sabbath-breaker"—Gertrude
is not going to church—is not "especially pretty"; of her eyes he says,
"they had the singularity of seeming at once dull and restless—differ-
ing herein, as you see, fatally from the ideal 'fine eyes,' which we always imagine to be both brilliant and tranquil" (2:23–24). He seeks to
define his unconventional young woman precisely through her difference from the ideal simplicity of her environment. The initial picture
of the innocent girl in the garden, a recurrent image in the iconography
of the James heroine, is presently succeeded by a more suggestive,
compelling picture of an unquiet young woman moving alone through
a deserted house. James describes Gertrude's restless spirit and her
longing for heroic action in words that look forward to Isabel Archer,
alone in the house at Albany: "It always seemed to her that she must
do something particular—that she must honor the occasion; and while
she roamed about, wondering what she could do, the occasion usually
came to an end" (2:32–33). When Gertrude presently takes up a book,
the resemblance to the heroine of *The Portrait of a Lady* is even more
striking.

Although James distinguishes Gertrude from the almost mythic simplicity of her surroundings and creates a possibility for a more complex drama of character development, he never fully exploits this opportunity, adopting instead the equally simple resolution of a fairy tale
for the problem of her destiny. After losing herself in a love story from
The Arabian Nights, the girl looks up to discover "a beautiful young
man [who] was making her a very low bow—a magnificent bow, such
as she had never seen before" (2:33). Gertrude takes the young man,
who proves to be her "European" cousin, Felix Young, for the prince
of her tale come to life, a phantasy benevolently fulfilled in the dénouement when Felix does in fact marry her and carry her off to Europe to live happily ever after.

If James decided to execute the potentially ambitious characterization of Gertrude Wentworth on a rather modest scale, it must be remembered that James planned *The Europeans* as "a very joyous little
romance,"[14] "a much slighter and shorter affair"[15] than *The Portrait of
a Lady*, upon which he proposed to stake his reputation. Describing

his conception of the narrative in a letter to Howells in 1877, he outlined the plot of a light and irresponsible comedy:

> I shall probably develop an idea that I have, about a genial, charming youth of a Bohemianish father, who comes back from foreign parts into the midst of a mouldering and ascetic old Puritan family of his kindred ([word illegible] imaginary locality in New England 1830), and by his gayety and sweet audacity smooths out their rugosities, heals their dyspepsia and dissipates their troubles. *All* the women fall in love with him (and he with them—his amatory powers are boundless;) but even for a happy ending he can't marry them all. But he marries the prettiest, and from a romantic quality of Christian charity, produces a picturesque imbroglio (for the sake of the picturesque I shall play havoc with the New England background of 1830!) under cover of which the other maidens pair off with the swains who have hitherto been starved out: after which the beneficent cousin departs for Bohemia (with his bride, oh yes!) in a vaporous rosy cloud, to scatter new benefactions over man—and especially, womankind!—(Pray don't mention this stuff to any one. It would be meant, roughly speaking, as the picture of the conversion of a dusty, dreary domestic circle to epicureanism.)[16]

Such a deliberately conventional story hardly suggests that James will develop the character of his heroine in any significant fashion; it is nevertheless James's novel treatment of the primary convention of his courtship fable that encourages the possibility of such an interest, for the inevitable process of conversion is to work the salvation here not of the idle expatriate hero but of a hopelessly virtuous set of native heroines. When, following the completion of "Daisy Miller," James wrote *The Europeans*, he retained the pattern of the earlier tale but reversed it: just as he used Winterbourne's discovery of Daisy in a garden in Vevey to set in motion his revelation of the young man's consciousness, so Gertrude's discovery of Felix in a garden in New England precipitates the drama of her inner life.

James speaks of his account of Gertrude's character and her "struggles" toward self-expression as "no small part of the purpose" (4:67–68) of *The Europeans*, and her story as he defines it turns upon the assertion or the suppression of the activity of her imagination. The imaginative Gertrude, alone of the Wentworth circle, responds to the opportunity for "European" experience offered by her cousins as a pleasure; her conscience-ridden mentors, her father, her sister Charlotte, and her suitor, Mr. Brand, react to it as "an extension of duty, of the exercise of the more recondite virtues" (4:67). The conservative Charlotte reflects the family consensus in her view that her sister's imagination is at the same time her most distinctive and her most dangerous attribute and that its enthusiasm in this instance ought to be checked. To the unimaginative, Calvinist outlook of her family, the plain, inexperienced young woman, different as she is from her exotic foreign cousin, Eugenia, is like her an eccentric and disturbing individual. Felix Young takes quite the opposing view of Gertrude, and he champions the emancipation of her imagination from the moral restraints of puritanism. He pictures the girl as a *belle au bois dormant,* whom he is to awaken into a wholly uninhibited, aesthetic appreciation of life. The narrative argues that the formation of her character can only be achieved through the opportunity for self-development offered by a life abroad, for "the angular conditions of New England life" (9: 192) prove no more accommodating as a field of action for Gertrude than for Eugenia. Reversing the pattern of Holgrave's union with Phoebe, James manipulates the relationship between the artist and the New England girl to achieve her freedom: Felix admires, paints, woos, and wins Gertrude with the greatest ease. The moral of this irreverent tale is that the New England girl must be saved from the morals of New England.

James had warned Howells that he would "play havoc with the New England background of 1830," and he kept his word. In this comic work he genially set aside the implications of the hereditary set of limitations that he uncovered in Gertrude's consciousness, limitations which determined the tragic destinies of Isabel Archer and Olive Chancellor. He did not, however, in dealing with the origins of Gertrude's consciousness, settle for an easy, unexamined identification of the girl as a novel national type on the order of Daisy Miller. Instead, for the first time, he locates the springs of her actions in a specific American background. James approaches Gertrude on the threshold of her career and presents the portrait of the New England girl of the generation before the Civil War, *prior* to her departure from her native setting, still surrounded, like any heroine of Mrs. Stowe, by an influential family circle. Later in this same year, in Bessie Alden of "An International Episode," he would portray the New England girl at a more advanced stage of self-development, the sole representative of the puritan world, a survival from an older America, moving virtually alone in alien, international settings. James linked Bessie's idealism to a Boston background off-stage; in *The Europeans* he presented for a firsthand view the physical and moral landscape of the region that has made Gertrude Wentworth what she is. James's New England girl turns from Sabbath-worship to *The Arabian Nights* because Calvinism no longer commands the energy of her restless imagination.

Gertrude's thirst for worldly experience is largely a reaction against the puritan rigor of her education. Having fallen under the spell of the attractive Felix, she is understandably impatient with the persistent attentions of her high-minded suitor, Mr. Brand. The Unitarian minister, with the blessing of the girl's father and sister, construes his courtship as a didactic process devoted to the formation of her character; to the restive girl the stiff young man symbolizes "an immense body of half-obliterated obligations" (5:110) which she is eager to forget. His version of romantic discourse as moral discipline, the familar pattern of affairs of the heart in the novels of Mrs. Stowe, fails to please the girl. Gertrude herself, however, is hardly a creature of passions. Her own capacity for feeling, like Bessie Alden's, Isabel Archer's, and many another Jamesian young woman's, is shown to be disturbingly limited, as James observes in the memorable aftermath of a trying scene between the minister and the New England girl: "There was something a little hard about Gertrude; and she never wept again" (5:113). Ironically, the girl's spirited rejection of Mr. Brand's plea for "the great questions of life" in favor of spontaneous self-expression—which sounds not a little like Grace Breen's repudiation of her mother's religion of duty—is fully as sontentious and conventional as any pronouncement delivered by the young man: "Why shouldn't I be frivolous, if I want? One has a right to be frivolous, if it's one's nature. No, I don't care for the great questions. I care for pleasure—for amusement. Perhaps I am fond of wicked things; it is very possible!" (8:165–66).

As an alternative to the orthodox instruction of Mr. Brand, Gertrude turns in pursuit of her bookish dreams of emancipation to Felix, the genial Bohemian; she throws off one apprenticeship, however, only to submit to another. Even an imaginative New England girl, if she is truly a daughter of the puritans, requires a formal program for the art of living: "To 'enjoy,' . . . to take life—not painfully, must one do something wrong? . . . What ought one to do? . . . To give parties, to go to the theatre, to read novels, to keep late hours?" (5:104–5). The artist urges an approach to experience as an "opportunity," an instinctive indulgence, an aesthetic pleasure, while Gertrude, in spite of her self-conscious rejection of her native "discipline," seeks to enter his world with all the seriousness and deliberation of her indelible New England formation.

For all her rebellious assertions of an emancipated self-expression and originality, Gertrude Wentworth is, like Olive Chancellor, an incorrigible New Englander with an inveterate compulsion to provide the license of her imagination with the sanction of higher laws.[17] The full extent of Gertrude's generous capacity for self-deception can be measured in her response to Felix's self-regarding scheme for the disposal of the troublesome Mr. Brand in a match with Charlotte Wentworth:

> "It seems as if it would make me happy," said Gertrude.
> "To get rid of Mr. Brand, eh? To recover your liberty?"
> Gertrude walked on. "To see my sister married to so good a man."
> Felix gave his light laugh. "You always put things on those grounds; you will never say anything for yourself. You are all so afraid, here, of being selfish." (7:161)

The girl's translation of Felix's proposition into the disinterested moral vocabulary of her New England heritage inevitably results in a loss of the spontaneity and frankness necessary to the ideal of self-culture that she pursues.

All of the characters, including Gertrude herself, may well agree that she is original, but James has revealed nonetheless that her "peculiarity" is in fact limited by certain hereditary characteristics of the New England mind. Gertrude, for all her difference, shares in the obliquity of motive and the oppressive sense of duty that govern the conduct of the rest of her family, particularly Charlotte and Mr. Brand. In *The Europeans* James makes a comedy of this characteristic of New England behavior which Mrs. Stowe, Howells, and he himself took so seriously elsewhere; he presents his characters here as a gallery of types. The reader remembers Charlotte Wentworth, "in her small, still way . . . an heroic sister" (5:99), as a quiet domestic figure, "sitting by a lamp, embroidering a slipper," "flanked on either side by an old steel engraving of one of Raphael's Madonnas" (11:245). "Poor" Charlotte nurses a secret love for her sister's fiancé, Mr. Brand. Although the girl submits to the inexorable duty of renunciation in the tradition of Mrs. Stowe's Mary Scudder, James's version of her trouble of the heart is lightly amusing: "It was not cheerful work, at the best, to keep giving small hammer-taps to the coffin in which one had laid away, for burial, the poor little unacknowledged offspring of one's own misbehaving heart" (12:254). As for the pompous Unitarian minister, James remarks that "he looked, as the phrase is, as good as gold" (2:29). With some prompting from Felix, the unimaginative young man perceives at last that his future lies with the prosaic Charlotte. Assured of solace for his wounded pride, he makes a "sublime" gesture of self-sacrifice, offering to unite Felix and Gertrude in his "ministerial capacity" (12: 268). Gertrude observes perceptively, "He wanted to be magnanimous; he wanted to have a fine moral pleasure. . . . It is better for him than if I had listened to him" (12:270–71). The passages portraying Charlotte and Mr. Brand read almost like a parody of *The Minister's Wooing*.

Supporting the bright satire of New England life in *The Europeans* is James's solid conviction of the determining impact of its Calvinist heritage upon the consciousness of its people There *is* something hard about Gertrude Wentworth, something perverse in the behavior of Charlotte and Mr. Brand, something cold and deathlike in the narrow, conscience-ridden Mr. Wentworth (James speaks, with irony, of his "spiritual mechanism" [3:52]). These are the qualities that find their climax in the figure of Olive Chancellor. In the environs of Boston, Felix Young believed that he had discovered a "primitive," "patriarchal" style of life which reflected "the *ton* of the golden age" (3:47). If he could describe the Wentworths as "a collection of angels" (3:45) living in a prelapsarian paradise, he was nevertheless puzzled by the presence of a pervasive shadow darkening the inner life of his American cousins: "They are sober; they are even severe. They are of a pensive cast; they take things hard. I think there is something the matter with them; they have some melancholy memory or some depressing expectation" (3:48). Latent in the symbolic picture of the Wentworths in *The Europeans* were the outlines of the most important passage of American intellectual history that James was ever to explore. He traced the pattern of these outlines in his book on Hawthorne in the following year, and in so doing he laid the foundations of the two great achievements of this American phase of his career, *The Portrait of a Lady* and *The Bostonians*. His revaluation of the New England past occasioned by his analysis of Hawthorne led at once to the recognition of an enduring and peculiarly American strain of moral values and to the affirmation of a continuous tradition in American literature as well.

III

In his remarkable essay on "The Hawthorne Aspect" of Henry James, T. S. Eliot defined James's American identity in terms of a specifically New England background associated with a cluster of villages in the neighborhood of Boston:

> When we say that James is "American," we must mean that this "flavor" of his, and also more exactly definable qualities, are more or less diffused throughout the vast continent rather than anywhere else; but we cannot mean that this flavor and these qualities have found literary expression throughout the nation . . . The point is that James is positively a continuator of the New England genius; that there is a New England genius, which has discovered itself only in a very small number of people in the middle of the nineteenth century . . . I mean whatever we associate with certain purlieus of Boston, with Concord, Salem, and Cambridge, Mass.: notably Emerson, Thoreau, Hawthorne, and Lowell.[18]

James, in his turn, had introduced his *Hawthorne* (1879) in a similar fashion, stressing the dual character of the writer as both an American and a New Englander, as at once the most eminent representative type of the American artist and at the same time an "intensely and vividly local" personality (1:429). More important, James further substantiates Eliot's portrait of the artist as New Englander in his assertion of the impact of the village world upon the formation of Hawthorne. In his opening remarks he observes that "Hawthorne's career . . . was passed for the most part in a small and homogeneous society, in a provincial, rural community" (1:427). In fact, James argues that the narrow confines of the New England village were to determine the limits of Hawthorne's experience throughout his life, including his residence abroad, as in this picture of him on the eve of his departure for Europe in 1853:

> His fifty years had been spent, for much the larger part, in small American towns—Salem, the Boston of forty years ago, Concord, Lenox, West Newton—and he had led exclusively what one may call a village life. This is evident, not at all directly and superficially, but by implication and between the lines, in his desultory history of his foreign years. In others words, and to call things by their names, he was exquisitely and consistently provincial. (6:538)

The picture of this village life which James presents in his *Hawthorne* provides a crucial document for the identification of the nature and sources of the consciousness of Isabel Archer and Olive Chancellor. Besides the brief, invaluably suggestive chapters which open *The Portrait of a Lady,* and the bright surfaces of *The Europeans* and the early portion of *Roderick Hudson,* James never left a detailed fictional account of the environment that produced his remarkable New England heroines. This village picture is important because James made it so. His commentators from his own day to this have been captured by the rhetoric of his well-known enumeration of the "negative aspects," that is, the absences, of the American scene. A few critics scruple to set this passage in its context. They point out that James not only dramatizes the power of a European angle of vision to diminish the substance of New World materials, but that he also designates the residue of this process of attrition as the great American "joke" (2:460). To be more exact, James devotes roughly half of the *Hawthorne* volume to a careful description of what remains of American life after the Continental subtraction has been performed. In fact, underlining the critical interdependence of character and setting, he claims that a knowledge of Hawthorne's New England is pivotal to an understanding of his art:

> Half of the interest that he possesses for an American reader with any turn for analysis must reside in his latent New England savor; and I think it no more than just to say that whatever entertainment he may yield to those who know him at a distance, it is an almost indispensable condition of properly appreciating him to have received a personal impression of the manners, the morals, indeed of the very climate, of the great region of which the remarkable city of Boston is the metropolis. (1:429)

This "impression" James seeks to supply through his descriptions of the series of small towns with which Hawthorne had at one time or another some connection—Salem, Raymond, Brunswick, West Newton, Lenox, Concord, and "the Boston of forty years ago."

James presents the New England consciousness before the Civil War as emerging from two centuries of Calvinist discipline to seek release for its reserves of mental energy in the creative activity of the imagination and the earnest drive toward self-culture. These are the directions in which the inner lives of Isabel Archer and Olive Chancellor were to move. James recreates each of these two manifestations of the puritan consciousness of the period in a symbolic picture of a community and its representative figure, the first with Hawthorne at Salem and the second with Emerson and the transcendentalist colony at Brook Farm. Before considering these two pictures in greater detail it is important to observe James's sense of both the difficulty of such an undertaking and of the resources that he could draw on to meet it. He clearly understood that the problem which he had set for himself centered in the act of consciousness, and he believed that in defining it he had to reckon with the fact of the Civil War: "One may say that the Civil War marks an era in the history of the American mind. It introduced into the national consciousness a certain sense of proportion and relation, of the world being a more complicated place than it had hitherto seemed, the future more treacherous, success more difficult" (5:536). In his effort to reach beyond the gap created by the war and to reestablish the vital line of continuity between himself and Hawthorne, whom he characterizes as "the last of the old-fashioned Americans" (6:549) and "the last specimen of the more primitive type of men of lettters" (6:550), James possessed an invaluable advantage in his personal experience of New England life. He figured himself in the role of "the initiated mind" (3:479,480). In *Hawthorne,* which originally appeared in the English Men of Letters series, he constantly indicates an awareness of his English audience, referring repeatedly to an American point of view as the "indispensable condition" for a penetration beneath the blankness of the American scene: "An American reads between the lines" (2:459). The value that James places upon native experience corroborates his view of the inadequacy of the expatriate observer in so many of his fables of the American girl.

In his portrait of Hawthorne at Salem, James identifies the artist as exclusively a man of imagination. He explicitly rejects "the general impression" that Hawthorne was "a somber and sinister figure," and more specifically he takes issue with the view that the New England writer was "*Un Romancier Pessimiste*" (2:446–47), a gloomy, brooding intellectual, offered by M. Emile Montégut in the *Revue des Deux Mondes* in 1860: "the development of Hawthorne's mind was not towards sadness; and I should be inclined to go still further, and say that his mind proper—his mind in so far as it was a repository of opinions and articles of faith—had no development that it is of especial importance to look into. What had a development was his imagination" (2: 448). This distinction is stressed at a time when the heroines of James's fiction—Bessie Alden, Gertrude Wentworth, Isabel Archer—are presented as particularly remarkable for the restless activity of their imaginations.

It is the "play" of Hawthorne's imagination, "always entertaining itself" (2:448), that engages James's attention, for his conception of the artist accords a primary role to pleasure: "I say he must have proposed to himself to enjoy, simply because he proposed to be an artist, and because this enters inevitably into the artist's scheme. . . . He proposes to give pleasure, and to give it he must first get it" (2:449). The requirements of the imagination, however, as Gertrude Wentworth and her cousin Eugenia so painfully learned, were not to be easily satisfied by the resources of "the large dry village picture" (2:448) of Salem which James reconstructs. The New England village might be "respectable, prosperous, democratic," but the novelist of manners could complain of a paucity of the historical and social detail necessary to create the desired "depth of tone" (1:438). He argues that to Hawthorne's contemporaries the very idea of aesthetic experience was itself unfamiliar and lay beyond the received Calvinist formulations of the inner life. "I imagine there was no appreciable group of people in New England at that time proposing to itself to enjoy life; this was not an undertaking for which any provision had been made, or to which any encouragement was offered" (2:449). Consequently, for the unexamined version of a comfortable relationship between Hawthorne and his native village presented by his biographer, George Parsons Lathrop, James substitutes a more discriminating reading of Hawthorne's ambivalent feelings, his "mingled tenderness and rancor" (1:437) towards Salem. While he asserts that the imagination of the New England artist necessarily found its subject in a *moral* consciousness, he insists that Hawthorne's relationship to his materials was aesthetic rather than moral or theological. Because James is as much interested in the dynamics of perception as he is in the content perceived, he can offer in a striking image an appreciation of Hawthorne's art which would have been undoubtedly repellent to Hawthorne's more high-minded, orthodox contemporaries: "His imagination—that delicate and penetrating imagination which was always at play, always entertaining itself, always engaged in a game of hide and seek in the region in which it seemed to him that the game could best be played—among the shadows and substructions, the dark-based pillars and supports, of our moral nature" (2:448).

James's study of the imagination of the New England artist, oriented

retrospectively toward a Calvinist past and its urgent sense of sin, is
complemented by his description of the emancipated conscience of
the self-reliant individual, pursuing the culture of a European present
and future. As a kind of preamble to his recreation of this second
major manifestation of the puritan consciousness in his account of the
transcendentalists at Brook Farm and their nonresident standard-
bearers, Margaret Fuller and Emerson, James considers Lathrop's account of an evening which Hawthorne spent at the home of the
Peabody sisters. His analysis of this occasion provides the clearest
example of his use of symbolic pictures in his effort to recapture the
New England mind of the pre–Civil War era, for he is able to make
this trivial event serve as a compact emblem of the larger passage of
intellectual history which he saw recorded in the annals of the West
Roxbury experiment. Focusing his attention on a single sentence,
"pregnant with historic meaning," in a passage from Lathrop, he subjects it to the insight of "the initiated mind": " 'His hostess brought
out Flaxman's designs for Dante, just received from Professor Felton,
of Harvard, and the party made an evening's entertainment out of
them.' " James makes this sentence yield a vision of "the early days
of 'culture' in New England":

> There was at that time a great desire for culture, a great interest
> in knowledge, in art, in aesthetics, together with a very scanty
> supply of the materials for such pursuits. Small things were made
> to do large service; and there is something even touching in the
> solemnity of consideration that was bestowed by the emancipated
> New England conscience upon little wandering books and prints,
> little echoes and rumors of observation and experience. . . . The
> initiated mind, as I have ventured to call it, has a vision of a little
> unadorned parlor, with the snow-drifts of a Massachusetts win-
> ter piled up about its windows, and a group of sensitive and
> serious people, modest votaries of opportunity, fixing their eyes
> upon a bookful of Flaxman's attenuated outlines. (3:479–80)

James was to recall this vision of the pursuit of culture in his portrayal of Olive Chancellor and her thirst for self-development within
the confines of her "strenuous parlor"[19] on Charles Street: " 'We will
work at it together—we will study everything,' Olive almost panted;
and while she spoke the peaceful picture hung before her of still
winter evenings under the lamp with falling snow outside, and tea on

a little table, and successful renderings, with a chosen companion, of Goethe."[20]

Instinctively James associates the personality of Margaret Fuller with the cultural complex latent in the Lathrop passage. Spiritual values are to be explored in terms of the consciousness that entertains them: "I mention Margaret Fuller here because a glimpse of her state of mind . . . helps to define the situation. The situation lives for a moment in those few words of Mr. Lathrop's." Identifying Fuller as "the apostle of culture, of intellectual curiosity," he presents "her vivacity of desire and poverty of knowledge"—a phrase that suggests his description of Isabel Archer as a young woman with "meagre knowledge" and "inflated ideals"[21]—as representative of the drive towards self-development. Turning to her *Memoirs* (1852) for an illustration of her pursuit of her ideal, James singles out her heightened response to the secondhand experience of art as she turns over portfolios of engravings at the Boston Athenaeum: "These emotions were ardent and passionate—could hardly have been more so had she been prostrate with contemplation in the Sistine Chapel or in one of the chambers of the Pitti Palace." Clearly "the very remarkable and interesting" (3:480) personality of Margaret Fuller had captured James's imagination. He declared his familiarity, indeed his fascination, with her *Memoirs* when he wrote in the *Hawthorne* monograph that it was "a curious, in some points of view almost a grotesque, and yet, on the whole, as I have said, an extremely interesting book" (4:485). The record of her imperfectly satisfied thirst for culture, epitomized by Lathrop's picture, undoubtedly served him as a major source of inspiration in his creation of the ardent and tortured heroine of *The Bostonians*.

In contrast to his dry picture of a confined inner life at Salem, James portrays the New England mind at Brook Farm as undergoing a liberating experience of intellectual discovery. The community at West Roxbury symbolizes the aspiration of the village world towards a society of greater depth and richness. He defines transcendentalism here as the response of "the strong and deep New England conscience" to "an imported culture" (4:489) from Europe, or again, in a formula which he was to quote with approval from James Elliot Cabot's *A Memoir of Ralph Waldo Emerson* (1887), as "that remarkable outburst of Romanticism on Puritan ground."[22] In his review of the *Memoir*, James regretted that Cabot had not taken advantage of his opportunity to illustrate "the primitive New England character, especially during the time of its queer search for something to expend itself upon." He expressed his own interest in the subject in the following arresting image: "Objects and occupations have multiplied since then, and now there is no lack; but fifty years ago the expanse was wide and free, and we get the impression of a conscience gasping in the void, panting for sensations, with something of the movement of the gills of a landed fish."[23] This statement from his review of Cabot illuminates his regret in his *Hawthorne* that the New England romancer had not been more involved with the transcendentalist movement, for James would have valued such "a pretext for writing a chapter upon the state of Boston society forty years ago" (4:489). The significance of his pages on Brook Farm lies in the extent to which his own response feeds into the discussion, in the extent to which he develops material *not* directly concerning Hawthorne's biography (as he acknowledges) but contemporaneous with him: the transcendentalist ideal of self-culture, with Emerson as its leading exponent and with Margaret Fuller as its most complete incarnation. He introduces and concludes his presentation of Brook Farm with commentary on passages drawn from Fuller's *Memoirs,* while he places at the heart of the section on the West Roxbury experience an account of the meaning of transcendentalist individualism derived from Emerson's thought.

As in the pictures of Salem and of the evening at the Peabodys', James's haunted sense of a barrier of elapsed time standing between him and the short-lived experiment at Brook Farm is offset by his privileged angle of vision as "the initiated mind." His knowledge of the transcendentalist milieu was extensive, ranging from an acquaintance with Emerson, the central personality of the movement, to a familiarity with its diverse literature, including O. B. Frothingham's *Transcendentalism in New England* (1876), the *Memoirs* of Margaret Fuller, and *The Blithedale Romance.* Highly conscious of ambivalent feelings toward the pre–Civil War generation, James pleads for a tactful approach to Emerson and his circle. He is fully aware of an alternative to filial piety, however, which would exploit the opportunities for irony and satire neglected by Hawthorne in *The Blithedale Romance.* He struggles repeatedly in these pages to control an impulse toward a more critical evaluation of the idealism of the Golden Day which could not fail to point out the provincial, the illusory, even the ridiculous aspects of the Emersonian philosophy.

James yields only momentarily to the spell of a vanished idealism, which was to lead Olive Chancellor into excesses of sentimentalism and self-deception. In his desire for an extension of his experience backward to the time of Brook Farm, he evokes a picture of the unworldly youth and goodness of the transcendentalists from the persistent aura still surrounding the figures whom he himself remembers:

> Something of its interest [the era of Brook Farm] adhered to them still—something of its aroma clung to their garments; there was something about them which seemed to say that when they were young and enthusiastic, they had been initiated into moral mysteries, they had played at a wonderful game. Their usual mark (it is true I can think of exceptions) was that they seemed excellently good. They appeared unstained by the world, unfamiliar with worldly desires and standards, and with those various forms of human depravity which flourish in some high phases of civilization

In the career of Isabel Archer, James was to subject this untested idealism to the experience of evil remarkable for its absence here. Once again he seeks the meaning of this symbolic picture in the personality of a representative figure: "The situation," he wrote, "was summed up and transfigured in the admirable and exquisite Emerson." "Emerson expressed, before all things, as was extremely natural at the hour and in the place, the value and importance of the individual, the duty of making the most of one's self, of living by one's own personal light and carrying out one's own disposition" (4:490). James understands the importance of this creed of individualism and self-culture in the possibilities that it discovered for the "play" of consciousness, for the release of mental energy denied other avenues of expression: "The doctrine of the supremacy of the individual to himself, of his originality and, as regards his own character, *unique* quality, must have had a great charm for people living in a society in which introspection, thanks to the want of other entertainment, played almost the part of a social resource." His version of Emerson's point of view applies equally to Isabel Archer's: "To make one's self so much more interesting would help to make life interesting, and life was probably, to many of this aspiring congregation, a dream of freedom and fortitude." In his analysis of Emerson's appeal, however, he suggests that such resources for self-knowledge lent themselves easily to self-deception. "There was therefore, among the cultivated classes, much relish for the utterances of a writer who would help one to take a picturesque

view of one's internal possibilities, and to find in the landscape of the
soul all sorts of fine sunrise and moonlight effects" (4:491). James
believed nevertheless in the value of the Emersonian impulse in its
original purity, and he concludes his discussion of Emerson with an
invocation of "the moral passion" (4:492) of the period which was
symbolized for him in his portrait of Emerson in his transcendentalist
prime: "When one remembers the remarkable charm of the speaker,
the beautiful modulation of his utterance, one regrets in especial that
one might not have been present on a certain occasion which made
a sensation, an era—the delivery of an address to the Divinity School
of Harvard University, on a summer evening in 1838" (4:492). Later
in the bright, hollow eloquence of Verena Tarrant in *The Bostonians*,
he recorded the decline of the strain of idealism which he cherished
here in the memory of Emerson.

Passing from this indulgent, retrospective vision of the American
Scholar living in a golden age, James concludes his portrait of Brook
Farm and the ideal of self-culture in a more critical vein, held until
then in abeyance. Adopting the reservations of Miles Coverdale,
Margaret Fuller, and Hawthorne—he interprets these three points of
view as roughly equivalent—toward the transcendentalist colony, he
stresses the illusions, the escapism, which lay behind the bright appearance of an Arcadian, Wordsworthian innocence.

James completes his survey of Hawthorne's New England with a
glowing account of the writer's residence at the Old Manse. There is
a strong accent of alienation present in the relationship which James
draws between Hawthorne and Salem, between Emerson and Brook
Farm (I draw here on James's review of Cabot's *Memoir*). Yet he captures their romantic revolt against the Calvinist domination of the
inner life in an image of ripeness and balance when he pictures these
two representative figures at Concord, "with 'a great original thinker'
at one end of the village, an exquisite teller of tales at the other, and
the rows of New England elms between" (4:502). The Concord equilibrium, however, "the perfect competence of the little society to
manage its affairs itself" (4:498), was not adequate to contain the
impulse toward self-expression of the emancipated puritan consciousness, and James devotes several passages of his *Hawthorne* to Margaret Fuller, who reached beyond the confines of New England toward
a larger destiny in Europe. Isabel Archer would follow in her steps,
for Fuller had cast a spell not only upon her contemporaries but upon
the "initiated mind" of James as well: "It was a strange history and

a strange destiny, that of this brilliant, restless, and unhappy woman—this ardent New Englander, this impassioned Yankee, who occupied so large a place in the thoughts, the lives, the affections, of an intelligent and appreciative society, and yet left behind her nothing but the memory of a memory" (4:485–86). Seeking an occasion to say more of her, he justifies the inclusion of her portrait in the Hawthorne monograph on two grounds, emphasizing the value of her personality not only as a representative type of the pursuit of self-culture but also as a source for Hawthorne's Zenobia. James recognized in Zenobia an exception to the general absence of realism in Hawthorne's fiction: "The finest thing in *The Blithedale Romance* is the character of Zenobia, which I have said elsewhere strikes me as the nearest approach that Hawthorne has made to the complete creation of a *person*. She is more concrete than Hester or Miriam, or Hilda or Phoebe; she is a more definite image, produced by a greater multiplicity of touches" (5:528–29). James, a dedicated realist himself, was impressed that Hawthorne had been able to achieve "the most vivid reflection of New England life that has found its way into literature" (1:430) without the technical resources of Balzac, Flaubert, and Zola. He turned to the presence of Margaret Fuller to account for the power of Hawthorne's conception of Zenobia, which transcended the limitation of the conventional types of character which were the stock in trade of romantic fiction: "The portrait is full of alteration and embellishment; but it has a greater reality, a greater abundance of detail, than any of his other figures, and the reality was a memory of the lady whom he had encountered in the Roxbury pastoral or among the wood-walks of Concord, with strange books in her hand and eloquent discourse on her lips" (4:487).

In his chapter on Brook Farm in the *Hawthorne* monograph James identified the addresses of Emerson and the "Conversations" of Margaret Fuller as the most characteristic manifestations of transcendentalist idealism, and he suggested in his concern with the problem of eloquence his awareness of the ambiguities of moral influence that lay at the heart of self-culture. While he expresses the greatest enthusiasm for Emerson's oratory, he is more cautious in his evaluation of the performance of Margaret Fuller. Defining her role as "a talker . . . *the* talker . . . the genius of talk," he describes her reputation as "singular, and not altogether reassuring." James does not explicitly state the nature of his reservation here, but it is immediately followed by observations on her egotism and the impact of her magnetic personality on others. He concludes that "her value, her activity, her sway (I am not sure that one can say her charm), were personal and practical" (4:486). A more substantial clue to the nature of James's misgivings occurs somewhat later in the same chapter (4:494–95), when he quotes at great length from the *Memoirs* a passage in which Fuller describes a series of conversations that she held at Brook Farm. In this glimpse of the priestess of self-culture, her intended display of disinterested moral passion is accompanied by an irrepressible drive for personal "sway." Interspersed with her account of the discussions that she led on such elevated and edifying subjects as education, impulse, and beauty are frequent complaints that her partners in self-development fail to treat her with the "deference" appropriate to her "genius." In particular she censures a young woman who was rude to her and notes with satisfaction the eventual submission of the wayward girl to her will. This by-play of personal power attracted James's attention, and he added to the passage a brief though inconclusive coda of his own in which he underlined the hero worship involved in Fuller's account. He proposes a comparison between Fuller and her disciples on the one hand and between Zenobia and Priscilla on the other, a comparison that suggests an affinity between his own reading of the experience of self-culture and Hawthorne's.

James was in fact in *The Bostonians* to pursue Hawthorne's insight into the "faulty parts in the Emersonian philosophy" (4:491), extending it to the whole of New England culture. Preoccupied like Hawthorne with the psychological dynamics of moral idealism, James may well have read the following passage (not mentioned in the *Hawthorne*), in which W. H. Channing relates the formation of his friendship with Margaret Fuller, in the light of the play of ego and Eros uncovered elsewhere by the editors of her *Memoirs:*

> By power to quicken other minds, she showed how living was her own. Yet more near were we brought by common attraction toward a youthful visitor in our circle, the untouched freshness of whose beauty was but the transparent garb of a serene, confiding, and harmonious soul, and whose polished grace, at once modest and naive, sportive and sweet, fulfilled the charm of innate goodness of heart. Susceptible in temperament, anticipating with ardent fancy the lot of a lovely and refined woman, and morbidly exaggerating her own slight personal defects, Margaret seemed to long, as it were, to transfuse with her force this nymph-like

form, and to fill her to glowing with her own lyric fire. No drop of envy tainted the sisterly love, with which she sought by genial sympathy thus to live in another's experience, to be her guardian-angel, to shield her from contact with the unworthy, to rouse each generous impulse, to invigorate thought by truth incarnate in beauty, and with unfelt ministry to weave bright threads in her web of fate. (Mem, II, 8)

This picture of the earnest, aspiring group of Cambridge youth who were to form the younger members of the transcendentalist circle brings together a variety of materials that James was to use in his exploration of self-culture in *The Bostonians:* a triangular relationship in which a young man and a young woman are both drawn to the same girl; and especially the attraction between the pleasing, inno-cent girl and the ambitious, slightly morbid young woman, who seeks not only to guide the spiritual development of her friend but indeed to live through her, transfusing the girl with her own "lyric fire."

James's outline of a New England consciousness in his recreation of Hawthorne's world provided him with a seminal formulation of the spiritual background of his own New England girls; more immediately to his purpose, he beheld an embodiment of this very consciousness in the heroines of Hawthorne's romances. In the *Hawthorne* James singled out Zenobia and Hilda for special notice: in Zenobia he wit-nessed the tragedy of self-culture which he associated with the puritan consciousness in its phase of revolt, while in Hilda he saw the ex-posure of the rigid moral innocence of New England's traditional ideals to the experience of evil. James's sense of Zenobia as a New England heroine deserves considerable emphasis, especially since, in dealing with the connection between Zenobia and Margaret Fuller that inevitably plays into such an identification, he shows himself properly conscious of the need for tact and discrimination. "It is idle," he writes, "to inquire too closely whether Hawthorne had Margaret Fuller in his mind in constructing the figure of this brilliant specimen of the strong-minded class and endowing her with the genius of conversa-tion; or, on the assumption that such was the case, to compare the image at all strictly with the model." He concludes his summary of the numerous points of resemblance between Zenobia and Margaret Fuller with the following observation: "The beautiful and sumptuous Zenobia, with her rich and picturesque temperament and physical aspects, offers many points of divergence from the plain and strenuous invalid who represented feminine culture in the suburbs of the New England metropolis" (5:529). Put in these terms, James's own portrait of Olive Chancellor in *The Bostonians* is much closer to the historical Margaret Fuller—at least as James presents her here—than Hawthorne's Zenobia. Still, despite the exotic aura surrounding Zenobia's personality—the rare flower, the dark hair, the suggestion of foreign blood—in short, the conventional attributes of the dark heroine of romantic fiction, James identified the drama that she had enacted in her turbulent career as a peculiarly New England one in its nature.

James regarded Hawthorne's presentation of the relationship between Zenobia and Hollingsworth as the major achievement of *The Blithedale Romance:* "The most touching element in the novel is the history of the grasp that this barbarous fanatic has laid upon the fastidious and high-tempered Zenobia, who, disliking him and shrinking from him at a hundred points, is drawn into the gulf of his omnivorous egotism" (5:530). In a brief introduction to Hawthorne which James published in 1897, he again stresses the interest of Zenobia's "baffled effort to make a hero of Hollingsworth," and he concludes that "nothing of the author's is a happier expression of what I have called his sense of the romance of New England." Earlier in the essay James defines this latent romance as "the secret play of the Puritan faith," that of "the restless individual conscience." It is a latent romance because "the large dry village picture" forced Hawthorne's imagination to assume "on the part of the society about him, a life of the spirit more complex than anything that met the mere eye of sense."[24] James is saying in effect that in Zenobia, Hawthorne had dramatized the play of a distinctively New England consciousness.

Now James concedes in this 1897 essay that this view of Zenobia, heightened by the tragedy of her death,[25] possibly reached beyond the intention of Hawthorne's conception of his heroine: "We fill out the figure, perhaps, and even lend to the vision something more than Hawthorne intended. Zenobia was, like Coverdale himself, a subject of dreams that were not to find form at Roxbury; but Coverdale had other resources, while she had none but her final failure."[26] It is, I would argue, entirely understandable that the author of *The Portrait of a Lady* should interpret Zenobia in this way, for he describes her appeal in phrases that strongly recall his own conception of Isabel Archer of some sixteen years before, as when he remarks that Hawthorne's "portrait" was "not least touching from the air we attribute to her of looking, with her fine imagination, for adventures that were hardly, under the circumstances, to be met." Zenobia, like Isabel, seeks in the man she loves the realization of the dreams of heroic action formed by her restless imagination, and despite her greater experience of the world, her capacity for self-deception is as great as Isabel's. Zenobia idealized Hollingsworth's "great heart," Isabel worshipped Gilbert Osmond's "beautiful mind"; when Zenobia denounced Hollingsworth at the last as "a cold, heartless, self-beginning and self-ending piece of mechanism"[27] she uttered the bitter fruits of knowledge that Isabel was to taste in Rome with pain. Zenobia and Hollingsworth, Isabel and Osmond—these are parallel versions of "the romance of New England." *The Blithedale Romance* offered to "the initiated mind" of Henry James the prototype of the tragedy of self-culture, a literary precedent of inestimable value for *The Portrait of a Lady* and *The Bostonians*.

Hawthorne's evaluation of this drama of consciousness in his romances was, as we have seen, decidedly ambivalent. James's biography of Hawthorne bears this out. He had occasion to emphasize the conservatism of the man Hawthorne in the simultaneous attraction and repulsion that Hawthorne experienced toward the Margaret Fuller–Zenobia figure: "Very much the same qualities that made Hawthorne a Democrat in politics—his contemplative turn and absence of a keen perception of abuses, his taste for old ideals, and loitering paces, and muffled tones—would operate to keep him out of active sympathy with a woman of the so-called progressive type" (4:487). He describes the play of the irrepressible imagination of Hawthorne the artist, however, as essentially heretical in its tendencies, heretical in so far as the pursuit of art proceeded in independence of moral constraints: "He speaks of the dark disapproval with which his old ancestors, in the case of their coming to life, would see him trifling himself away as a story-teller. But how far more darkly would they have frowned could they have understood that he had converted the very principle of their own being [the puritan consciousness with its urgent sense of sin] into one of his toys!" (3:471). James himself, uninhibited by the Calvinist formulation of spiritual experience to which he saw Hawthorne as necessarily subject, was free to value the act of consciousness as an end in itself, and hence he believed that he did not need to advance any further justification for his view that it must inevitably provide the primary subject of a work of art: "I confess I never see the *leading* interest of any human hazard but in a consciousness (on the part of the moved and moving creature) subject to fine intensification and wide enlargement."[28] Hawthorne's expedient had been to pair the dangerous development of his dark heroines with the safe fixity of his fair New England girls, whose chief article of faith was well expressed by James's Mary Garland when she said, "It seems to me very frightful to develop." Abandoning this distribution of qualities and capacities between two different and complementary heroines, a separation that Hawthorne had found increasingly difficult to maintain, James advanced beyond the limitation of Hawthorne's strategy. Hawthorne, interestingly enough, may well have helped him to do so. When James endowed Isabel Archer with both the innocence of Hawthorne's New England girls and the imagination of his mature women and proceeded to trace her self-development toward the deeper knowledge available in Hawthorne only to heroines of the dark persuasion, he could look to Hawthorne's Hilda for a crude but suggestive precedent.

After Zenobia, James apparently found Hilda to be the most interesting of Hawthorne's women. Following the judgment articulated by Miriam and Kenyon, Marius Bewley has observed that in the New England heroine of *The Marble Faun* (1860) Hawthorne created the type of an ethereal womanhood incompatible with evil. He points out the extent to which the idealized girl is presented as a redemptive figure by Hawthorne, and he suggests that the "positive apotheosis of New England girlhood"[29] that she represents provided James with a prototype for Milly Theale. What particularly captured the attention of James, however, was that Hawthorne had subjected Hilda to the discovery of evil, documenting rather extensively the moral confusion of her response to this knowledge. He writes in *Hawthorne:*

> The character of Hilda has always struck me as an admirable invention—one of those things that mark the man of genius. . . . This pure and somewhat rigid New England girl, following the vocation of a copyist of pictures in Rome, unacquainted with evil and untouched by impurity, has been accidentally the witness, unknown and unsuspected, of the dark deed by which her friends, Miriam and Donatello, are knit together. This is *her* revelation of evil, her loss of perfect innocence. She has done no wrong, and yet wrongdoing has become a part of her experience, and she carries the weight of her detested knowledge upon her heart. (6:554)

Hawthorne in fact had not carried out this conception of Hilda to its logical conclusion in *The Marble Faun*. He drew back finally from the unsettling implications of so severe a challenge to the New England girl's fragile powers of moral agency, preferring to send her home again, affirming that her innocence remained unchanged, the lesson of her experience of evil unlearned. (It is interesting to note in this connection that James spoke of Emerson's "ripe unconsciousness of evil" as "one of the most beautiful signs by which we know him.")[30] Isabel Archer, however, could only refuse Caspar Goodwood's offer to realize her dream of freedom in America at the last; following her "loss of perfect innocence," there was to be no return from Rome.

Chapter 6

THE TRAGEDY OF SELF-CULTURE:
THE PORTRAIT OF A LADY

IN HIS PREFACE to the New York edition, James defined the literary achievement of *The Portrait of a Lady* as the success with which he had been able to endow "the mere slim shade of an intelligent but presumptuous girl" with "the high attributes of a Subject" for a novel. Here for the first time he located "the centre of the subject in the young woman's own consciousness."[1] In none of the narratives discussed previously, except possibly *The Europeans*, had he assigned to his heroine so dominant a role. Instead she had usually been presented from the point of view of an expatriate American, frequently an artist, and potentially her lover. Characteristically, his courtship of her had dramatized his attempt to achieve a mature self-awareness by comprehending a complex, contemporary American reality symbolized by the girl; James had suggested that the young man might even establish, with luck, a solid identity as an American artist. In *The Portrait of a Lady* the author's conception of courtship as a process of self-definition remained constant, but he transferred the interest of this drama and the artist's role in it to the character of the young woman herself.

Prior to his creation of Isabel Archer, when James sought to fill out the characters of his American heroines, he did so in two ways: through his choice of a particular setting (as for Mary Garland or Gertrude Wentworth), and more important, especially for those of his rootless young women who move principally abroad, through his suggestion of their complex inner lives (Bessie Alden and Christina Light). In his biography of Hawthorne and in the heroines of "An International Episode" and *The Europeans*, James laid the foundations of his characterization of Isabel Archer. He presented the restless activity of the imagination as the force that drove both Bessie Alden and Gertrude Wentworth. In his portrait of Bessie, James described the play of her consciousness in a single episode, but he offered little account of the nature and origin of its ideals. His rendering of Gertrude can be said to complement his picture of Bessie, for he beheld in her inner life a characteristically New England drama of innocence in which her imagination, ambitious to realize her vague aspirations for self-development, struggled to free itself from the moral restraints of puritanism into an uninhibited aesthetic appreciation of experience. In *Hawthorne* James documented these same tendencies of his heroines in his investigation of the New England consciousness: in James's belief, the development of the New England artist was limited by the grip of his Calvinist heritage, while the American Scholar's pursuit of self-culture, dangerously unfamiliar with evil in the world, became a source of potentially tragic illusions.

Abandoning the use of paired heroines which had been central to Hawthorne's explorations of the New England mind, James pursued his critique of Emersonian individualism in *The Portrait of a Lady* through his presentation of the entire career of a single character. Endowing her with the qualities of a New England consciousness and with a set of ideals of a distinctly transcendentalist cast,[2] he proceeded to expose her to an experience in which the design of her inner life was to be tested and transformed. In his description of her spiritual landscape James was drawing on his knowledge of Emerson, Margaret Fuller, Hawthorne, and their contemporaries, and on his sense of these three as representative figures of his usable past, of the most important native moral and literary tradition available to him as an American artist.

I

In the first major event of *The Portrait of a Lady*, Isabel Archer's refusal of Lord Warburton, James demonstrates the inadequacy of a conventional reading of the drama of courtship, as a simple affair of the heart, to account for the conduct of his heroine. "Poor" Warburton is baffled by his failure to lead Isabel, by the usual logic of the emotions, to accept his proposal, for the girl not only attempts to express her belief in the truth of his love for her, but she speaks freely of her own high esteem for him as well. On the basis of some unexpressed view of herself, incomprehensible to Warburton, she rejects not so much her lover but rather an imagined version of herself as "the heroine of the situation," the central figure of a conventional romance that would feature "the park of an old English countryhouse, with the foreground embellished by a local nobleman in the act of making love to a young lady who, on careful inspection, should be found to present remarkable analogies with herself."[3] However "remarkable" the "analogies" may be, they remain only superficial, pictorial correspondences, for Isabel is convinced that she is to have an original story of her own. Warburton's direct appeal to the heart fails because he has not captured the girl's imagination which controls her emotions. At the close of their inconclusive interview both Warburton and Isabel recognize that it is her "remarkable mind" that separates them.

In this first phase of the courtship of Isabel Archer, then, James makes it clear that the heroine's self-absorption leaves no room for a second and complementary figure to love her: she is in love with the romantic pictures she has fashioned of her self. Convinced that "she had a system and an orbit of her own," Isabel shrinks from Warburton because his presence challenges the autonomy of her imagination. She fears in the entry "into the system in which he lived and moved" a new and unfamiliar order of experience where her own resources, which she so highly esteems, might lose their application:

> She herself was a character—she could not help being aware of that; and hitherto her visions of a completed life had concerned themselves largely with moral images—things as to which the question would be whether they pleased her soul. Lord Warburton loomed up before her, largely and brightly, as a collection of attributes and powers which were not to be measured by this simple rule, but which demanded a different sort of appreciation— an appreciation which the girl, with her habit of judging quickly and freely, felt that she lacked the patience to bestow. (12:87)

Her thoughts, instead of moving forward to explore Warburton's character, turn inward upon herself: the girl rehearses her preferred means of self-expression, the exercise of her taste, which James describes as a "simple rule" of perception and judgment on the basis of the aesthetic pleasure produced in her imagination by "moral images." Isabel's feelings are not only disciplined by her imagination but they are directed toward the expression of the ideals to which it is devoted. Preoccupied with the play of her own consciousness, she can only regard as "an aggression" the possibility of a love that might interfere with her enjoyment of herself. Only a man she took to be her own ideal reflection could find a place in the crowded mirror of the young woman's imagination.

When Isabel fails to recognize in Warburton's proposal the chance to realize "her visions of a completed life," she has rejected the usual opportunity offered by the conventions of courtship in nineteenth-century fiction for a heroine to shape her destiny, and she is left to her own devices. Accordingly the girl feels that she is placed upon her mettle to vindicate her vision of herself as a superior individual by the performance of some heroic action: "Who was she, what was she, that she should hold herself superior? What view of life, what design upon fate, what conception of happiness, had she that pretended to be larger than this large occasion? If she would not do this, then she must do great things, she must do something greater." Isabel's meditation, however, concludes in a darker vein. Her earlier alarm, that love for Warburton might interfere with the superior sensibility of a girl with "an orbit of her own," is supplanted by a new and unanswerable fear of an alternative version of herself as the exceptional, insensitive girl in twenty, "a cold, hard girl" (12:95) unable to feel anything at all.

The upshot of the Warburton episode is to dramatize decisively the degree of Isabel Archer's commitment to the life of her own consciousness, confirming in her observers and in the young woman herself the high expectations concerning her character which her initial appearance in England aroused. At the outset Ralph Touchett remarked, "It's her general air of being some one in particular that strikes me. Who is this rare creature, and what is she? Where did you find her, and how did you make her acquaintance?" James makes this issue of her identity the question that his readers are to ask, for it is the subject of his narrative; and in Mrs. Touchett's reply to her son he points out the direction of the answer he means to give: "I found her in an old house at Albany, sitting in a dreary room on a rainy day, reading a heavy book, and boring herself to death" (5:34–35). It is then to the remarkable Albany chapters that we must turn if we are to improve on Mrs. Touchett's knowledge of her niece; there is no parallel in any of James's earlier work to the complex and searching characterization of his heroine's consciousness in these pages.

In his own initial evocation of Isabel at Albany, James also presents his heroine as a figure alone with a book, but to Mrs. Touchett's unexamined, literal interpretation of this image as one of spiritual deprivation, he supplies an informed, alternative reading of her solitary attitude as a symbol of her involvement in a drama of the inner life, a drama that I shall argue is distinctively Emersonian in its inspiration: "To say that she had a book is to say that her solitude did not press upon her; for her love of knowledge had a fertilising quality and her imagination was strong. There was at this time, however, a want of lightness in her situation" (3:17). Isabel's deliberate choice of this

attitude and setting reflects her attempt to express a relationship between the two leading drives of her personality, her desire for knowledge and her allegiance to the independence of her imagination. In
accordance with the design that she has chosen for her character,
Isabel pursues her reading, which James describes as "the foundation
of her knowledge," within the confines of "the office," "a mysterious
apartment which lay beyond the library." Her act represents a symbolic withdrawal from an unstructured world of reality into a theater
of the inner life governed by a theory of her imagination. Although the
office has an entrance which opens on the street, an unused door
whose sidelights have been blocked off with green paper, Isabel even
as a child had "no wish to look out, for this would have interfered with
her theory that there was a strange, unseen place on the other side—
a place which became, to the child's imagination, according to its
different moods, a region of delight or of terror" (3:19). In her reading
in the office the girl balances her ambivalent feelings toward experience against each other, for if she has "a great desire for knowledge," "an immense curiosity about life," preferring "almost any
source of information to the printed page" (4:28), she has nevertheless
continued to observe the convention of the office which she established in her childhood: "She had never assured herself that the vulgar
street lay beyond it" (3:19). James takes up the story of his heroine,
however, at a turning point in the history of her consciousness, when
her ordering of her world, no longer able to satisfy the requirements
of her restless imagination, is on the point of losing its inveterate
equilibrium.

James brings his retrospective portrait of Isabel at Albany to a climax in his extended analysis of her character in the sixth chapter,
which he introduces with this proposition: "Isabel Archer was a young
person of many theories; her imagination was remarkably active." In
his exposition of this statement James attributes to his heroine the
same peculiar complex of moral preoccupations and aesthetic perceptions that he, as an initiated observer, recognized as characteristic of
the New England mind in his biography of Hawthorne. He takes as
his point of departure Isabel's sense of herself as a "superior" individual which played so decisive a role in her conduct in the Warburton
episode. Like Margaret Fuller, who once observed, "I now know all
the people worth knowing in America, and I find no intellect com-
parable to my own,"[4] Isabel confidently believes in the fineness of her
mind. Instinctively she seeks occasions to indulge her self-esteem, and

accordingly she invests her notion of the superior self with the dignity
of an ideal of heroic action: "She had a theory that it was only on this
condition that life was worth living; that one should be one of the
best, should be conscious of a fine organization (she could not help
knowing her organization was fine), should move in a realm of light,
of natural wisdom, of happy impulse, of inspiration gracefully chronic" (6:42).[5] In its emphasis upon an approach to knowledge through
intuition and feeling, in its assumption of a benevolent universe, and
above all in its highly self-conscious dedication to the spontaneous realization of self, Isabel's buoyant theory resembles Emerson's doctrine
of self-reliance as James defined it in the chapter devoted to "Brook
Farm and Concord" in his *Hawthorne:* "Emerson expressed, before all
things, as was extremely natural at the hour and in the place, the value
and importance of the individual, the duty of making the most of one's
self, of living by one's own personal light and carrying out one's own
disposition" (4:190).

Isabel's preoccupation with the ideas of genius and self-reliance,
following the characteristic movement of transcendentalist thought,
leads her to the formulation of a program of self-culture. The girl from
Albany subscribes to this version of "the duty of making the most of
one's self" embraced by the Concord sage: "It was one of her theories
that Isabel Archer was very fortunate in being independent, and that
she ought to make some very enlightened use of her independence"
(6:43). Like Margaret Fuller, Isabel "was always planning out her
own development, desiring her own perfection, observing her own
progress." She sees in the career of her friend, Henrietta Stackpole, an
irrepressible type of the new woman, a vindication of her theory that
"a woman might suffice to herself and be happy." If her own conception of a role beyond the conventional resource of marriage is as yet
unformed, her self-trust reinforces nevertheless her belief in the unfolding of her character as a beneficent process: "If one should wait
expectantly and trustfully, one would find some happy work to one's
hand" (6:44).[6]

James sought an understanding of Isabel's theories of moral action in
the dynamics of her imagination.[7] In his development of this central
insight into the design of her character he placed what he had identified as the leading tendencies of transcendentalist New England
thought, the moral preoccupation of the imagination and the pursuit
of self-culture, in direct relationship to each other, and he proceeded
to reconstruct in the inner life of his heroine the workings of an eman-

cipated puritan consciousness. In so doing he explored the impulse
that had determined the characteristic acts of self-expression of Emerson, Hawthorne, and their contemporaries, and he laid the groundwork for the "chapter upon the state of Boston society forty years ago"
which Hawthorne had regrettably omitted from *The Blithedale Romance* and which he was himself to write obliquely in *The Bostonians.*
In fiction James could transcend the limits of his own experience and
meet the requirement, which he had set for the historian who would
undertake the recreation of such a passage of intellectual history, that
"the biographer's own personal reminiscences should stretch back to
that period and to the persons who animated it."[8]

Reflecting on the popularity of Emerson's orations, James observed
in his *Hawthorne* that the pursuit of self-culture might end in self-
deception, that "the moral passion . . . of the most poetical, the most
beautiful productions of the American mind" might encourage a shal-
low taste for the moral picturesque: "There was therefore, among the
cultivated classes, much relish for the utterances of a writer who would
help one to take a picturesque view of one's internal possibilities, and to
find in the landscape of the soul all sorts of fine sunrise and moonlight
effects" (4:491–92). For all her high seriousness of purpose, her stout
determination "not to be superficial," Isabel has a marked taste for just
such "sunrise and moonlight effects" of the soul. James traces her idealization of herself and of her intellectual life to its source in her imagination: "Her nature had for her own imagination a certain garden-like
quality, a suggestion of perfume and murmuring boughs, of shady
bowers and lengthening vistas, which made her feel that introspection
was, after all, an exercise in the open air, and that a visit to the re-
cesses of one's mind was harmless when one returned from it with a
lapful of roses" (6:44). Implicit in the girl's flattering description of
herself in terms of an untroubled, orderly, sheltering landscape, redolent of softness and sweetness, is an Emersonian assumption of an
identity between the mind and nature in which the beauty of the world
is interpreted as a guarantee of the morality of the self.[9] The basis of
this assumption, however, has been altered by the agency of her imagination: instead of a correspondence between the reality of the self
and an external reality beyond, there is a correspondence between two
pictures which are both equally the products of her imagination.[10] In
any event, the girl derives her greatest pleasure from experiences of
her imagination which tend to vindicate her interest in herself: "She
carried within herself a great fund of life, and her deepest enjoyment

was to feel the continuity between the movements of her own heart and the agitations of the world. For this reason she was fond of seeing great crowds and large stretches of country, of reading about revolutions and wars, of looking at historical pictures" (4:28). This is Isabel's highly self-conscious application of Emerson's theory that the most private thought of the American Scholar possessed the value of a public act.

The sanguine cast of Isabel Archer's imagination is at once the source of her ideals and the instrument of her self-deceptions:

> She spent half her time in thinking of beauty, and bravery, and magnanimity; she had a fixed determination to regard the world as a place of brightness, of free expansion, of irresistible action; she thought it would be detestable to be afraid or ashamed. She had an infinite hope that she should never do anything wrong. . . . Sometimes she went so far as to wish that she should find herself some day in a difficult position, so that she might have the pleasure of being as heroic as the occasion demanded. (6:42–43)

It is revealing to observe here the extent to which James has reproduced in Isabel's utterance his sense of the characteristic note of Emersonian rhetoric. This can be suggested by comparing the opening lines in the above quotation to his paraphrase in *Hawthorne* of a typical passage of Emerson's thought:

> He talked about the beauty and dignity of life, and about everyone who is born into the world being born to the whole, having an interest and a stake in the whole. . . . He insisted upon sincerity and independence and spontaneity, upon acting in harmony with one's nature, and not conforming and compromising for the sake of being more comfortable. (4:490–91)

Isabel in her innocence responds not directly to experience but rather to a series of ideal pictures of it formed by her imagination. Her faith in her imagination encourages her belief that in pleasing herself she would perform an heroic action: aesthetic perception yields an infallible moral knowledge, for good can be easily distinguished from evil on the basis of feeling, and hence, in a universe of such benevolent clarity, moral conduct presents itself as a pleasurable opportunity for self-expression. Such for James was "the Emersonian philosophy" in its pristine state, in which beauty was one with goodness and with truth, and his reading of its flaws applies to the limitations of Isabel's theories of the self.

In contrast to Isabel's complacent sense of the order of her inner life, her "biographer" is acutely aware of her "errors and delusions": "Her thoughts were a tangle of vague outlines, which had never been corrected by the judgment of people who seemed to her to speak with authority. In matters of opinion she had had her own way, and it had led her into a thousand ridiculous zigzags" (6:42). Significantly, James chooses the girl's reflections on the problem of evil as the occasion for his revelation of the dangers latent in her theory of herself. He was to write of Emerson that his especial distinction lay in his "vivid conception of the moral life," and he believed that his "ripe unconsciousness of evil" helped to account for the beautiful simplicity, the serenity, and the inadequacy of his "direct, intimate vision of the soul itself."[11] Lacking any substantial knowledge of evil, Isabel imagines its existence in pictures of "dusky, pestiferous tracts, planted thick with ugliness and misery" (6:44). Following a logic of her own, however, she jealously guards against any intrusion of such unpleasant realities that might interfere with the unfolding idyl of self culture which her imagination has conceived for her "garden-like" soul:

> What should one do with the misery of the world in a scheme of the agreeable for oneself? It must be confessed that this question never held her long. She was too young, too impatient to live, too unacquainted with pain. She always returned to her theory that a young woman whom after all every one thought clever, should begin by getting a general impression of life. This was necessary to prevent mistakes, and after it should be secured she might make the unfortunate condition of others an object of special attention. (6:45)

The girl's conception of the life of self-culture, her appeal to an ideal of moral education from which the disagreeable presence of evil is deliberately, if temporarily, excluded, shows clearly as a rationalization for a peculiar program of self-indulgence.[12] This her cousin, Ralph Touchett, shrewdly discerned when he told her, "You want to see, but not to feel" (15:130). If there is "something pure and proud," "something cold and stiff," in Isabel's indefinite postponement of marriage in favor of her self-reliant determination "that a woman ought to be able to make up her life in singleness," James insists nevertheless that at the very heart of her character lay an untested capacity for self-surrender, which helps to explain her reluctance to move beyond the safety of her world of theories into the uncertainty of a world of feeling beyond her own control: "Deep in her soul—it was the deepest thing there—lay a belief that if a certain light should dawn, she could give herself completely; but this image, on the whole, was too formidable to be attractive" (6:44). When Isabel accepts Mrs. Touchett's offer of "a chance to develop" in Europe, she has deferred for the time being any serious confrontation with this "formidable image" which she recognizes in the person of her unrelenting suitor, Caspar Goodwood, a businessman from Boston whom she regards variously as the "finest," the "cleverest," and the "strongest" gentleman of her acquaintance. The choice between self-culture and self-surrender is repeated when, immediately following the Warburton episode, she again refuses Goodwood and in the company of her aunt proceeds at last to the Continent. In her reiterated determination to resist the principle of masculine "energy" which Goodwood so abundantly expresses she tastes an exhilarating sense of the power of her selfhood: "She had done what she preferred." However, when James emphasizes the "theoretic" aspect of Isabel's "love of liberty" (17:142) which her commitment to self-culture expresses, he clearly distinguishes her from American girls like Daisy Miller and in so doing offers a more complex definition of the problem of American individualism. In her uninhibited enjoyment of experience, Daisy possessed the beautiful simplicity of a natural fact; she was an unreflecting incarnation of the very freedom to which Isabel self-consciously aspires.

In his *Hawthorne* James urged that there was "only one possible tone" which could do justice to the idealism of the transcendentalists (4:489), the major source of inspiration for his conception of "a certain young woman affronting her destiny."[13] Conceding that "the Emersonian philosophy" had its "faulty parts," he yet admired its "magnificent" "moral passion,"[14] and he sought to strike precisely that delicate balance of criticism and compassion which Hawthorne had achieved in his rendering of Margaret Fuller as Zenobia. When he paused to summarize his own portrait of Isabel Archer at Albany, he explicitly urged the reader to view his heroine in a spirit as generous as his own:

Altogether, with her meagre knowledge, her inflated ideals, her confidence at once innocent and dogmatic, her temper at once exacting and indulgent, her mixture of curiosity and fastidiousness, of vivacity and indifference, her desire to look very well and to be if possible even better; her determination to see, to try, to know; her combination of the delicate, desultory, flame-like spirit and the eager and personal young girl; she would be an easy victim of scientific criticism, if she were not intended to awaken on the reader's part an impulse more tender and more purely expectant. (6:43)

II

In *The Portrait of a Lady* James delegates to Ralph Touchett the responsibility of arranging for his self-reliant heroine the opportunity to act out her Emersonian ideal of self-culture. Imaginative and idealistic himself, Ralph recognized Isabel's rejection of Lord Warburton as a "remarkable" act which distinguished her from "nineteen women out of twenty" (15:128–29) who would have jumped at the chance to marry an English lord. Easily identifying himself with "this spontaneous young woman from Albany" (6:52), he seeks, by endowing her imagination with an unrestricted sphere of action, to gratify the desires of his own. By means of this strategy of identification the expatriate American proposes, in this version of the fable of the American girl, to express both his artistic sensibility and his love without abandoning the security of his passive, spectatorial role. In order to persuade his father to leave a fortune of seventy thousand pounds to the girl, he urges the morality of his belief in self-reliance: "When the person is good, your making things easy is all to the credit of virtue. To facilitate the execution of good impulses, what can be a nobler act?" To this question Mr. Touchett, and James, can only reply: "Isabel is a sweet young girl; but do you think she is as good as that?" (18:161).

Isabel herself is troubled by the moral implications of her newly-acquired fortune and freedom. Her conversations with Ralph on this subject recall those between Gertrude Wentworth and Felix Young. "Do you think it good for me suddenly to be made so rich?" (21:193) she asks her cousin. Characteristically, the girl finds an aesthetic resolution to these troublesome moral uncertainties. Placing the idea of her wealth in the redemptive company of her other theories, her resourceful imagination proceeds, in a series of flattering pictures, to demonstrate that her fortune simply enhances the beauty of that very ideal of herself which it might otherwise have seemed to challenge: "She lost herself in a maze of visions; the fine things a rich, independent, generous girl, who took a large, human view of her opportunities and obligations, might do, were really innumerable. Her fortune therefore became to her mind a part of her better self; it gave her importance, gave her even, to her own imagination, a certain ideal beauty." James adds dryly, "What it did for her in the imagination of others is another affair" (21:195).

Isabel's first meeting with Madame Merle at Gardencourt marks a turning point in her career, for she imagines her friend to be a model of the great self that she would like to become. She believes that Madame Merle has been able to discipline "in admirable order" the "quick and liberal impulses" of "a rich nature" (18:152) much like her own, and when Isabel speaks of her as "rare," "superior," and "pre-eminent" (19:163), it is to this "ideal combination" of thought and feeling, the measured, commanding expression of a fine sensibility, that she refers. The inexperienced girl views the life of the older woman as an exemplary existence, an "aristocratic situation" in which the vague possibilities of her theory of the superior individual have been fulfilled: " 'That is the great thing,' Isabel reflected; 'that is the supreme good fortune: to be in a better position for appreciating people than they are for appreciating you.' And she added that this, when one considered it, was simply the essence of the aristocratic situation. In this light, if in none other, one should aim at the aristocratic situation" (19:165–66). In his commentary on this passage James explicitly refrains from giving a full account of Isabel's view, which is quite at variance with the reality of Madame Merle's position; implying nevertheless that a "fatuous illusion" (19:166) is involved, he refers for only answer to the workings of the girl's imagination. Fully as naive, serious, and impressionable as Gertrude Wentworth was in her response to the worldly Eugenia, Isabel seeks to imitate the manner, the art, which has made of her distinguished friend "a great lady," "an image of success" (19:174).

Isabel's zealous dedication to her relationship with Madame Merle recalls the romantic cult of friendship practiced by Margaret Fuller and her disciples. The two women engage in grave conversations concerning the nature of the self, the exercise of its power, the realization of its greatness, and other "matters of high and low philosophy."[15] Although the girl soon realizes that she is, "as the phrase is, under an influence," her untroubled rationalization of this difficulty resembles Fuller's initial acceptance of the dangers of hero worship in her devotion to Goethe: " 'What is the harm,' she asked herself, 'so long as it is a good one? The more one is under a good influence the better. The only thing is to see our steps as we take them—to understand them as we go. That I think I shall always do' " (19:165). In her passionate desire to be understood, Isabel thirsts for confidences and communion. She impulsively displays her "spiritual gems" ("the only ones of any magnitude that Isabel possessed" [19:163], James adds with gentle irony) for the admiration of the flattering priestess of experience, and she treasures in return such a reciprocal sign of intimacy in their conversations as "her companion's preference for making Miss Archer herself a topic" (19:170). Whatever influence Madame Merle might exert for the good of her young friend is prevented by the girl's infatuation with herself. Isabel is unable to heed such wisdom as the older woman, in the supposed freedom of her aristocratic situation, is prepared to offer: "There is no such thing as an isolated man or woman; we are each of us made up of a cluster of appurtenances. What do you call one's self? Where does it begin? where does it end? . . . One's self— for other people—is one's expression of one's self" (19:175).

To Isabel, with her untried Emersonian faith in the existence of an independent theater of action for the self, Madame Merle, speaking as a scarred veteran of experience, as a woman without position, disappointed in her ambitions for greatness, offers a darker reading of the possibilities of such freedom: "A woman, perhaps, can get on; a woman, it seems to me, has no natural place anywhere; where-ever she finds herself she has to remain on the surface and, more or less, to crawl" (19:171). Nevertheless, like Ralph Touchett and Isabel herself, Madame Merle possesses a restless imagination which takes fire when the girl becomes an heiress. All three dream of "the fine things a rich, independent, generous girl, who took a large, human view of her opportunities and obligations, might do" (21:195). For Ralph, ever the spectator standing in the wings, it is enough simply to encourage his cousin to give herself freely, as he has never done, to the life of the imagination: "Spread your wings; rise above the ground. It's never wrong to do that" (21:194). It occurs to Madame Merle, however, to provide her young friend with a more definite object worthy of her concern—and her fortune—in the person of Gilbert Osmond, whom she describes as "one of the cleverest and most agreeable men it was possible to meet" (23:213). Thoroughly familiar with Isabel's theory of the superior individual, she deliberately uses her "influence" with the girl to prime her imagination for her first meeting with Osmond by dwelling on his cleverness, his brilliance, his distinction, his taste, "a taste which was quite by itself" (23:214).

By means of an extended metaphor of the theater which he uses to describe Isabel's initial encounter with Osmond, James emphasizes that she responds to Madame Merle's distinguished friend as she would to an artistic performance, to a concert or a play, and he demonstrates in the most complete rendering of Isabel's consciousness prior to her marriage, the sequence of chapters (24–26) concerning her first visit to Osmond's villa on a hilltop outside Florence, the extent to which the moral conduct of this imaginative American girl is determined by her aesthetic perceptions. Repeating the pattern of her friendship with Madame Merle, Isabel, who believed that one "should be conscious of a fine organization," who "spent half her time in thinking of beauty, and bravery, and magnanimity" (6:42), is predisposed to recognize Osmond as yet another model of the great self, an exemplary figure who enjoys the privilege of the aristocratic situation to which she aspires. With that instinctive confidence in the testimony of appearances which had drawn her to Madame Merle, she interprets Osmond's "fine" features, his clear voice, for example, with its utterance like "the tinkling of glass" (28:216), or the "light, smooth, slenderness of structure which made the movement of a single one of his fingers produce the effect of an expressive gesture," as "the signs of an unusual sensibility" (24:228). Natural facts for Isabel Archer are the signs of spiritual truth.

Although she admits that he stands beyond the range of her customary appraisal of character by type as "a specimen apart" (24:228) and that she "was certainly far from understanding him completely" (24:229), Isabel is convinced nonetheless of a correspondence between Osmond's "intelligence" and her own, and she is determined to avoid any "grossness of perception" which would discredit in his eyes her claim to the distinction of "the truly initiated mind" (24:230). For all that he was to tell her, "No, I am not conventional. I am convention itself" (29:273), she believes that behind his observance of convention lies an unspoken originality: "Mr. Osmond had the interest of rareness. It was not so much what he said and did, but rather what he withheld, that distinguished him" (24:228). Despite the meagerness of her knowledge of him, based on her reading of signs superficial and disconcerting and even more on her intuitive sense of the unexpressed, Isabel is confident in her estimate of Osmond. Characteristically she forms a theory of him as "a shy personage" which allows her to place the most favorable construction possible upon his leading traits. Thus his fastidious sensibility, "the shyness of ticklish nerves and fine perceptions," is "consistent" with "the best breeding" and it even becomes "almost a proof of superior qualities," which include "an inquiring mind" (24:229) and, significantly, an interest in her own feelings.

Turning to the familiar problem of self-esteem, she proceeds: "Mr. Osmond was not a man of easy assurance, who chatted and gossiped with the fluency of a superficial nature; he was critical of himself as well as of others, and exacting a good deal of others (to think them agreeable), he probably took a rather ironical view of what he himself offered: a proof, into the bargain, that he was not grossly conceited" (24:229). These reflections possess the logic of Isabel's self-analysis at Albany. If the girl leaps easily from "proof" to "proof," it is because certain aspects of Osmond's manner of self-expression, more even than Madame Merle's, lend themselves to the requirements of her imagination, that is, they permit her to believe of his nature what she would like to believe of her own.

Isabel is convinced that she has never met "a person of so fine a grain" (24:228), and Osmond's attractions are further enhanced when, in order to explain to her what he has made of himself, he adopts the language of her own idealism. In the course of their conversation Isabel has announced with characteristic ardor her conception of the deliberate life as a salutary discipline for her "frivolous" tendency to act impulsively: "One ought to choose something very deliberately, and be faithful to that" (24:231). Osmond proceeds to measure his character by this "rule" of value which the girl has proposed. If, earlier in the afternoon, he referred to his life in Italy in a tone of gracious disparagement, acknowledging that the complacencies of such an existence encouraged an "idle," "dilettantish," "second-rate" aestheticism (24:225), he now urges nevertheless that he has acted according to a "plan" which redeems his conduct from the "frivolous":

> "It was very simple. It was to be as quiet as possible."
> "As quiet?" the girl repeated.
> "Not to worry—not to strive nor struggle. To resign myself. To be content with a little."

Puzzled by this refusal of aspiration, this passive, possibly ascetic inversion of her theory of moral action, Isabel presses for a more complete explanation:

> "Do you call that simple?" Isabel asked, with a gentle laugh.
> "Yes, because it's negative."
> "Has your life been negative?"

Observing that she hangs upon his words ("quiet?" "simple?" "negative?"), and sensing perhaps that such a statement hardly suggests the kind of "plan" of which she has spoken, Osmond obliges her by defining his life as the decisive consequence of a considered act of will:

> "Call it affirmative if you like. Only it has affirmed my indifference. Mind you, not my natural indifference—I had none. But my studied, my wilful renunciation."
>
> Isabel scarcely understood him; it seemed a question whether he were joking or not. (24:231)

Although Osmond has by now so turned her words around and played upon his own that she is bewildered, Isabel perseveres in her attempt to understand why, given the freedom to choose, he has chosen to renounce. In the first words of his lengthy reply Osmond tells her all:

> "Because I could do nothing. . . . I was simply the most fastidious young gentleman living."

And yet he manages successfully to engage the activity of her imagination in his own behalf by making of her prescription for moral success a rationale for his failure:

> "So I have passed a great many years here, on that quiet plan I spoke of. . . . The events of my life have been absolutely unperceived by any one save myself; getting an old silver crucifix at a bargain (I have never bought anything dear, of course), or discovering, as I once did, a sketch by Correggio on a panel daubed over by some inspired idiot!"

James observes that "this would have been rather a dry account of Mr. Osmond's career if Isabel had fully believed it." So great is her conviction in the reality of her ideals of freedom and feeling, however, that Isabel cannot see Osmond's "dry," candid confession of limitations, of thwarted ambitions, for what it is. Instead, "her imagination supplied the human element which she was sure had not been wanting." Thus reassured about the nature of his renunciation, she determines "to express considerable sympathy for the success with which he had preserved his independence" in her bland formulation of his "plan" which concludes their exchange of "confidences":

> "That's a very pleasant life," she said, "to renounce everything but Correggio!" (24:231–32)

High on a hilltop outside Florence, in a garden which seems to cor-

respond to the gardens of which her "virginal soul" (6:44) dreamed
at Albany, Isabel Archer believes that she has discovered an incarnation of the aristocratic situation. Her experience of Gilbert Osmond's
show, his things and his words, during that first memorable afternoon
visit to his villa soon crystallizes into an "image" of his existence in
which she beholds the exemplary figure of the superior individual who
has embraced her ideal of the deliberate life:

> She had carried away an image from her visit to his hill-top which
> her subsequent knowledge of him did nothing to efface and which
> happened to take her fancy particularly—the image of a quiet,
> clever, sensitive, distinguished man, strolling on a moss-grown ter-
> race above the sweet Val d'Arno, and holding by the hand a little
> girl whose sympathetic docility gave a new aspect to childhood.
> The picture was not brilliant, but she liked its lowness of tone,
> and the atmosphere of summer twilight that pervaded it. It
> seemed to tell a story—a story of the sort that touched her most
> easily; to speak of a serious choice, a choice between things of a
> shallow, and things of a deep, interest; of a lonely, studious life in
> a lovely land; of an old sorrow that sometimes ached to-day; a
> feeling of pride that was perhaps exaggerated, but that had an
> element of nobleness; a care for beauty and perfection so natural
> and so cultivated together, that it had been the main occupation
> of a lifetime of which the arid places were watered with the sweet
> sense of a quaint, half-anxious, half-helpless fatherhood. (26:242)

With an effortlessness that resembles the peroration of so many of
Emerson's lectures, Isabel's imagination has resolved the discordant
aspects of Osmond's character, the "negative" qualities of his act of
renunciation and the signs of his "exaggerated" pride, into a harmony
of its own in which the potential aridity of aesthetic pursuits is redeemed by the presence of feeling. Osmond's devotion to his daughter
Pansy, symbolized in the charming image, provides "the human element which she was sure had not been wanting." All of her doubts
about the nature of Osmond's inner life (whether or not, as she puts
it, "a person was sincere") are eclipsed by her enthusiasm for the beauty of his expression, the "extraordinary subtlety" of his discourse and
the "quick-flashing" movement of his wit (26:242). As for Pansy, she
beholds in the child's performance the perfection of "an *ingénue* in a
French play," the purity of "the ideal *jeune fille* of foreign fiction" (26:

243). If Isabel admires the art that father and daughter display, the
creative activity of her own imagination, for all her pretensions to
originality, shows here as extremely conventional. She savors the halftones and twilight in her picture which lend themselves to the pleasure of a sentimental revery on the sweetness of fatherhood and childhood, on the pathos of "an old sorrow." Her idealized vision of "a
lonely, studious life in a lovely land" is a pretty exercise in the moral
picturesque, a diminished, homely version of the Emersonian landscape of the soul.

In this passage James offers the most important instance of his heroine's taste for "moral images," a taste which not only determined her
refusal of Warburton but eventually her acceptance of Osmond as well.
At Albany, at Gardencourt, in Florence, he consistently portrays Isabel's restless imagination as seeking confirmation for its theories of the
self and the world, of good and evil, in images of beautiful gardens
and pestiferous tracts. When James refers to Isabel during the Warburton episode as "a person of great good faith" (12:88), he means
precisely to insist on the trust of this self-reliant girl in the moral authority of her imagination, that is to say, her trust in her ability to recognize such images intuitively and to distinguish between them. After
Isabel rejected Warburton's proposal because the picture that it suggested had failed to measure up to "her visions of a completed life"
(12:87), she contemplated with alarm the possibility of latent egotism
in her act of judgment: "The isolation and loneliness of pride had for
her mind the horror of a desert place" (12:95). If her imagination is
exacting, however, it is self-indulgent as well. The flattery of its art
prevents her recognition of Osmond's garden as one of the desert places
of pride; for her interpretation of her picture she settles upon "a story
of the sort that touched her most easily." When Osmond proposes to
Isabel in Rome, however, she instinctively retreats from him, partly
from her sense of the seriousness of an act of moral choice and partly
from her reluctance to surrender to her own feelings. Significantly, it
is while the flight of her imagination is suspended that she becomes
acutely aware of "dusky, pestiferous tracts" otherwise ignored, dis-
pelled, or transformed by its agency: "Her imagination stopped, as I
say; there was a last vague space it could not cross—a dusky, uncertain tract which looked ambiguous, and even slightly treacherous, like
a moorland seen in the winter twilight. But she was to cross it yet"
(29:274). So confident is Isabel, however, in the truth of the beauti-

ful picture which she entertains of Osmond's life that she soon proceeds once more with her sanguine inferences about the moral character of the artist whom she is to choose for her husband.

In the early days of the friendship between Isabel and Madame
Merle, the older woman warned the girl of the dangers of an expatriate existence, choosing Ralph Touchett and Gilbert Osmond, whom
she disparagingly described as faceless nonentities, for her leading examples of Americans ruined by a life of indolent aestheticism in Europe. Isabel herself observed an affinity between the two men in their
"appearance of thinking that life was a matter of connoisseurship," yet
she distinguished between them: "In Ralph it was an anomaly, a kind
of humorous excrescence, whereas in Mr. Osmond it was the key-note,
and everything was in harmony with it" (24:229). Nowhere does James
make a more telling distinction between these two, between an ideal of
consciousness and its perversion, than in his analysis of the value that
each of them places upon the imagination of the American girl from
Albany. As much in love with Isabel's theories as he is with the girl
herself, Ralph interferes in her destiny in an attempt to provide her
imagination with an unlimited freedom of creative activity in which
they may be fulfilled. Osmond, on the other hand, declares with brutal
emphasis to Madame Merle that it is precisely the independence of
Isabel's imagination—for him her only "fault" is that "she has too many
ideas" (26:249)—that he will not tolerate in their marriage. In Osmond's egotistical conception of their union, Isabel's imagination,
which Ralph had idealized as a bird in flight, is to become "a silver
plate" in which he will display "the ripe fruits" of his own mind: "He
found the silvery quality in perfection in Isabel; he could tap her
imagination with his knuckle and make it ring" (35:307). Osmond's
ruling ambition is "to make himself felt," and he proposes to make of
Isabel's character a theater for self-expression: "A single character
might offer the whole measure of it; the clear and sensitive nature of
a generous girl would make space for the record. The record of course
would be complete if the young lady should have a fortune" (29:267).
James concludes this anatomy of Osmond's art on a distinctly Hawthornian note which recalls Miles Coverdale's fears for Priscilla at the
hands of Hollingsworth, when he observes that, for want of the "superior" material that Madame Merle has at last placed within his grasp,
he has been limited in the exercise of his power to the passive, diminu-
tive nature of his daughter: "If he wished to make himself felt, there

was soft and supple little Pansy, who would evidently respond to the slightest pressure" (29:268). Such is Osmond's regard for "the human element."

James brings the first section of his narrative to a climax when his heroine finally determines to express herself completely in an act of deliberate choice. When Isabel tells Caspar Goodwood of her engagement to Gilbert Osmond, she asserts once more that freedom of the will which she had so jealously guarded from the assaults of her suitor from Boston twice before. Isabel attempts to persuade Ralph, however, that her decision to marry represents a realistic acceptance of the inescapable limitations of her independence. During the year of restless travel which followed Osmond's proposal in Rome, she explored the possibilities of Ralph's vision of her destiny and her own and found them wanting; she was unable to locate a satisfactory opportunity for action and feeling—for her the two ought to be inseparable—beyond the conventional theater of marriage which she had, in her inexperience, rejected at Albany and later at Gardencourt. Yet curiously, for all her pretensions to the contrary, the impossible idealism of the girl from Albany with her many theories and her active imagination is clearly symbolized—if not to herself, then at least to Ralph—in her decision to marry Osmond. Shortly before her marriage Isabel tells her cousin, "I have only one ambition—to be free to follow out a good feeling" (34:304). She means in fact to be free to feel as she chooses and to choose freely to feel. If she refused Warburton because she feared the confinement of a "system" alien to the requirements of her imagination, and Goodwood because he had no "system" at all, she accepts Osmond because she mistakenly identifies his "system" as an embodiment of her own most fundamental beliefs. Her self-reliant step in pursuit of her vision of the deliberate life betrays her and provides in effect the most devastating criticism possible of the vision itself. Ralph, disillusioned, contemplates the "passionate good faith" of his cousin. In despair he realizes that she has lived up to their shared ideal of individualism with a vengeance:

She was wrong, but she believed; she was deluded, but she was consistent. It was wonderfully characteristic of her that she had invented a fine theory about Gilbert Osmond, and loved him, not for what he really possessed, but for his very poverties dressed out as honours. Ralph remembered what he had said to his father about

wishing to put it into Isabel's power to gratify her imagination. He
had done so, and the girl had taken full advantage of the privilege.
(34:305)

Although she was to be cruelly disappointed in her expectations, Isabel was destined in the course of her disastrous marriage to achieve
herself the distinction of the aristocratic situation which she had believed Osmond to possess.

III

In the second half of *The Portrait of a Lady* James explores the consequences of his heroine's act of deliberate choice as Isabel, with her
glowing creed of Emersonian individualism, makes her way in a Hawthornian world of shadows. Two years after her marriage, Ralph Touchett is troubled to observe striking changes in the character of his
cousin: "The free, keen girl had become quite another person; what
he saw was the fine lady who was supposed to represent something."
Isabel as a girl resembled Margaret Fuller in her serious quest for
"comprehensiveness of development"; now, as Osmond's "lady," she
has become strangely indifferent and lacking in direction, yet given to
a restless activity, a "crudity" and even "violence" in her impulses
which recalls the fitfulness of Zenobia's temperament following her
unfortunate marriage to Westervelt. Isabel's ambitious pursuit of self-
culture has been succeeded by the apparent suppression of any characteristic marks of her individuality. Perplexed, Ralph is driven to ask
himself, " 'What did Isabel represent?' . . . and he could only answer by
saying that she represented Gilbert Osmond" (39:344). He realizes
that Osmond has indeed made himself felt, that Isabel herself has become a figure in the picture of his life. Osmond's art, which had been
to the trusting girl the emblem, in fact the "proof," of "a superior morality," shows as a sham to Ralph's discerning eye, which divests Isabel's cherished image of its charming halftones and twilight, of its
feeling and its truth: "Everything he did was *pose*—*pose* so deeply
calculated that if one were not on the lookout one mistook it for impulse. . . . His life on his hill-top at Florence had been a *pose* of years.
His solitude, his ennui, his love for his daughter, his good manners,
his bad manners, were so many features of a mental image constantly
present to him as a model of impertinence and mystification" (39:345).
 If Isabel Archer beheld an enlightened and deliberate self-reliance

in what was in reality the calculated refinement of egotism, her imagination was to blame. When she achieves an understanding of her imagination, however, during the course of what James was later to describe as her "extraordinary meditative vigil" before the fire of the Casa Osmond on a winter night in Rome, she gains a knowledge not only of her self-deception but of the limitations of her character and her ideals as well, which raises her consciousness at the last high above the fineness of intelligence whose worship, in Osmond, in Madame Merle, and indeed in herself, brought her low. James conceived of Isabel's vigil as an experience of "searching criticism"[16] in which she creates a new picture to represent the moral reality of her marriage. While this meditation provides a characteristic example of the play of Isabel's imagination, of her preoccupation with her theories, and especially of her inveterate tendency to think in terms of images, images of beautiful gardens and pestiferous tracts, recalling the movement of her inner life at Albany, at Gardencourt, and later, in Florence, it differs from all those passages of introspection which precede it in one crucial respect. Isabel here approaches for the first time a complete knowledge of herself and consequently of Osmond because she now perceives the agency of her imagination as the determining force in their marriage: "He admired her—he had told her why; because she was the most imaginative woman he had known. It might very well have been true; for during those months she had imagined a world of things that had no substance" (42:373).

By means of a review of her earlier picture of Osmond in which she demonstrates an awareness of the process by which it was formed, Isabel proceeds to analyze the workings of her imagination which Ralph, James, and the reader have already explored at length themselves in the brilliant sequences of her courtship, first by Warburton and then by Osmond:

She had a vision of him—she had not read him right. A certain combination of features had touched her, and in them she had seen the most striking of portraits. . . . He was like a sceptical voyager, strolling on the beach while he waited for the tide, looking seaward yet not putting to sea. It was in all this that she found her occasion. She would launch his boat for him; she would be his providence; it would be a good thing to love him. And she loved him—a good deal for what she found in him, but a good deal also for what she brought him. (42:373)

As Isabel begins to appreciate the activity of her imagination she recognizes that her enthusiasm for this "portrait" of Osmond has been in part the result of her eagerness to locate, even to create, to invent, an occasion for significant moral action, an opportunity "to do something finely appreciable with her money." Although she concedes the importance of this "factitious theory" as a motive for her marriage, she is quick to reassure herself that the life of the heart has played an equal part in her conduct: "a certain feeling took possession of her," she urges, "a sense of the earnestness of his affection and a delight in his personal qualities" (42:374).

Even Isabel's feeling, however, for all its sincerity and strength, contains in it more than a little of the "factitious," as James suggests when he describes her "devotion" to this "finest individual" with his "beautiful mind" (42:374–75). Feeling for Isabel is really another name for the pleasure taken in ideas; her emotions are governed by and directed towards her theories. Hawthorne's passionate Zenobia, desiring "the stroke of a true, strong heart against [her] own," discerned in Hollingsworth "not so much an intellectual man . . . as a great heart";[17] James's intellectual Isabel, who drew back from the figure of Goodwood because "it was deficient in the social drapery which muffles the sharpness of human contact" (48:425), has aspired in her love for Osmond to a union of quite another order. She believed that in marrying him she was giving herself not to a man with a great heart but to a man with a beautiful mind with whom she might share her ideas, her "spiritual gems": "She had not been mistaken about the beauty of his mind; she knew that organ perfectly now. . . . A mind more ingenious, more subtle, more cultivated, more trained to admirable exercises, she had not encountered; and it was this exquisite instrument that she had now to reckon with" (42:374). James traces Isabel's deception to its source here, for although Osmond's mind *was* beautiful, the girl's confidence in this recognition was misplaced. Assuming that the beauty of his mind guaranteed the goodness of its works, she proceeded to make it the subject of the edifying picture of his life with which she fell in love. She now discovers in this portrait the presence of his egotism, which "lay hidden like a serpent in a bank of flowers" (42:376). Osmond's "rigid system, . . . draped though it was in pictured tapestries" (42:377), was not only conventional but "hideously unclean" (42:378). The beautiful mind, as this daughter of the transcendentalists painfully learns, is in itself morally neutral, a source from which either good or evil may spring.

If Isabel "had thrown away her life" (42:379)—this is now her despairing version of the self-reliant act of deliberate choice which was to have given her career a heroic turn—it was because she had attributed to the imagination a moral authority which it did not possess. Her marriage to Osmond demonstrated beyond any doubt that two "fine" individuals, speaking of renunciation and of the aristocratic situation, could yet entertain conceptions of these ideals so totally different and opposed that "the vital principle of the one was a thing of contempt to the other" (42:371): "Her notion of the aristocratic life was simply the union of great knowledge with great liberty; the knowledge would give one a sense of duty, and the liberty a sense of enjoyment. But for Osmond it was altogether a thing of forms, a conscious, calculated attitude" (42:377). For all their claim to fineness of perception, both were greatly deceived: neither expected the imagination of the other to interfere with the autonomous life of his own. Isabel's "real offence" for Osmond, in fact, was "her having a mind of her own at all" (42:378). If as an American girl in Albany Isabel relished introspection, which she regarded as "an exercise in the open air," if as a young heiress in Europe she dreamed of the pursuit of self-culture in an ideal marriage, "the infinite vista of a multiplied life" (42:371), which might have claimed *Woman in the Nineteenth Century* as its inspiration, now, as Osmond's lady in Rome, she finds that her inner life has become an intolerable oppression. A memorable image of suffocation within a darkened prison now replaces her earlier picture of a garden as the emblem of her consciousness: "When, as the months elapsed, she followed him further and he led her into the mansion of his own habitation, then, then she had seen where she really was. . . . It was the house of darkness, the house of dumbness, the house of suffocation. Osmond's beautiful mind gave it neither light nor air; Osmond's beautiful mind, indeed, seemed to peep down from a small high window and mock at her" (42:375).

In the light of such knowledge, the mystery of Osmond's art, his manipulation of her imagination and its moral ideals, becomes for Isabel increasingly transparent, and she places herself accordingly in unmistakable opposition to Osmond's "malignant" will when she impulsively announces to her husband her intention to go to Gardencourt to be with her dying cousin in his final hours. Osmond seizes this occasion as an opportunity to exact his wife's compliance—if only before the world—with his own conception of their marriage. Although he now knows that deception is played out between them, acknowledging that his "reason" for forbidding her journey is one of displeasure pure and simple, he proceeds nonetheless to accompany his ultimatum in the rhetoric customary to his specious displays of a superior morality:

> "I take our marriage seriously; you appear to have found a way of not doing so. . . . It may be a disagreeable proximity; it's one, at any rate, of our own deliberate making. You don't like to be reminded of that, I know; but I am perfectly willing, because—because—" And Osmond paused a moment, looking as if he had something to say which would be very much to the point. "Because I think we should accept the consequences of our actions, and what I value most in life is the honour of a thing!" (51:471)

Although Isabel recognizes this speech as an appeal to her imagination against her judgment, it yet retains sufficient force to cause her to renounce for the time being her contemplated journey. For all "her sense of her husband's blasphemous sophistry," his calculated invocation of her cherished theory of the deliberate life, his words still represent for her "something transcendent and absolute, like the sign of the cross or the flag of one's country." If he can still influence her conduct, he can no longer command the allegiance of her imagination, for his appeal only serves to deepen her understanding of her own beliefs. Osmond regards the lacerated feelings which fester at the heart of their marriage as merely a "drawback" to the observance of their life together as "a magnificent form." For Isabel, however, the failure of the correspondence between ideal and conduct completely destroys the value of their union as an act of self-expression. Taking up the issue of her journey and its bearing on their marriage once more, she returns Osmond's ultimatum with interest, disturbing his composure at last:

> "I suppose that if I go you will not expect me to come back," said Isabel.
> He turned quickly round, and she could see that this movement at least was not studied. He looked at her a little, and then— "Are you out of your mind?" he inquired.
> "How can it be anything but a rupture?" she went on; "especially if all you say is true?" (51:472)

Observing that his customary strategy, designed to enslave his wife, has led finally to her spiritual emancipation, Osmond's only recourse is to bring their interview to a close.

The vital principle of Isabel Archer's moral life, her belief in her value as a superior individual, is shaken when, later in the same afternoon, the Countess Gemini reveals to her the nature of the connection between Osmond and Madame Merle. Isabel is left face to face with "the dry, staring fact that she had been a dull, unreverenced tool" (52:484): "When," she is presently to wonder, "had it ever been a guarantee to be valuable?" (53:492). She does not regard her subsequent journey to England, however, as a considered decision concerning the future of her marriage; it expresses only an instinctive search for sanctuary, a recoil from suffering. Once at Gardencourt, Isabel experiences the pull of two forms of surrender which seem to offer refuge from the exigencies of her situation and from the act of moral choice which it requires: to lose herself in death like Ralph or in love with Caspar Goodwood. When Isabel shares the fullness of her knowledge with her cousin, the dying apostle of the creed of Emersonian idealism upon which they have both staked their lives, these two expatriate Americans, in the remote isolation of an English country house, enjoy for a poignant hour the privilege of the aristocratic situation, "the knowledge that they were looking at the truth together": "You wanted to look at life for yourself—but you were not allowed; you were punished for your wish. You were ground in the very mill of the conventional!" (54:506).

James concludes the last half of his narrative of Isabel's history as he has the first, when his heroine moves once more to shape her destiny in an act of deliberate choice;[18] she replaces her earlier identification with Osmond's renunciation which has proved to be false with a genuine renunciation of her own. In his account of Isabel's life during six years of courtship and marriage, James consistently associated each important decision of her career with an encounter between her and Caspar Goodwood. He has shown Isabel at Albany and again in London as preferring "an almost exclusively theoretic" (17:142) conception of her liberty to a surrender to love for Goodwood who "seemed to take from her the sense of freedom" (13:98). Isabel has continued to postpone a final reckoning with the indomitable Bostonian, although she allowed that his very "limitations" might "some day prove a sort of blessing in disguise—a clear and quiet harbour, inclosed by a fine granite breakwater" (21:196). Now, in the last of the series of confrontations between Isabel and Goodwood, she experiences in the shock of his kiss the expansive, overpowering reality of passion which she earlier dismissed as a limiting and conventional harbor. Her chastened imagination, however, draws back from the "mighty sea" (55:518), the uncharted ocean of freedom offered by her lover: what dream of emancipation can she possibly embrace? Isabel prefers the painful knowledge that choice is necessarily limited to such an unrestricted freedom as Goodwood's, one which might in fact deny her the exercise of choice altogether, a kind of freedom which, in any event, she had never desired. Although her decision to return to Italy, her election of "a very straight path" (55:519), must be read as a confession of limitations, it is for all that an act of choice.

In the characteristic version of James's fables of the American girl, courtship promised either to her expatriate lover or to the American girl herself an emancipation from the social restrictions of Continental conventions or the moral confinement of New England's Calvinist heritage into the ennobling freedom of a contemporary New World reality. *The Portrait of a Lady* marks a turning point in James's exploration of the redemptive possibilities of American courtship: Isabel Archer, free of her illusions at last, deliberately renounces Goodwood's love. If certain readers, continuing to seek a revelation of Isabel's character in what Madame Merle had called "the whole envelope of circumstances" (19:175), are perplexed by Isabel's return to Osmond, they fail to apply the lesson of the self-knowledge for which Isabel has paid so great a price. She was right, after all, when she told her older friend, "I don't know whether I succeed in expressing myself, but I know that nothing else expresses me" (19:176). Determined to locate a theater beyond the self where she might express her imagination and her theories, she pursued her search into narrower and narrower spheres of action. She has failed to find in either her restless movement across the open stage of Europe or her commitment to domestic life a satisfactory opportunity for self-expression, and she enters at the last the final bastion of the believing individual, the isolated self. Isabel's idealism is to survive the tragic consequences of her career of self-reliance, but in a darker world, different from the one that she conceived of at Albany as "a place of brightness, of free expansion, of irresistible action" (6:42). In *The Bostonians* James pursued his study of the idealism of the American girl to its logical conclusion.[19]

Chapter 7

NEW ENGLAND IN EXTREMIS:
THE BOSTONIANS

THE LATE EDMUND WILSON regarded the year 1886 as a turning point in the career of Henry James, the moment when James, "having gone to live in England, had definitely abandoned the United States as a subject or background for his fiction." He made of *The Bostonians*, appearing serially at that time, the emblem of this shift, emphasizing that it was "the last long novel (till *The Ivory Tower* at the end of his life)" to be set in his native country. In support of this view he read James's article on William Dean Howells in *Harper's Weekly* of June 19, 1886, as "a kind of farewell" in which the novelist entrusted to the care of his friend "the nice young American girl, so 'innocent,' so 'extraordinarily good,' with her suitors, her engagements, and her moral dilemmas."[1] It was entirely natural that James should make such a gesture, for it was Howells whom he credited with the discovery of the American girl in his early novels of the 1870s. In a letter that James wrote to Thomas Sargeant Perry in January of 1886, probably referring to *The Bostonians*, he clearly expressed his feeling that he had investigated the entire range of possibilities of the heroine with whom he had been preoccupied ever since the success of Daisy Miller years before. He confessed to Perry that he had had enough of the eternal young woman, that he was restless and eager to explore pastures new: "But I mean to surpass it, *de beaucoup*. I mean also to 'quit' for awhile paying so much attention to the young unmarried American female— to stop, that is, making her the central figure; which is of necessity a limitation."[2] This sense of the limitations of his star performer was undoubtedly deepened by the cool reception of *The Bostonians* by both the public and the critics, and James was not to return to the American girl as a major subject of inquiry until *The Wings of the Dove* (1902) and *The Golden Bowl* (1904), novels in which she was to undergo transformations that lie beyond the scope of this study.

In his biography of Hawthorne, James regretted that the author of *The Blithedale Romance* had not pursued a full-scale critique of "the Emersonian philosophy," and he proceeded to outline its flaws in extended commentaries on Emerson and Margaret Fuller when he treated Hawthorne's residence at Brook Farm and Concord. In *The*

Portrait of a Lady he continued to read the lesson of this chapter of the past, creating a heroine of the pristine Emersonian stamp whose indulgence in "fine sunrise and moonlight effects . . . in the landscape of the soul"[3] led her into a tragic experience of self-culture. Now in *The Bostonians* he brought his anatomy of the passionate aspirations of the New England Arcadia up to date, studying the legacy of the romantic cult of friendship and its twin ideals of renunciation and self-culture in a final, decadent phase. With Olive Chancellor's determination to possess Verena Tarrant to the exclusion of family and marriage, the Emersonian drama of self-culture, pushed to the last extreme, has become an alternative form of courtship, designed to supplant the conventional variety which had always been the theater of action for James's heroines in the past.

I

James's preliminary description in his notebook of the relationship between Olive and Verena suggests that he had a lively sense of the contemporary significance of a subject so rooted, as we shall see, in American intellectual and literary history:

> The subject is strong and good, with a large rich interest. The relation of the two girls should be a study of one of these friendships between women which are so common in New England. The whole thing as local, as American, as possible, and as full of Boston: an attempt to show that I *can* write an American story. . . . At any rate, the subject is very national, very typical. I wished to write a very *American* tale, a tale very characteristic of our social conditions, and I asked myself what was the most salient and peculiar point in our social life. The answer was: the situation of women, the decline of the sentiment of sex, the agitation on their behalf.[4]

The language of this passage, with its linking of the recent manifestations of the feminist insurgents to the familiar tradition of the friendship among New England women, the national to the local, the new to the old, suggests the dialogue between the present and the past that is central to James's understanding of American "social conditions" in the 1880s. In order to enter into the spirit of James's historical purpose in *The Bostonians*, I shall attempt to read the novel much as James himself read George Lathrop's biography of Hawthorne. James proposed that "the initiated mind" of a reader familiar with the New England past could not help responding to a single sentence in Lathrop, an account of an evening which Hawthorne spent at the home of the Peabody sisters, as "pregnant with historic meaning," evoking a vision of "the early days of 'culture' in New England."[5] Similarly evocative of the age of Emerson, Hawthorne, and Margaret Fuller is James's characterization of the American girl in the first major scene of the novel.

A motley evening gathering of feminists that draws all of the central characters into a single bare room in Boston's South End, the scene is cleverly designed to demonstrate the presence of the past in the present. James announces this theme in a prefatory exchange between the fiction's two rival centers of force: Olive Chancellor, apostle of the new, promises Basil Ransom, her handsome southern cousin, that the party at Miss Birdseye's will be an introduction to the "new ideas"; reactionary Ransom, genial but skeptical, expecting only the "old truths" in disguise, welcomes the occasion nevertheless as "a chance to see Boston."[6] Olive would seem to be right, for the initial impression of the evening's events is distinctly novel. In this latest fable of the American girl, James's heroine is discovered by the southern gentleman and the New England girl, her destined suitors, not in the pastoral setting customary to the unfolding of courtship in James's earlier treatments of this figure—not abroad on the piazza of a resort hotel, on the lawn of a country estate, or even at home alone with a book—but in a different theater altogether, the world of reform where woman's very nature is in question. Further, the circumstances of the encounter, however shabby, would seem to be auspicious, for Miss Birdseye, sponsor of the contemporary, is herself unquestionably respectable, an authentic abolitionist relic whose tireless energies in the years following the Civil War seek a fresh outlet in the agitation for the emancipation of women. However, when the Tarrants unexpectedly appear at her house to display their gifted daughter Verena to the guests assembled in the name of the feminist cause, this "old survivor of the New England Reform period"[7] finds herself at the end of her long career a host not to any dispensation of the new but to a debased, popularized version of the old transcendentalist idealism. Doctor Selah Tarrant, a seedy impresario of mesmerist and spiritualist séances, has in fact got up his daughter in the image of a Zenobia, an ardent advocate of women's rights, but it is no longer possible to distinguish clearly between the sincerity of a Zenobia's passionate radicalism and the meretricious show contrived by a Westervelt at the expense of a Priscilla. In the performance of Verena at Miss Birdseye's gathering of latter-day Bostonians, James stages a séance of his own, raising the old New England ghosts of the world of Emerson, Hawthorne, and Margaret Fuller to make them rap and squeak. Basil Ransom was right—it was to be a great chance to see Boston.

The remarkable young woman with the flame-red hair strikes Ransom as "an odd mixture of elements" (8:58), and his keen sense of the past is primed to pick them out for recognition, one by one. Familiar with the literature of romanticism, he realizes that Verena's plastic qualities have lent themselves to a cultivation of no ordinary sort. She has been formed, as he later observes, to resemble the model of flamboyant womanhood celebrated by Madame de Staël, and, he might have added, admired by Hawthorne and Margaret Fuller: "He had read, of old, of the *improvisatrice* of Italy, and this was a chastened, modern, American version of the type, a New England Corinna, with a mission instead of a lyre" (38:270). The particular nature of Verena's gift, her "genius" for oratory, strengthens her identification with this tradition of romantic individualism. Having singled out in his *Hawthorne* the eloquence of Emerson's addresses and Margaret Fuller's "Conversations" as the most characteristic examples of transcendentalist self-expression, James emphasizes that Verena, as an offshoot of "old Abolitionist stock" (4:32), has a talent for public speaking. The gospel of woman's redemptive love which the girl preaches at Miss Birdseye's, however, fails to vindicate her repuation for "a new style, quite original" (7:52); what she offers is a kind of parody of the exalted rhetoric of Margaret Fuller's feminist manifesto, *Woman in the Nineteenth Century*:

> "Why shouldn't tenderness come in? Why should our woman's hearts be so full of it, and all so wasted and withered, while armies and prisons and helpless miseries grow greater all the while? I am only a girl, a simple American girl, and of course I haven't seen much, and there is a great deal of life that I don't know anything about. But there are some things I feel. . . . It is what the great sisterhood of women might do if they should all join hands, and lift up their voices above the brutal uproar of the world." (8:63)

Ransom easily distinguishes between "the visible freshness and purity" of Verena herself and the emptiness of "the little effort," which "was full of schoolgirl phrases, of patches of remembered eloquence, of childish lapses of logic" (8:61). "She didn't know what she meant," he concludes, "she had been stuffed with this trash by her father, and she was neither more nor less willing to say it than to say anything else" (8:62).

Verena's performance as a New England Corinne with its echoes of Margaret Fuller sets in motion a second series of associations that link her to the heroines of Hawthorne's romances. There is, first of all, an aura of the histrionic and the exotic that colors her presence for Ransom as much as it ever had Zenobia's for Coverdale, and he imagines her variously as ropedancer, trapeze artist, and mountebank, an Oriental, or an Esmeralda without a goat. If Ransom makes fun of Verena's girlish counterfeit of the dark heroine's romantic spell, he is prepared to take her resemblance to the fair heroine in jeopardy much more seriously. He beholds in the girl a misplaced innocent moving in a decadent milieu alien to the purity of her nature, and he instinctively resents Selah Tarrant's influence over his daughter, much as Coverdale and Hollingsworth abhorred Westervelt's over Priscilla, because it seems to threaten "a dishonor to the passive maiden" (8:60). These inescapable parallels with *The Blithedale Romance*, like the allusions to Corinne, place the character of James's heroine in a diminishing perspective. If the girl seems to possess the leading attributes of each member of Hawthorne's pair of heroines, she has nonetheless little or nothing of the spiritual qualities of either. James insists that Verena is not the source, but only the expression, of the ideals to which she is nominally dedicated. Thus while she has something of Zenobia's richness, of the theatrical glamor of the romantic heroine, while she is, like her, a crusader for women's rights, the inexperienced, "melodramatic" girl with "her flat young chest" (8:59) has none of Zenobia's passionate womanhood and awakened consciousness. Although she resembles Priscilla in the pallor of her beauty, in her unreflecting, virginal innocence and in her susceptibility to the influence of a stronger will, Verena, lively and gregarious, possesses nothing of Priscilla's shrinking girlhood and the rarified, redemptive love with which it is endowed by Hawthorne.

The strangeness of James's engaging picture of Verena's innocence is in fact largely superficial. Behind the borrowed mask of New England's Corinne, beneath the overlay of Hawthornian attributes which suggest a kinship between her and each of the *Blithedale* heroines dark and fair, James and Ransom discern the real identity of "this attractive but ambiguous young person" (8:58), none other than that of the American girl in the fable of his own novels and tales.[8] It is not Verena's portrayal of a schoolgirl Margaret Fuller but the ideal qualities of her girlhood itself that capture Ransom's imagination: "the necessity of her nature was not to make converts to a ridiculous cause, but to emit those charming notes of her voice, to stand in those free young attitudes, to shake her braided locks like a naiad rising from the waves, to please every one who came near her, and to be happy that she pleased" (8:62). Verena is, of course, yet another version of the pretty American girl, audacious and innocent, a direct descendant of Daisy Miller; Olive Chancellor explicitly identifies her as the type of the innocent American girl (15:124). James celebrates her very being in that familiar language of paradox which determined the unfolding of Winterbourne's ill-fated study of the girl from Schenectady some years before:

> The girl herself would have been the most interested person in the world if she had not been the most resigned; she took all that was given her and was grateful, and missed nothing that was withheld; she was the most extraordinary mixture of eagerness and docility. Mrs. Tarrant theorized about temperaments and she loved her daughter; but she was only vaguely aware of the fact that she had at her side the sweetest flower of character (as one might say) that had ever bloomed on earth. (14:108)

There is a substantial body of evidence which suggests that "the initiated mind" would—and did—see in Basil Ransom's analysis of "the odd mixture of elements" in Verena Tarrant a series of connections, however misleading, between James's American girl and the likes of Priscilla, Zenobia, and Corinne. To begin with, James himself in his biography of Story years later formulated the kind of question that his allusions to the "Margaret-ghost" and her ideals in his treatment of Verena were designed to provoke: "Would she [Margaret Fuller], in other words, with her appetite for ideas and her genius for conversation, have struck us but as . . . a culture-seeker without a sense of proportion, or, on the contrary, have affected us as a really attaching, a possibly picturesque New England Corinne?"[9] While James does not mention Hawthorne by name in the course of his presentation of Verena as "the passive maiden" threatened with "dishonor," he may not have felt it necessary to do so, for the ground had, interestingly enough, been prepared by Howells in *The Undiscovered Country*

(1880). The opening scene of Howells's novel provides a striking analogue, possibly even a source of inspiration, for James's conception of
the American girl in the guise of the Boston sibyl.[10] Howells, as we
have seen, had his observer-figure, the counterpart of James's Ransom,
remark that the spectacle of Egeria Boynton as girl-child "Pythoness,"
an "innocent in the midst of fraud," was "worthy of Hawthorne."[11]

Whether or not Ransom had any thought of Margaret Fuller when
he recognized Verena as a version of Corinne, whether or not James
had Howells in mind as a precedent for the similarly allusive texture
of *The Bostonians,* James's readers were quick to fall in with the
spirit of the proceedings.[12] A number of his contemporaries, including
his Aunt Kate, James Russell Lowell, and especially William James,
saw in Miss Birdseye a portrait—and not a complimentary one at
that—of Hawthorne's sister-in-law, Elizabeth Peabody, who was still
living, an inveterate lecture-goer who had continued to thrive in her
old age on curiosity and culture in the best Boston tradition, which she
herself had helped to establish. Writing in protest to William, Henry
claimed that he had never intended such an identification, although
he "freely" admitted that "my creation would perhaps be identified
with Miss Peabody." He urged that "Miss Birdseye was evolved entirely from my moral consciousness, like every other person I have
ever drawn," that his conception had "originated in my desire to make
a figure who should embody in a sympathetic, pathetic, picturesque,
and at the same time grotesque way, the humanitary and *ci-devant*
transcendental tendencies which I thought it highly probable I should
be accused of treating in a contemptuous manner in so far as they
were otherwise represented in the tale."[13] James was clearly taken
aback by this naming of names, for he insisted in his fiction that public
life had obliterated Miss Birdseye's individuality altogether; her face
had been "soaked, blurred, and made vague" (4:27) by her career as a
philanthropist. The connection of this representative figure with such
a woman as Elizabeth Peabody was in any case entirely appropriate
to James's purpose, for she had been closely involved with the activi-
ties of the transcendentalist circle, and her West Street bookshop had
been a favorite meeting place for its gatherings, especially for the celebrated "Conversations" of Margaret Fuller. James's Miss Birdseye is,
of course, no more literal a portrait of Elizabeth Peabody than Hawthorne's Zenobia was of Margaret Fuller. The comparison, however,
is instructive, for both writers grounded their critiques of New England's "transcendental tendencies" in allusions to historical fact that

proved to be highly charged. Readers from then until now have stubbornly insisted on a narrow construction of these two characterizations, attributing to Hawthorne and James a personal animus that has in part discredited the serious historical purpose behind their scrutiny of the past.

James's stance in *The Bostonians* then was clearly retrospective. In this novel about post–Civil War New England he was looking back to the prewar era, systematically measuring the one against the other. Now Verena Tarrant was only partly suited to this end. Her talent for impersonation, her very possession of a chameleon identity which allows her to take on the coloration of the leading archetypes of the nineteenth-century American heroine, raise extremely disturbing questions, both moral and psychological, about the integrity of her personality. These doubts James himself reluctantly acknowledged when he observed that Ransom's patronizing analysis of Verena's posturing "attributed to Miss Tarrant a singular hollowness of character" (8:62). Even if we accept James's own praise of his heroine at face value, it is nonetheless true that the delicate reality of this pretty American girl is very much at odds with the cultural situation at whose center she so strangely stands. The intrinsic simplicity of an innocent girl, which easily harmonized with James's conception of New England in its golden age in *The Europeans*, could only seem incongruous in his vision of New England after the Fall in *The Bostonians*. James's sense of the lapse that separated the sheltered, limitless idealism of the Emersonian consciousness from the worldly, self-conscious skepticism of his own generation had been the governing theme of his biography of Hawthorne. He had even gone so far as to make out in Hawthorne himself, ironically, for all his searching criticism of "the Emersonian philosophy," a characteristic specimen of its illusions, "an American of the earlier and simpler type—the type of which it is doubtless premature to say that it has wholly passed away, but of which it may at least be said that the circumstances that produced it have been greatly modified."[14] To account for the gap between Hawthorne's generation and his own, James had turned to the Civil War, which he believed marked "an era in the history of the American mind": "It introduced into the national consciousness a certain sense of proportion and relation, of the world being a more complicated place than it had hitherto seemed, the future more treacherous, success more difficult."[15] In the perspective of history the great creation of James's first mature work, the innocent American girl, shows as obsolete.

II

When James came to write *The Bostonians,* he found that a single American figure, an Isabel Archer or a Christopher Newman, was no longer adequate to express his deepening sense of the complexity, the ambiguity, of the national character. The inability of the American girl to enact by herself the drama that he wished to explore is certain, for Verena never stands forth alone but always in the shadow of some dependency, whether that of her father, of Olive, or at the last of Ransom. This incompleteness seems to have necessitated the creation of a second heroine. Olive Chancellor is surely the most remarkable and the most peculiar of all of James's New England girls, and she surpasses even the morbidity of Howells's Alice Pasmer, the perversity of his queer young Dr. Breen:

> This pale girl, with her light-green eyes, her pointed features and nervous manner, was visibly morbid; it was as plain as day that she was morbid.(2:11)
> Her white skin had a singular look of being drawn tightly across her face but her features, though sharp and irregular, were delicate in a fashion that suggested good breeding. Their line was perverse, but it was not poor. The curious tint of her eyes was a living color; when she turned it upon you, you thought vaguely of the glitter of green ice. She had absolutely no figure, and presented a certain appearance of feeling cold. (3:18–19)

In Verena Tarrant James expressed those qualities of Isabel Archer which had captured the imagination of her admirers—her innocence, her vivacity, her spontaneity—while he embodied her capacity for an inner life in Olive Chancellor, in whom he pursued his study of the New England consciousness into the final decadent stage of its evolution from the pastoral simplicity and purity of the Emersonian vision.[16]

Tracing the connection between James and Margaret Fuller, Perry Miller suggested that James's conception of Verena as a late American mutation of the Corinne-figure owed more than a little to "the nearsighted, ungainly, doomed Margaret-ghost,"[17] but it is Olive Chancellor, possessed as she is of "the advantages as well as the drawbacks of a nervous organization" (3:19), who bears the closest resemblance of all of James's heroines to the historical Margaret Fuller. Fuller had dreamed of being a Muse figure, an inspired *improvvisatrice,* a Mariana or a Corinne, but she was herself, to borrow a distinction from

Woman in the Nineteenth Century, much more the Minerva figure,
"the plain and strenuous invalid"[18] whom James described as the
apostle of self-culture in New England, the restless intellectual whom
W. H. Channing portrayed as a potentially tragic individual, driven
by "the morbid influence of affections pent up to prey upon themselves."[19] James's account of Olive's impassioned response to Verena's
speech at Miss Birdseye's heightens her likeness to the Margaret Fuller
of the *Memoirs:* "the girl had moved her as she had never been
moved, and the power to do that, from whatever source it came, was
a force that one must admire. . . . She found here what she had been
looking for so long—a friend of her own sex with whom she might
have a union of soul" (11:80). From the very beginning Olive seeks
to form with Verena a relationship which recalls the romantic cult of
friendship practiced by Fuller and her friends: "Will you be my
friend, my friend of friends, beyond every one, everything, forever
and forever?" (11:81). As for Verena, James reports: "She knew too
little of the world to have learned to mistrust sudden enthusiasms. . . .
She never held back" (11:83).

If Olive is moved by Verena, she is moved especially by the girl's
"inspirational" speaking on the rights of women. In placing such an
emphasis upon Verena's gift—"Verena, for Olive, was the very type
and model of the 'gifted being'" (15:117)—Olive borrows a further
justification for their relationship from the now venerable tradition of
New England individualism, for a preoccupation with genius was always central to the transcendentalist experience of self-culture. Olive
brings her first meeting with Verena to a climax when she proposes
that they devote their friendship to the development of her gift, which,
in a heroic gesture of renunciation, is to be dedicated to the redemption
of women. As she makes this plea, Olive takes up an elevated strain,
quoting from the great German master whom Margaret Fuller worshiped for a time as the incarnation of her creed:

"I wonder if you know what it means, young and lovely as you
are—giving your life!"
Verena looked down for a moment in meditation.
"Well," she replied, "I guess I have thought more than I ap-
pear."
"Do you understand German? Do you know 'Faust'?" said
Olive. "'*Entsagen sollst du, sollst entsagen!*' . . . 'Thou shalt

renounce, refrain, abstain!' That's the way Bayard Taylor has translated them," Olive answered. (11:87)

Olive anticipates her intimacy with Verena in a cosy vision of Goethe and tea to be consumed in the shelter of her Charles Street parlor on snowy winter evenings. "The initiated mind" of James would surely have recognized this vision as a hothouse version of the traditional New England pursuit of self-culture, an aspiration that for him was symbolized in its classic purity by Lathrop's picture of an evening that Hawthorne and the Peabody sisters spent studying Flaxman's illustrations of Dante.

Olive's grandiose proposal is not without ambiguities, ambiguities which recall those that troubled the editors of Fuller's *Memoirs* and the author of *The Blithedale Romance* that Fuller so largely inspired. Her parade of duty shows increasingly as a rationalization for an intensely personal program of action, an oblique expression of psychological drives and sexual desire. The history of the friendship of Olive and Verena was to be, as Olive projected, that of a series of renunciations, but the disparity between the ostensible meaning of these acts and the real motivation behind them serves as a measure of the moral confusion regarding this ideal in the minds of the two young women. If Olive spoke to Verena solemnly of the necessity for self-sacrifice, it soon becomes plain that what she requires is that her friend "give up" her present ties with her family and with the young gentlemen of her acquaintance in order that she may devote herself exclusively to the cause of women, that is, to Olive. In the chill of a New England winter night Olive makes the meaning of renunciation abundantly clear to her friend, pleading, "Promise me not to marry!" (10:137).

Olive's "sublime," indeed megalomaniac, vision of reform springs from an insatiable egotism and lust for power which threaten the pretty American girl with complete loss of any individuality of her own. When Verena observes to Olive that "it would be very nice . . . just to take men as they are, and not to have to think about their badness" (18:158), she is led to recognize the extent to which her commitment to feminism is dependent on Olive:

"Do you know, Olive, I sometimes wonder whether, if it wasn't for you, I should feel it so very much!"

"My own friend," Olive replied, "you have never yet said any-

thing to me which expressed so clearly the closeness and sanctity
of our union."

"You do keep me up," Verena went on. "You are my conscience."

"I should like to be able to say that you are my form—my envelope. But you are too beautiful for that!" (18:159)[20]

Given the unlimited generosity of Verena, together with the demoral-
ized state of Olive's conscience and her unscrupulous drive for possession, the picture of their union which this remarkable exchange
evokes has in it not a little of the Hawthornian sinister, for James has
set the stage for a drama of hero worship reminiscent of the world
of *The Blithedale Romance*. This portentous scene between the morbid
New England girl and her yielding friend leads James to the very
heart of the world that he wished to explore.

Following the insight of James Freeman Clarke, W. H. Channing,
Emerson, and Hawthorne, who saw in Margaret Fuller's friendships the
most characteristic mark of the apostle of self-culture, James makes
Olive's friendship with Verena the medium for displaying the legacy
of transcendentalist individualism in the New England mind. In his
analysis of the three joys of the course of self-development that the
two young women pursue, their taste for music, for the society of
Miss Birdseye, and for the suffering of women in history, James records
the perversion of the venerable tradition of idealism for which he expressed a measured admiration in *Hawthorne*. He finds an appropriate
symbol for the spiritual dislocation that has taken place in the Bostonian universe in the first of the three joys of their spiritual discipline, the extravagance of their response to concerts at the Music
Hall, for their worship of the ideal of a feminist culture to the strains
of Beethoven and Bach takes on the proportions of a surrogate religion. Thus Olive tells herself that she is preoccupied with the salvation of her friend, and she invariably speaks of their "holy work" as a
priesthood of self-sacrifice.

Olive enshrines poor old Miss Birdseye, the second joy of her program of self-culture, in the place of honor in her church militant of
reform, and she savors a martial glamour in the abolitionist exploits
performed before the war by her aging patron saint, who "carrying
the Bible to the slave," "had been so nearly scorched by penal fires."
Although Miss Birdseye sustains "the unquenched flame of her transcendentalism" in her reading of Emerson, in her "frequentation of
Tremont Temple" (20:183), and in her reminiscences of Concord "as

it used to be" (20:185), Olive is acutely aware of the precarious and diminished New England tradition that the cherished older woman represents: "It struck Miss Chancellor (more especially) that this frumpy little missionary was the last link in a tradition, and that when she should be called away the heroic age of New England life—the age of plain living and high thinking, of pure ideals and earnest effort, of moral passion and noble experiment—would effectually be closed" (20:183). In his own tender evocation of Brook Farm in *Hawthorne*, James too recalled the line from Wordsworth, "plain living and high thinking" (4:494), but his knowledge of the intellectual provincialism and the moral illusions of the period prevented any sentimental surrender to its Arcadian appeal. Olive Chancellor knows no such restraint. While she candidly acknowledges that "one never pretended that [Miss Birdseye], poor dear, had the smallest sense of the real" (5:34), she yearns nonetheless for a lost sphere of heroic action, and she seeks, accordingly, to absorb her historic friend into the private world of her own imagination, her refuge from an unaccommodating contemporary reality. Transfigured by Olive's "sunrise-mist of emotion which made danger as rosy as success" (5:38), the old lady takes her place as an exemplary figure in Miss Chancellor's book of martyrs.

Within the sanctuary of her private life with Verena, Olive lavishes all the resources of her heated imagination upon "the history of feminine anguish" (20:185); this last of their joys is the heart of their cult, the obsession of their curriculum of self-culture, the guarantee, strangely, of the survival of their beautiful union. Her morbid consciousness is preoccupied with images of pestiferous tracts rather than of such beautiful gardens as Isabel Archer's from which suffering was to have been excluded altogether: "The world was full of evil, but she was glad to have been born before it had been swept away, while it was still there to face, to give one a task and a reward. When the great reforms should be consummated, when the day of justice should have dawned, would not life perhaps be rather poor and pale?" (18:160). If Margaret Fuller conceived of her career as a quest for the fulfillment in her nature of an eternal law of growth, Olive seeks in hers to satisfy a feverish thirst for martyrdom. Hers is a nature at war with itself, in which a principle of creativity and a drive toward self-destruction, endlessly striving for mastery, are simultaneously expressed in her preoccupation with self-sacrifice as an ideal of heroic action: "The most secret, the most sacred hope of her nature was that she might some day have such a chance, that she might be a martyr and die for something" (2:13). When it comes to Olive's relish of the painful, the vital principle of her liturgy of reform, James is devastating: "The prospect of suffering was always, spiritually speaking, so much cash in her pocket" (14:112–13). If Olive is fully as aggressive, demanding, and emotional as the Margaret Fuller portrayed by the editors of her *Memoirs* in the sections on "Friendship," she is, in her "fits of tragic shyness" (2:10), in her paralyzing fear of self-expression in public, quite unlike the leader of the "Conversations." Although in his rendering of her aspirations James demonstrates that his New England heroine is not without the gift of eloquence, he reveals that she has devoted this characteristic attribute of the transcendentalist artist to strange exercises which neither Emerson nor Margaret Fuller could have accepted as legitimate. She exploits her imagination, her art, to meet the requirements of her personal inadequacies, the fastidious inhibitions of a class-conscious proper Bostonian heightened by a violent, indeed mortal antipathy to men. Her apocalyptic vision of woman's historical mission, the quintessential expression of her decadent moral consciousness, shows as a curious blend of the sentimental and sado-masochistic, of tears and suffering, of cruelty and revenge, which contrasts strikingly with Verena's mild gospel of the redemptive power of woman's love:

> The unhappiness of women! The voice of their silent suffering was always in her ears, the ocean of tears that they had shed from the beginning of time seemed to pour through her own eyes. Ages of oppression had rolled over them; uncounted millions had lived only to be tortured, to be crucified. They were her sisters, they were her own, and the day of their delivery had dawned. This was the only sacred cause; this was the great, the just revolution. It must triumph, it must sweep everything before it; it must exact from the other, the brutal, blood-stained, ravening race, the last particle of expiation! It would be the greatest change the world had seen; it would be a new era for the human family, and the names of those who had helped to show the way and lead the squadrons would be the brightest in the tables of fame. They would be names of women weak, insulted, persecuted, but devoted in every pulse of their being to the cause, and asking no better fate than to die for it. (5:37–38)

It is with such an exalted strain as this that James concludes his

account of the winter of self-culture in which the two young women
are engaged. Although Verena is theoretically in training to become
the leader of a movement, she is in fact being drawn into Olive's private world where, subordinated in a "fine web" of dependency to the
indomitable personality of her friend, she moves like "some gently
animated image" (20:177) within the confines of Miss Chancellor's
"strenuous parlor" (20:180). If the girl is to be displayed before the
public as a standard-bearer of feminism, it is as an incarnation of Saint
Olive's vision. This victimization of Verena, however, which results
from the pursuit of self-culture, is not tragic in its consequences, as
Isabel Archer's was, because the experience, foreign to her nature,
is wholly imposed from without rather than sought in the fulfillment
of an inner need, and it never takes a deep hold upon her. The tragedy
lies with her friend, for Olive Chancellor contains within her tangled
personality at once the aspiration of an Isabel and the perversion of
an Osmond. For all her sincerity of purpose, which James is careful to
distinguish from the superficiality of Gilbert Osmond's *pose*, Olive has
so transformed self-culture, originally an expression of an impulse
toward spiritual emancipation, that it has become a closed system like
that of the sterile dilettante who sought to reduce the infinite vistas of
Isabel's idealism to the blank wall of a prison. Just as Ralph Touchett
realized with a chill that Isabel, after her marriage, has come to represent Osmond, so Verena's individuality is threatened by Olive's determination to make of their relationship an extension of her own ego,
a theater for her thwarted urge toward self-expression. At the close
of this first section of his narrative, James writes that imaginative
Verena was "immensely wrought upon" (20:186). The American girl
for the time being has been completely captured by the spell of her
New England friend: "The fine web of authority, of dependence, that
her strenuous companion had woven about her, was now as dense as
a suit of golden mail" (20:170).[21]

III

In the polemical world of *The Bostonians* where private lives are
governed by the logic of sexual politics, a feminist requires a male
chauvinist for an opponent, an Olive Chancellor a Basil Ransom, and
so it is that the captive Verena has captured in her turn the heart of
the handsome southerner. James promised in his notebook that the
novel would be at once local and national, and he exploited his knowl-

edge of the reigning archetypes of American cultural mythology in order to make that promise good. He fashioned a brilliant series of satiric parallels between the rival suitors for the hand of the American girl to demonstrate the larger, representative significance of his diagnosis of the aberrations of the New England mind after the Civil War. James's southern gentleman is indeed psychologically and morally, the cousin of his New England girl.

Ransom's initial impression of the girl who made a speech at Miss Birdseye's was vivid and disturbing, for the image of "the strange, beautiful, ridiculous, red-haired young *improvisatrice*" (22:206) struck his imagination as a perversion of the honest, natural qualities of a charming young woman. Convinced that "she was meant for something divinely different—for privacy, for him, for love" (28:275), he determines to rescue the girl from "the pernicious forces which were hurrying her to her ruin" (26:253) and place her in her proper sphere. The southerner's amatory campaign takes the form of an attack on the "preposterous puppet" (34:339) of the feminist identity that Miss Chancellor has forged for her, arguing that hearth and home provide the appropriate theater for the expression of her gift.[22] The role that Olive termed, with a bluestocking's contempt, that of "the ordinary pusillanimous, conventional young lady" (15:123) presents from Ransom's male angle of vision a glowing opportunity for Verena to become "in conversation, the most charming woman in America" (38:402).

For all that Ransom attempts to persuade Verena that his love offers her a return to normalcy from the lunatic fringe of the reform movement, his articulated version of their courtship is freighted with theory and rhetoric, suggesting that his wooing of the girl is in fact the mirror image of Olive's. With her professional ear for the quality of discourse, Verena laughs nervously at Ransom's phrasemaking, at his glib delivery of such slogans as "the realm of family life and the domestic affections" (34:348), but she is quick to see that he is not "piling it up satirically" when he speaks in a "religious tone" of saving his own sex "from the most damnable feminization": " 'The whole generation is womanized; the masculine tone is passing out of the world; it's a feminine, a nervous, hysterical, chattering, canting age, an age of hollow phrases and false delicacy and exaggerated solicitudes and coddled sensibilities, which, if we don't soon look out, will usher in the reign of mediocrity, of the feeblest and flattest and the most pretentious that has ever been' " (34:343). While Ransom is genuinely convinced that woman's natural happiness—and man's—is to be achieved in the expression of her love for him and in her docile acceptance of an inferior position in society, he is led, in the highly charged ideological environment in which courtship takes place in *The Bostonians*, to endow the traditional version of relations between the sexes with a larger significance. Thus when he champions submission to masculine authority as a safeguard against the debilitating feminization of his generation, Ransom himself becomes sententious in his very protest against the falseness of a "canting age." Ransom, like Olive, is full of talk about Verena's vocation, and James's unsparing account of Olive's pretentious, self-indulgent carrying-on about self-culture primes us to observe the "thread of moral tinsel" in "the Southern idea of chivalry" (33:328) that makes up Ransom's line.

Rhetoric finally cannot fill the vacuum left by the atrophy of role, for Basil Ransom and Olive Chancellor find their inherited parts as the southern gentleman and the New England girl no longer viable in the present. Their professed allegiance to such outworn creeds as a chivalric code or a quest for self-culture show as anachronisms in the hard, commercial reality of the new age. Both share in the loss of an heroic theater of action, which vanished, they believe, with the passing of the Civil War. Ransom is deeply stirred by the memorial to the Union dead at Harvard, and even Olive, reflecting on Ransom's experience as a soldier in the war, can find herself filled with admiration and envy for a man when he is one who "had fought and offered his own life, even if it had not been taken" (2:13). Each of them aspires to the position of leadership which is part of his identity as traditionally defined, and each fails to carve out such a role in the postwar era. Both condemn that version of the world of reform which thwarts their personal ambitions or offends their fastidious taste, yet each covets a public success. Olive dreams of being "a representative woman, an important Bostonian," and she contemplates a vicarious fulfillment of this destiny as "the prompter, colleague, associate of one of the most original girls of the time" (30:292). As for Ransom, James observes that he "had always had a desire for public life; to cause one's ideas to be embodied in national conduct appeared to him the highest form of human enjoyment" (21:193). Significantly, however, the only substantial achievements of Ransom and Olive that James records are narrowly private, the relationships—such as they are—that they form with Verena Tarrant, who provides each of them with a receptive, captive audience of one for his views.

Although Ransom's formulation of Verena's character differs radical-

ly from Olive's, his polemical strategy is the same that she has used
to implement her friendship with the gifted girl. Each exploits his
ideal of love, whether it be a transcendental union of soul in a friendship between women or an ultraconservative version of patriarchal
marriage, in order to win possession of Verena as a home for his
homeless ego. With a toughness worthy of Osmond, the southerner
means to require as the condition of their union that the girl abandon
her career, the display of her gift, the practice of her art, altogether:
"If he should become her husband he should know a way to strike
her dumb" (33:329). In accomplishing his end Ransom reverses the
course of James's development of the American girl in his fiction. From
the moment of her very first appearance in his tales, the expatriate
artist consistently valued her bright presence as representative national fact, an incarnation of freedom and spontaneity, an emblem of
the artistic possibilities of American life. In the subsequent narratives
which James devoted to a more intensive exploration of the consciousness of the girl herself, the imaginative young woman tended to
acquire an artistic sensibility of her own. Ransom's plea for Verena's
emancipation from an enslavement to Olive and to the feminist cause,
however, shows increasingly as a disguise for his unrelenting determination to make her submit to his will. In the future that Ransom projects for this American girl, she is to be neither a free spirit nor an
artist.

Olive would appropriate Verena as a beautiful "envelope," Ransom
her "engaging exterior," each equally willing to sacrifice in the American girl that core of Emersonian selfhood that had always been the
vital principle of the James heroine since the days of Daisy Miller. As
the Hawthornian drama of the violation of innocence proceeds apace,
it becomes harder and harder to believe that the American girl has
any substance of her own, for all of James's generous effusions to the
contrary. Olive intended to transform Verena into a militant feminist
armed at all points against inevitable encounters with the male sex,
and Verena herself assured her friend that she took only a polemical
interest in Ransom as "the type of the reactionary" (30:296). In the
course of a single spring afternoon in Central Park, however, the seductive southerner manages to subvert the conception of Verena's
mission which his New England cousin had devoted more than a year
of self-culture to forming. Because "it was in her nature to be easily
submissive, to like being overborne" (33:337), Verena abandons her
effort to "convert" Ransom to the cause of women, preferring instead

to acknowledge the irresistible power of the unreconstructed male. As she lingers with Ransom in the park, her behavior, in spite of her convictions, testifies to the truth of Ransom's view of woman's nature, that "what is most agreeable to women is to be agreeable to men!" (34:345). It is the conversion of the gifted girl herself that has begun.

IV

That Basil, Olive, and Verena should conceive of courtship as a drama of conversion aligns *The Bostonians* with the fiction of Stowe, Hawthorne, and Howells. James's satire in *The Bostonians*, however, like Howells's in *April Hopes*, celebrates the death of courtship as a redemptive process. In book three, as Ransom and Olive struggle to win possession of Verena with the ascendancy of the southerner definitely established at the last, James offers what is surely the most curious account of the wooing of the American girl in all of his fiction. After the meeting with Ransom in Central Park, Verena flees with Olive to a seaside retreat on Cape Cod where they pass the summer in the company of Miss Birdseye. Tracing the two young women, Ransom lays a veritable siege to this feminist stronghold where Verena daily rehearses the address, "A Woman's Reason," which is to inaugurate her mission in Boston in the fall. As a pretext for granting regular interviews to her insistent suitor, Verena professes a high-minded desire "to prove (the picture Olive had held up from the first), that a woman *could* live persistently, clinging to a great, vivifying, redemptory idea, without the help of a man" (37:393). The "redemptory idea," which had been invariably associated with the power of a woman's love in the world of Stowe and Hawthorne, has become oddly divorced from its traditional expression in the relations between the sexes, and James paints a comic picture of the curious inversion of courtship which Verena, with her divided allegiances and her confused ideals, attempts to enact: "With her watch in her hand" (37:395), the girl devotes an hour a day to her lover in order "to see, for the moral satisfaction of the thing," as she tries to persuade Olive, and herself as well, "how good a case, as a lover, he might make out for himself and how much he might touch her susceptibilities" (37:391).

And so the American girl joins her suitors in the rhetoric of dissimulation that is the hallmark of moral discourse in the fallen world of *The Bostonians*. More and more self-conscious about the seriousness of her concern with the dignity of womanhood which Ransom

systematically ridicules, Verena instinctively substitutes her eloquence
for her waning commitment to the feminist cause. As her conversations
with Olive take on the quality of her public utterances, of "speeches"
filled with "phrases" and buttressed by "arguments" and "proof," Olive
is increasingly aware of a want of sincerity in her friend's exercise of
the very gift that she had originally reverenced as a guarantee of the
girl's integrity: "She could no longer be put off with sophistries about
receiving visits from handsome and unscrupulous young men for the
sake of the opportunities it gave one to convert them" (37:387). James
traces the origins of Verena's innocent, "artlessly artful" evasions to
the decadent public tradition of idealism in which she had been nurtured, pointing to "her habit of discussing questions, sentiments, moral-
ities, her education, in the atmosphere of lecture-rooms, of *séances*, her
familiarity with the vocabulary of emotion, the mysteries of 'the spiritual life'" (37:391–92). Further, he suggests that Olive may have
confronted her own responsibility for fostering "the abundant eloquence" of which she finds herself, to her dismay, not the guardian
but the victim: "Did she say that Verena was attempting to smother
her now in her own phrases?" (37:392). Thus Olive reaps with a
vengeance the fruits of her program of self-culture. She has educated
Verena to a language of humanitarianism which her friend now uses
to justify her response to the very force that destroys their friendship.

Sustained by endless pledges of renunciation, by extravagant ex-
hortations, by all the machinery of mutual self-deception at the disposal of those who have made a profession of the arts of persuasion,
the sacred union of the two young women begins to dissolve under
the strain of Ransom's steady attack, and the moral poverty of their
pursuit of self-culture is painfully exposed by the death of their
mentor, Miss Birdseye. Just as Fenimore Cooper commemorated in
the death of Natty Bumppo the passing of the wilderness ideal, so
James in the death of the tutelary genius of reform celebrates the last
rites of the tradition of New England idealism which had flourished
in the age of Emerson, Hawthorne, and Margaret Fuller. Verena,
Olive, and Ransom, for all their differences, are equally quickened
with a solemn sense that the opportunities for moral heroism in American life are slipping away from them into an unrecapturable past.
Chastened by her recognition that she herself "had come too late for
the heroic age of New England life" (38:408), Verena makes a brave
effort to sustain Miss Birdseye in her sanguine illusions, allowing her
to believe that Ransom has been won to the cause. In fact, a classic

version of the familiar paradigm of nineteenth-century courtship had become central to the old woman's rosy vision of progress, for she saw in the love of Ransom for Verena the conversion of an unregenerate antagonist to the redemptive value of "Boston ideas" (28: 279): "It warmed her heart to see the stiff-necked young Southerner led captive by the daughter of New England trained in the right school, who would impose her opinions in their integrity" (36:378). As Miss Birdseye yields up "her philanthropic soul" (38:406), she looks blindly forward to the fulfillment of all of her millennial hopes in the work of the two young women and their southern "convert" whom she regards as her successors: " 'Good-by, Olive Chancellor,' Miss Birdseye murmured. 'I don't want to stay, though I should like to see what you will see' " (38:412). Olive, however, is too stricken to go along with Verena's well-meant deception in this laying-on of hands, for she faces the loss not only of the little old lady in whose "displaced spectacles" "the whole moral history of Boston was reflected" (5:35), but of her dearest friend as well. She realizes that the union of Verena and Ransom represents a conversion indeed, but of a sort fatally other than that which Miss Birdseye envisioned, a conversion that unmistakably spells the destruction of her friendship with Verena. To Miss Birdseye's affirmation of faith, she shrieks out, in reply, "I shall see nothing but shame and ruin!" (38:412).

In the last extended view of Olive's consciousness in *The Bostonians,* James portrays the New England girl in her darkest hour in nineteenth-century American fiction. With redemptive courtship reduced to an empty charade and their own relationship no better, Olive confronts her failure to transform Verena into a feminist heroine. Ironically, her obsessed imagination and the rhetoric of its arsenal of cherished images govern her perception of Verena to the last: if the girl is not destined to be the invulnerable, military figure of feminine resistance, then she is to be the type of the frailty of women, a fulfillment of Olive's all-consuming vision of the suffering of women at the hands of men. When Verena, determined to refuse Ransom once and for all, prolongs the would-be final interview with her lover to include an all-day excursion in a boat, Olive realizes that her friend "was now not to be trusted for an hour." Wounded by Verena's desertion, Olive gives herself up to a series of "hideous recognitions" (39:419) which pierce the very heart of her self-conception. "Did she ask herself why she should give up her life to save a sex which, after all, didn't wish to be saved?" (39:422). Shaken by killing doubts of the value of such a renuncia-

tion, she mourns her ruined ideals of friendship and self-culture which
had been consecrated in its name:

> The splendor of the vision over which the curtain of mourning now
> was dropped brought to her eyes slow, still tears, tears that came
> one by one, neither easing her nerves nor lightening her load of
> pain. She thought of her innumerable talks with Verena, of the
> pledges they had exchanged, of their earnest studies, their faith-
> ful work, their certain reward, the winter nights under the lamp,
> when they thrilled with previsions as just and a passion as high
> as had ever found shelter in a pair of human hearts. The pity of
> it, the misery of such a fall after such a flight, could express itself
> only, as the poor girl prolonged the vague pauses of her unnoticed
> ramble, in a low, inarticulate murmur of anguish. (39:423)

In the extremity of her despair, Olive imagines the death of Verena
herself, the guarantee of the precarious equilibrium of her moral life:
"She saw the boat overturned and drifting out to sea, and (after a week
of nameless horror) the body of an unknown young woman, defaced
beyond recognition, but with long auburn hair and in a white dress,
washed up on some faraway cove" (39:424). This image, conventional as it is, deserves a special place in the iconography of nineteenth-
century American fiction, for it is the conception of a heroine, the innocent garden girl dressed in white whom Stowe and Hawthorne had
made a force for life, that is "defaced beyond recognition." In the
moving twilight vigil which follows the girl's return from her outing
with Ransom at dusk, the dying friendship of the two young women
passes for a brief moment from the betrayals of rhetoric into the silence and purity of inexpressible feeling: "[Olive] would just sit there
and hold her hand; that was all she could do; they were beyond each
other's help in any other way now" (39:425).

In the unaccommodating moral universe of *The Bostonians* James
makes it clear that neither of his heroines is to find the place of honor
of which she dreamed. In the melodramatic finale Ransom at last takes
complete possession of Verena at the Music Hall by wresting the girl
from Olive's grasp minutes before she is to deliver the address on the
rights of women which was to have been the glorious dawn of her
feminist career. Hurried from the hall by her lover toward a future of
uncertain happiness, Verena is, significantly, no longer recognizable in
the cloak and hood with which he has sought "to conceal her face
and her identity" (42:464). As for Olive, she is almost reduced by Ran-

som to the abject weakness that she had dedicated her life to resist. "There was a moment during which she would have been ready to go down on her knees to him, in order that the lecture should go on" (42: 456). At the last, however, she moves from desperation to a posture of strength, willing to sacrifice herself for the sake of the redemption of women. As she turns to mount the platform alone to announce the definitive departure of the pretty American girl from the stage forever, she believes herself defeated utterly, and she hopes to achieve the apotheosis of suffering womanhood, meeting at the hands of an outraged throng the martyrdom of her fanatical visions. Ransom, unrelenting yet compassionate, beholds in a single moment of revelation the presence in his doomed New England cousin of heroic possibilities destined never to be fulfilled:

> She had straightened herself again, and she was upright in her desolation. The expression of her face was a thing to remain with him forever; it was impossible to imagine a more vivid presentment of blighted hope and wounded pride. Dry, desperate, rigid, she yet wavered and seemed uncertain; her pale, glittering eyes straining forward, as if they were looking for death. Ransom had a vision, even at that crowded moment, that if she could have met it there and then, bristling with steel or lurid with fire, she would have rushed on it without a tremor, like the heroine that she was. (42:461–62)

Cheated of her dream of success by the defection of her friend, Olive is ironically deprived of even "the fierce expiration" (42:462) that has been the obsession of her morbid imagination, for the announcement of Verena's desertion fails to incite the audience to violence. At the close of the novel James has completely tested his heroines, exhausting for the time being the literary possibilities of the types of womanhood that they represented; no one could look to either for moral inspiration any more. The spontaneity and freedom of the pretty American girl, her career as a gifted being abandoned, have been eclipsed; and the perverted transcendentalist idealism of her New England friend, with her anguished consciousness and her broken ideals of friendship, self-culture, and renunciation, has been destroyed.

Conclusion

Conclusion

THROUGH THE INNER LIVES of their representative heroines Harriet Beecher Stowe, Nathaniel Hawthorne, William Dean Howells, Henry James, and others (among them John William DeForest, Henry Adams, Oliver Wendell Holmes, Sarah Orne Jewett and Mary Wilkins Freeman) unfolded the history of a single moral tradition; they dwelt—such was their shared attraction to the play of abnormal psychology—on its every involution. Their fiction offers an anatomy of puritanism and of the reaction against it, the flood of romantic individualism and the flowering of transcendental idealism. The redirection of moral energy previously contained in the Calvinist formulation was signalled in their novels by the emergence of new heroines to replace the once and former queen. In the succession the crown passed from the puritan maiden to the romantic rebel and finally to the American girl. When Hawthorne, for example, taking up the domestic savior worshipped by Mrs. Stowe, found her ideals and her health eroded, he introduced an alternative conception of womanhood, a mature figure whose sexuality and consciousness endowed her with a vitality requisite to challenge yet never quite usurp the ailing throne. Inspired by Howells's discovery of the American girl, James championed the claim of a fresh pretendor to the title of reigning heroine. The touted freedom and originality of this new dynasty proved illusory, however; the paradoxical power of the girl's "audacious innocence" was revealed at the last as an improbable crossing of earlier lines of descent, an unstable synthesis of the rebel's dangerous pursuit of self-culture and the maiden's indulgence in morbid renunciations.

On the whole, the most satisfactory strategy adopted by these writers to dramatize the shifting dialectic of intellectual history was the invention of a brand new heroine rather than the rehabilitation of an obsolete model. James's *The Portrait of a Lady* is the rare exception to this rule, a successful effort to mature a girlhood nurtured on the simple ideals of the Emersonian philosophy to a stature commensurate with the complexity of the Gilded Age, while the Hilda of Hawthorne's *The Marble Faun* is a more characteristic example of an author's failure to make his innocent complete the education set in motion by her experience of suffering and evil. A heroine usually demonstrated her power most convincingly in the absence of competing types of womanhood, as with the solo appearance of Hawthorne's progressive Hester in *The Scarlet Letter*, or even with his reversion to the emphatically old-fashioned Phoebe in *The House of the Seven Gables* of the following year. The revelation, however, of a community engaged in altering its image of itself was most strikingly captured in novels with two rival heroines, each testifying to the incompleteness of the other. Thus the hopes still possible to the solitary heroines of *The Scarlet Letter* and *The Portrait of a Lady* yield to the pronounced disillusionment portrayed in the hopelessly divided pairs of *The Blithedale Romance* and *The Bostonians* with their separation of action from thought, of body from soul. In the age of disjunction the capacity for moral action either shriveled to an empty gesture or succumbed to a morbid paralysis of the will. Ironically, at the very moment when the new heroine displayed her obvious superiority—variously defined—to her opposite, orthodox number, she betrayed her own limitations as well. The triumph of a full-blown womanhood over a perpetual virginity, for instance, was qualified sharply by the failure of the emancipated woman to find an accepted place in society through marriage. At the same time, the tragedy of the romantic rebel was balanced by the frigidity of the New England girl, the futility of Zenobia's suicide by the desolation of Priscilla's union with Hollingsworth, the emblem of her perfunctory maturity.

Although the attempted redefinition of the community ideal ended, more often than not, in an impasse, the vicissitudes of the cult of womanhood nevertheless preserved in its very excesses and distortions the aspirations of a society in flux, hankering after strange gods. Changes in the location of the worship of "the divine presence" were accompanied by shifts in the quality of belief as the sacred hope of the puritan community of visible saints came to be exploited as the idol of the masses. She who was to have been the inspiration of every village hearth and home provided in the cities the dubious excitement of "conversations," the titillation of séances. The ideal woman was not to be looked for in the girl next door but searched out as a museum piece, revered on the Lyceum stage as a peerless platform exhibit, cherished as an objet d'art in a villa abroad. The hero's redemptive veneration of

the heroine, equivalent to the confession of his "evidences," was succeeded by the debilitating adulation of the profane, the shrewd cash
appraisal of the showman, and the sterile appreciation of the expatriate
connoisseur.

Some such summary as the preceding might be made of the progress
of the New England girl in American fiction. I have argued that the
cumulative study of her role in all these novels yields a privileged
insight into the spiritual history of New England in the nineteenth
century. Yet even the most committed student of intellectual history
must draw up short in his undertaking, soon or late, to ask, as Perry
Miller conscientiously did, "Do words like 'New England tradition' and
'Puritan heritage' mean anything concrete and tangible? Do they 'explain' anything? Do habits of thought persist in a society as acquired
characteristics, and by what mysterious alchemy are they transmitted
in the blood stream? I am as guilty as Emerson himself if I treat ideas as
a self-contained rhetoric."[1] The novels of Stowe, Hawthorne, Howells,
and James answer Miller's questions with a resounding yes; but have
we not in the sequence of these fictions precisely such a self-contained
rhetoric as Miller speaks of? These novels of the matter of New England may well confirm the existence of a literary tradition, but has their
analysis of the moral life of a culture a larger, historical value as well?
There are, of course, moments when the unfolding of intellectual history and the destiny of the heroines of fiction converge; the life of
Margaret Fuller, as we have seen, is one of these and affords some
measure of the fidelity of Hawthorne and James as observers of the
New England scene.

The issues that troubled Miller, however, are not likely soon to be
resolved. It is altogether fitting that Howells should have made what
is surely the finest statement of the problem before us when he wrote
in "Puritanism in American Fiction": "The question whether the fiction
which gives a vivid impression of reality does truly represent the conditions studied in it, is one of those inquiries to which there is no very
final answer. The most baffling fact of such fiction is that its truths are
self-evident; and if you go about to prove them you are in some danger
of shaking the convictions of those whom they have persuaded." Where
indeed, beyond the covers of such books as those that we have studied
in these pages, is the New England mind of the nineteenth century on
display? Howells asserts that "the life of New England . . . is not on
the surface, or not visibly so, except to the accustomed eye,"[2] while
"the initiated mind" of Henry James, as we have seen, located "the

latent romance of New England" in "the secret play of the Puritan faith," "a life of the spirit more complex than anything that met the mere eye of sense."[3] Howells values the stories of Mary Wilkins Freeman, James the romances of Hawthorne, precisely because such literature makes visible the elusive if fundamental realities of the New England mind and character. Howells proceeds to relate a charming anecdote to illustrate "the sense of reality" imparted by the picture of New England life in fiction. He relates the story of an impressionable young girl from New York, driving with her mother along the North Shore of Massachusetts, who refused to look at the houses in the villages as they passed. The girl confided to her mother that the houses "were terrible, and she knew that in each of them was one of those dreary old women, or disappointed girls, or unhappy wives, or bereaved mothers, she had read of in Miss Wilkins's stories." Howells's sympathy clearly lies with the overly susceptible young girl; "if one has not the habit of experiencing support in tragedy itself," he observes, "one gets through a remote New England village, at nightfall, say, rather limp than otherwise, and in quite the mood that Miss Wilkins's bleaker studies leave one in. . . . To the alien inquirer, however, I should be by no means confident that their truth would evince itself, for the reason that human nature is seldom on show anywhere. . . . Types are very backward and shrinking things, after all; character is of such a mimosan sensibility that if you seize it too abruptly its leaves are apt to shut and hide all that is distinctive in it." If we are prepared to accept, as I am, the authority of Howells's and James's experience of New England life, then we may rest with Howells when he observes at the end of his essay, "I should not blame any one who brought the portrait to the test of reality, and found it exaggerated, overdrawn, and unnatural, though I should be perfectly sure that such a critic was wrong."[4]

Notes

Notes

The following notes supply complete bibliographical information for all works cited in the text and for secondary sources relevant to my argument; I have accordingly omitted a formal bibliography.

CHAPTER 1

1. *Victorian Mode* (East Lansing: Michigan State Univ. Press, 1965), pp. vii, 16, viii, 15. When several references to the same text occur within a single paragraph, they have been grouped in a summary note appended to the final reference in the series.

2. *American Scene*, ed. W. H. Auden (New York: Scribners, 1946), p. 346.

3. *Heiress* (Minneapolis: Univ. of Minnesota Press, 1959), p. vii. In his recent study *The American Eve in Fact and Fiction, 1775–1914* (Urbana: Univ. of Illinois Press, 1974), Ernest Earnest seeks to test the authenticity of the portrait of American women in fiction, by examining "actual girls and women as they are revealed in diaries, memoirs, and biographies" (p. 4). Earnest concludes that American women "were vastly more lively, able, full blooded, and interesting human beings than we have been led to suppose" (p. 270) by the fiction of James, Howells, and others. This interesting book appeared too late to receive the consideration it deserves in my own; I can only comment here that Earnest strikes me as setting up a rather simplistic opposition between the heroines of fiction and "actual girls and women." For the cultural historian the two categories represent equally important kinds of cultural fact, since each influences and is influenced by the other in a demonstrable and determining way.

4. Patricia Thompson's formulation of her study, *The Victorian Heroine: A Changing Ideal, 1837–1873* (London: Oxford Univ. Press, 1956), is characteristic: "I am interested principally in assessing the effect of the feminist movement on the heroine of the novel, in indi-

cating how far the novelists' ideal of womanhood was affected by contemporary trends" (p. 11).

5. "Inner and Outer Space," *Daedalus*, 93 (1964), 598, 599.

6. *Wooing*, the Riverside Edition of *The Writings of Harriet Beecher Stowe* (Boston, 1896), 42:410. All references to novels quoted in the text give first the chapter and then the page.

7. *Heroines* (New York: Harper, 1901), i, 112.

8. *In Defense of Historical Literature: Essays on American History, Drama, and Fiction* (New York: Hill, 1967), pp. 13, 31.

9. *The Scarlet Letter*, the Centenary Edition of *The Works of Nathaniel Hawthorne* (Columbus: Ohio State Univ. Press, 1962), pp. 28, 29, 32.

10. *Historical Literature*, pp. 14–31.

11. *William Wetmore Story and His Friends* (Boston: Houghton, 1903), i, 129.

12. *Hawthorne*, in *The Shock of Recognition*, ed. Edmund Wilson (New York: Modern Library, [c. 1955]), 1:430. All citations of *Hawthorne* refer to this edition.

13. *Literary Friends and Acquaintance: A Personal Retrospect of American Authorship*, ed. David F. Hiatt and Edwin H. Cady (Bloomington: Indiana Univ. Press, 1968), p. 102.

14. See Austin Warren, "The New England Conscience, Henry James, and Ambassador Strether," *Minnesota Review*, 2 (1962), 149–61, for a suggestive treatment of the place of Strether in the literature concerned with the "high and morbid ethicality" (149) of the New England conscience. Warren singles out Stowe, Hawthorne, Howells, and James as the foremost analysts of this New England phenomenon.

15. *The Art of the Novel: Critical Prefaces*, ed. Richard P. Blackmur (New York: Scribners, 1934), preface to "The Reverberator," pp. 186–93, preface to "Daisy Miller," pp. 272–80.

16. *Art of the Novel*, pp. 267, 270, 268.

17. *The Complete Tales of Henry James*, ed. Leon Edel (Philadelphia: Lippincott, 1962), iv, 206. All citations from "Daisy Miller" refer to this edition.

18. James W. Gargano has correctly emphasized the extent to which "Daisy Miller" is really Winterbourne's story in his article, "*Daisy Miller*: An Abortive Quest for Innocence," *South Atlantic Quarterly*, 59 (1961), 114–20.

19. *The Reverberator* (London, 1888), pp. 223, 220, 224–25.

20. *Complete Tales*, IV, 442–43. "The Pension Beaurepas" (1879) offers a more extended dramatization of this state of mind.

21. Christof Wegelin, in *The Image of Europe in Henry James* (Dallas: Southern Methodist Univ. Press, 1958), similarly distinguishes between two kinds of stories about the American girl, those of conduct and those of consciousness, "either of the struggle against the limitations on her freedom imposed from without, or—if the freedom is granted—of the growth of her awareness" (p. 69).

22. *Art of the Novel,* p. 51.

23. *Complete Tales,* IV, 276. All citations from "An International Episode" refer to this edition.

24. *Henry James: The American Essays,* ed. Leon Edel (New York: Vintage, 1956), p. 19.

CHAPTER 2

1. Alice C. Crozier's recent study, *The Novels of Harriet Beecher Stowe* (New York: Oxford Univ. Press, 1969) does deal extensively with Mrs. Stowe as a writer of fiction. See her discussion of the observer figure in Mrs. Stowe's social novels, which she compares with those of Howells and James (pp. 187–92).

2. Praised by James Russell Lowell and Vernon L. Parrington, *The Minister's Wooing* has not shared in the contemporary revival of interest in *Oldtown Folks* (1869), reissued in the John Harvard Library series (Cambridge: Harvard Univ. Press, 1966) with an introduction by Henry F. May. The only extended commentary on the novel is Charles Howell Foster's article, "The Genesis of Harriet Beecher Stowe's *The Minister's Wooing,*" *New England Quarterly,* 21 (1948), 493–517, an inquiry into the origins of this fiction in Mrs. Stowe's personal life and spiritual history. See also Foster's expansion of this material in *The Rungless Ladder: Harriet Beecher Stowe and New England Puritanism* (Durham, N.C.: Duke Univ. Press, 1954), pp. 86–128. It has seemed to me unnecessary to rehearse in my own discussion of Mrs. Stowe the biographical background of *Wooing,* given Foster's thorough and judicious investigation of this involved subject. He reads the novel as a "symbolic action" in which Mrs. Stowe resolves her tangled feelings about the spiritual fate of her eldest son, Henry, who drowned at sea in 1857 before he had experienced conversion.

3. *The Minister's Wooing,* in the Riverside Edition of *The Writings of Harriet Beecher Stowe* (Boston, 1896), 2:15. All citations from *Wooing* refer to this edition.

4. This passage confirms the appropriateness of Crozier's designation of the Stowe heroine as "angelic" (p. 134). When Crozier observes that "Mrs. Stowe's sentimental heroine has affinities with Lucy Gray" (p. 143), she places the Stowe heroine, for all her distinctive New England traits, in the mainstream of the romantic movement.

5. I would suggest that the springs of the ideal of renunciation that both ennobled and deceived James's Isabel Archer and Olive Chancellor, the source of the vague notion of self-sacrifice over which Howells had the daughters of Silas Lapham shed such idle, sentimental tears, lie in Mary Scudder's belief in predestination, the divine original of the act of moral choice. Cf. Crozier, p. 224, n. 80.

6. Mrs. Stowe was not, of course, the first American writer to present courtship as a redemptive process. The practice is common in the fiction of the period, with Cooper's popular romances probably offering the most familiar examples. In *The Sea Lions* (1849), the pious heroine refuses to accept her lover until he experiences conversion, abandoning his rationalistic skepticism to embrace her own true faith in the divinity of Christ.

7. For a characteristic example of Mrs. Stowe's effusive utterances on the meaning of love, reminiscent of the impassioned, exalted vein of so much of the writing of Margaret Fuller, see *Wooing,* 8:90–91; here, as always, she emphasizes the essentially religious nature of love and its expression in the interrelated acts of hero worship and self-sacrifice.

8. Mrs. Stowe preferred to explore the victimization of the loving woman by hero worship in minor characters who were to be distinguished from native American womanhood by their alien blood (Madame de Frontignac, for example, or Cassy, the unfortunate octoroon in *Uncle Tom's Cabin* [1852]).

9. Crozier comments: "[Mrs. Stowe] is obviously very fond of this passage, and has, equally clearly, modeled her heroine on Edwards's ideal" (p. 125).

10. Crozier reads the upshot of the confrontation between Burr and Mary as follows: "She has made the ice-cold cynic cry; that is, she has made the renegade grandson submit to his own better nature and acknowledge the truth of Mary's doctrine of the holiness of love" (p. 124). See Kenneth S. Lynn's fine introduction to *Uncle Tom's Cabin,*

reissued in the John Harvard Library series (Cambridge: Harvard Univ. Press, 1962), for a treatment of "the Calvinistic causes of romantic sickness" (p. xxi) which afflicts the Byronic hero in Mrs. Stowe's fiction. His brief discussion of her religion of love, with its emphasis on womanhood, the family, and domestic values as an alternative to the unwholesome burden of romanticism, has been valuable to me in the formulation of my own thinking about *The Minister's Wooing*.

11. Mrs. Stowe herself provides a gloss for this cherished image in the following observation: "The greatest moral effects are like those of music,—not wrought out by sharp-sided intellectual propositions, but melted in by a divine fusion, by words that have mysterious, indefinite fullness of meaning, made living by sweet voices, which seem to be the out-throbbings of angelic hearts. So one verse in the Bible read by a mother in some hour of tender prayer has a significance deeper and higher than the most elaborate of sermons, the most acute of arguments" (*Wooing*, 25:288).

12. *The Europeans* (Boston, 1879), 3:48.

13. That this pivotal event of death should eventually stand revealed as a mistake casts a strange light on the action arising from it. I think of the freeing of the already free Jim in the final section of *Huckleberry Finn*. Reflected in the imposition of these deceptions upon their unwitting and suffering characters there is, it seems to me, an analogous desire on the part of both authors to undercut the existence of the seemingly insoluble problems which they face.

14. Following Perry Miller, Crozier argues persuasively that "Mrs. Stowe's sentimental heroines convey a mysticism [similar to Emerson's transcendentalism] in their many rapturous visions of Christ and an analogous pantheism in their instinctive rapport with flowers and natural beauty" (p. 131).

15. Further evidence of her view of the exalted position of women in the life of the spirit is advanced by John R. Adams in *Harriet Beecher Stowe* (New York: Twayne, 1963). Observing that she preferred to think of Jesus as "his mother's boy," he writes: "As He was the union of the feminine and the divine, He had an understanding of women that other men cannot approach; and moreover, He is understood better by women, pure women, than by crude masculine creatures." He proceeds to quote from Mrs. Stowe's *Footsteps of the Master* (New York, 1877) as follows: "We can see no image by which to represent the Master but one of those loving, saintly mothers, who in leading

along their little flock, follow nearest in the footsteps of Jesus" (Adams, pp. 81–82).

16. Lillie Ellis of *Pink and White Tyranny, A Society Novel* (1871) presents an important exception to this pattern. John Seymour, mistaking pretty, empty Lillie, the frivolous product of Newport and New York, for the embodiment of all the virtues of his New England mother, marries her and brings her back to live in idyllic Springdale. The antithesis of Mary Scudder, Lillie is the idol of the watering place, "the daughter and flower of the Christian civilization of the nineteenth century" (the Riverside Edition, 4:303). She is exactly the type of girl whom such a narrative as *The Minister's Wooing* would have failed to interest. In Lillie Mrs. Stowe dared to entertain the conception of a young woman wholly lacking in the capacity for feeling, for love, oblivious to the sacraments of courtship, marriage, and family. With the bankruptcy of this representative of contemporary girlhood the Stowe heroine has reached the end of the road.

CHAPTER 3

1. "From Edwards to Emerson," *Errand into the Wilderness* (Cambridge: Harvard Univ. Press, 1956), pp. 184–85, 192, 201.

2. *Margaret Fuller: American Romantic,* ed. Perry Miller (Garden City, N.Y.: Doubleday, 1963), pp. xii–xiii. Citations from this edition will appear in the text, preceded by the abbreviation MF.

3. *Heroines of Fiction,* i, 179.

4. *The Collected Works of Ralph Waldo Emerson,* ed. Alfred R. Ferguson and Robert E. Spiller (Cambridge: Harvard Univ. Press, 1971), i, 45.

5. *Memoirs of Margaret Fuller Ossoli,* ed. W. H. Channing, J. F. Clarke, and R. W. Emerson, 2 vols. (Boston, 1852), i, 194–95. Citations from the *Memoirs* will appear in the text, preceded by the abbreviation Mem.

6. "Thoughts on Modern Literature," *Dial,* 1 (1840), 146.

7. "Bettina Brentano and Her Friend Gunderode," *Dial,* 2 (1842), 314.

8. See also Mem, i, 65–66.

9. *The Blithedale Romance,* the Centenary Edition of *The Works of Nathaniel Hawthorne* (Columbus: Ohio State Univ. Press, 1964), 12:103. All citations from Hawthorne's romances refer to the Centenary Edition.

10. Mason Wade, *Margaret Fuller: Whetstone of Genius* (New York: Viking, 1940), p. 112.

11. *The American Notebooks,* ed. Randall Stewart (New Haven: Yale Univ. Press, 1932), p. 176. (The recent Centenary edition of the notebooks omits some of the material on the Hawthorne-Fuller relationship offered by Stewart in his elaborate notes; for this reason I have chosen to refer to Stewart's edition.) James quotes the first sentence of this passage from the journal in *Hawthorne* and observes, in his guise as the "initiated" reader, "There is probably a great deal of Concord five-and-thirty years ago in that little sentence" (4:506).

12. Louise Hall Tharp, *The Peabody Sisters of Salem* (Boston: Little, 1950), pp. 137, 87–89.

13. *American Notebooks,* p. 315.

14. Ibid., pp. 293–94.

15. Ibid., p. 160.

16. Ibid., p. 293.

17. Wade, p. 111.

18. Ibid., p. 113.

19. Ibid., pp. 281–82. Wade's presentation of the Hawthorne-Fuller relationship is to my mind the most satisfactory, and it has guided my own approach to this problem. See chap. 7, "Brook Farm and Hawthorne," esp. pp. 113–18.

20. See also the passages in Fuller's *Memoirs* where Clarke and Emerson observe that the narrow circumstances of her situation seemed ill-suited to the generous dimensions of her character (i, 135, 232).

21. See Wade, pp. 115–18, for a review of points of resemblance between Zenobia and Margaret Fuller.

22. See Zenobia's observation on the nature of women: "Our virtues, when we have any, are merely impulsive and intuitive" (25:217).

23. See James's *Hawthorne,* 5:530, and Bewley, *The Complex Fate* (London: Chatto and Windus, 1952), pp. 21–23.

24. *American Essays,* p. 19.

25. I was first introduced to the romantic convention of paired heroines by Perry Miller in his course on American romanticism at Harvard University. My discussion of Hawthorne's women is indebted to his lively treatment of this subject.

26. Virginia Ogden Birdsall, in "Hawthorne's Fair-Haired Maidens: The Fading Light," *PMLA,* 75 (1960), 250–56, has traced Hawthorne's "steady loss of faith in the redemptive qualities of his New England

girl" as a manifestation of the deepening pessimism of his final years. James thought of Hawthorne's "exquisite" New England girls as a related group of characters, referring to Hilda as the "sister" of Phoebe and Priscilla (*American Essays*, p. 21).

27. Hawthorne's contemporaries and certain of his later critics have regarded his wife, Sophia, as a possible prototype or at least a significant source of inspiration for the fair heroines of his romances, especially for Phoebe and Hilda. Among the most suggestive correspondences are Mrs. Hawthorne's activity as a painter and her invalidism (she was treated for her chronic headaches at one point by a mesmerist healer, Dr. Fiske, her father's partner in his medical practice). One of Hawthorne's pet names for Sophia was Phoebe.

28. In his discussion of *The House of the Seven Gables* in the *Hawthorne* James quoted this passage with warm approval.

29. For an alternative reading of Phoebe, emphasizing her growth into womanhood through her initiation into an adult knowledge of sex and death, see Joel Porte, *The Romance in America: Studies in Cooper, Poe, Hawthorne, Melville, and James* (Middletown, Conn.: Wesleyan Univ. Press, 1969), pp. 121–25.

30. See 9:71–72, 78–79 for explicit statements of Coverdale's fear that Priscilla's hero worship of Hollingsworth will lead to her destruction by his ruthless egotism.

31. *Hawthorne*, 6:554.

32. Cf. Mrs. Stowe's initial picture of little Eva: "Always dressed in white, she seemed to move like a shadow through all sorts of places, without contracting spot or stain; and there was not a corner or nook, above or below, where those fairy footsteps had not glided, and that visionary, golden head, with its deep blue eyes, fleeted along" (*Uncle Tom's Cabin*, the Riverside Edition of *The Writings of Harriet Beecher Stowe* [Boston, 1896], 14:192).

CHAPTER 4

1. *Literary Reviews and Essays by Henry James on American, English, and French Literature*, ed. Albert Mordell (New York: Twayne, 1957), p. 207.

2. Reprinted in F. O. Matthiessen, *The James Family: Including Selections from the Writings of Henry James, Senior, William, Henry, and Alice James* (New York: Knopf, 1947), p. 499.

3. In his article "Howells' Irrational Heroines," *University of Texas*

Studies in English, 35 (1956), 64–80, John Roland Dove surveys the Howells heroine in nine different novels, emphasizing her prominence in the fiction of the 1880s and asserting that "she plays a more important role in his novels than any other of his characters" (64). He seeks to distinguish two types of the irrational heroine, "the romantic enthusiast" whose misguided ideals of conduct are derived from literature, and "the moral enthusiast," "a descendent of generations of New England Puritans" with "an almost pathological sense of duty" (73). In practice these categories tend to be overly schematic: thus Alice Pasmer of April Hopes is identified as a representative of the first type although she fits the description of the second as well. Curiously, Marcia Gaylord, surely Howells's finest study of the irrational heroine, is omitted from this discussion.

4. Literary Reviews, p. 211.

5. Ibid., p. 207.

6. In In Quest of America: A Study of Howells' Early Development as a Novelist (Cambridge: Harvard Univ. Press, 1958), Olov W. Fryckstedt speaks of Howells's discovery in the late 1870s of the role of puritanism in New England life and character as "a major event in [his] literary development" (p. 218). He observes that women became the focus for this new concern, stating that Howells believed that "women were more instilled by the stern spirit of Puritanism" (p. 220) than men.

7. Literary Reviews, p. 204. This version of the story, which tells all in capsule form, is a conversational quip that James quotes in his first review of the novel.

8. The Lady of the Aroostook (Boston, 1879), 19:219. Citations from Howells's novels in this chapter refer to the following editions, listed in order of their appearance in the text:

The Lady of the Aroostook.
The Undiscovered Country (Boston, 1880).
Dr. Breen's Practice (Boston, 1881).
A Modern Instance, ed. William M. Gibson (Boston: Houghton, 1957).
Indian Summer, ed. Scott Bennett and David J. Nordloh (Bloomington: Indiana Univ. Press, 1971).
The Rise of Silas Lapham, ed. Walter J. Meserve and David J. Nordloh (Bloomington: Indiana Univ. Press, 1971).
April Hopes, ed. Kermit Vanderbilt, Don L. Cook, James P. El-

liott, and David J. Nordloh (Bloomington: Indiana Univ. Press, 1974).

Annie Kilburn (New York, 1889).

9. Staniford deliberately rejects for his Lydia-Lurella the conventional destiny of the intellectual magazine heroine which he formulates as follows in something like a parody before-the-fact of *The Portrait of a Lady:* "If she were literary, she would be like those vulgar little persons of genius in the magazine stories. She would have read all sorts of impossible things up in her village. She would have been discovered by some aesthetic summer boarder, who had happened to identify her with the gifted Daisy Dawn, and she would be going out on the aesthetic's money for the further expansion of her spirit in Europe. Somebody would be obliged to fall in love with her, and she would sacrifice her career for a man who was her inferior, as we should be subtly given to understand at the close" (9:91).

10. *Discovery of a Genius: William Dean Howells and Henry James,* ed. Albert Mordell (New York: Twayne, 1961), pp. 93–94.

11. Ibid., pp. 92–93.

12. Ibid., pp. 95–96.

13. *The James Family,* p. 503.

14. In *The Achievement of William Dean Howells: A Reinterpretation* (Princeton: Princeton Univ. Press, 1968), Kermit Vanderbilt observes that Boynton was "Howells' distillation of New England's historical search for spiritual reality" (p. 43). He offers a carefully elaborated argument, however, that Egeria is the victim not simply of her father's crisis of belief but of a repressed, incestuous transferrence of his love for his dead wife. Here and in his treatment of the relationship between Squire Gaylord and his daughter Marcia in *A Modern Instance,* he suggests that Howells studied the troubled moral climate of his age in the sexual as well as the religious confusion experienced by his characters.

15. Years later, in his essay "Puritanism in American Fiction" in *Literature and Life* (New York: Harper, 1902), Howells made the following inventory of the unexploited resources of New England life for fiction:

There was, however, always a revolt against Puritanism when Puritanism was severest and securest; this resulted in types of shiftlessness if not wickedness, which have not yet been duly studied, and which would make the fortune of some novelist who cared to do a fresh thing. There is also a sentimentality, or pseudo-emotionality (I have not the right phrase for it), which awaits full recognition in fiction. This efflorescence from the dust of systems and creeds, carried into natures left vacant by the ancestral doctrine, has scarely been noticed by the painters of New England manners. It is often a last state of Unitarianism, which prevailed in the larger towns and cities when the Calvinistic theology ceased to be dominant, and it is often an effect of the spiritualism so common in New England, and, in fact, everywhere in America. . . . But as yet little hint of all this has got into the short stories, and still less of that larger intellectual life of New England, or that exalted beauty of character which tempts one to say that Puritanism was a blessing if it made the New-Englanders what they are. (p. 282)

Howells's insistence that these striking features of the life of the region have yet to be captured by American writers seems to me surprising. Modesty may have played its part in his willingness to set aside, by implication, the by-no-means negligible achievement of *The Undiscovered Country* in dealing with the "revolt against Puritanism" and the "pseudo-emotionality" of spiritualism. The complex of issues in his outline, however, especially the emphasis on "that larger intellectual life" and the "exalted beauty of character," so closely matches the central concerns of the New England novels of Harriet Beecher Stowe that one can only wonder to what extent he was familiar with her work exclusive of *Uncle Tom's Cabin* and what he thought of it.

16. The striking resemblances between *The Undiscovered Country* and *The Blithedale Romance* have been discussed by George N. Bennett, in *William Dean Howells: The Development of a Novelist* (Norman: Univ. of Oklahoma Press, 1959), p. 104, and Howard Kerr, in *Mediums, and Spirit-Rappers, and Roaring Radicals: Spiritualism in American Literature, 1850–1900* (Urbana: Univ. of Illinois Press, 1972), pp. 142–43.

17. I do not mean to suggest that Howells neglects the woman question. Grouped with narratives like Mrs. Stowe's *My Wife and I* (1871), Henry Adams's *Esther* (1884), Sarah Orne Jewett's *A Country Doctor* (1884), James's *The Bostonians* (1886), *Dr. Breen's Practice* has often been regarded as a symptom of the crisis of contemporary American womanhood in this period, and Howells makes the ambiguities attending his heroine's position as a woman physician, a "doctress," a con-

stant subject of conversation in the novel, recording with a wealth of psychological insight the interplay of professional and sexual motivation in the relationship between Dr. Breen and Dr. Mulbridge.

18. It may be well that the writing of *A Fearful Responsibility,* which appeared just before *Dr. Breen's Practice* in 1881, recalled the character of Florida to Howells, for this short novel, with its innocent American girl, its expatriate American consul, its European lovers, its concern with the conventions of courtship and the eternal issue of chaperonage, and finally, its setting in Venice at the outbreak of the Civil War, reads like a warmed-over version of *A Foregone Conclusion.* The only fresh source of interest in this otherwise undistinguished revival resides in Howells's anatomy of the delicate conscience of the self-preoccupied college professor, Owen Elmore, who shares with Dr. Breen the asceticism and the painful introspection which for Howells were characteristic of the puritan sensibility.

19. See Vanderbilt's sharp anatomy of decadent Equity as "a counterfeit of a village America" (*Achievement,* pp. 89–90).

20. Suggesting that James's portrait of Isabel Archer may have provided Howells with a hint for his own conception of an American heroine who "throttles her emotional life in a marriage to a passionless egotist," Vanderbilt points out that a contemporary reviewer of *A Modern Instance* "noticed that Isabel Archer's sickly admirer Ralph Touchett prefigures the role of serviceable and guilt-ridden Ben Halleck" (*Achievement,* p. 73, n. 20).

21. Fryckstedt describes Howells's attitude toward the residual puritanism of his own day as "a mixture of admiration and censure" (*Quest,* p. 220).

22. Richard Watson Gilder, editor of *The Century Magazine,* where the novel was published as a serial, apparently shared Howells's original sense of the heroine as the central figure in the story when he proposed the title, *Marcia: A Modern Tragedy.* See Edwin H. Cady, *The Road to Realism: The Early Years 1837–1885 of William Dean Howells* (Syracuse, New York: Syracuse Univ. Press, 1956), p. 212.

23. Robert Falk in *The Victorian Mode in American Fiction* has stressed this shift in Howells's treatment of his heroines as an indication of his growth as a novelist (p. 123). He makes no connection, however, between this shift and Howells's concern in these years with the decline of Calvinism in New England and of the village culture that it had sustained. Fryckstedt, on the other hand, has suggested a

reading which parallels my own (*Quest*, p. 227). For a valuable biographical approach to this turning-point in Howells's career, see Vanderbilt's investigation of the origins of Howells's growing sense of determinism in human affairs (*Achievement*, pp. 75–86 passim).

24. Fryckstedt, for example, is willing to accept Howells's portrait of Alice Pasmer as "a penetrating study of [the] morbid side of New England psychology" (*Quest*, p. 222). William Wassertrom, in "William Dean Howells: The Indelible Stain," *New England Quarterly*, 32 (1959), 486–95, rejects this interpretation as an inadequate explanation for the girl's peculiarities. In his view it is sex, not conscience, that makes Alice Pasmer sick.

CHAPTER 5

1. An observation made by William James suggests that an affinity between the two writers was operative from the very earliest years of Henry's creative activity. He wrote to Henry from Cambridge on January 19, 1870: "That you and Howells with all the models in English Literature to follow, should needs involuntarily have imitated (as it were) this American [Hawthorne], seems to point to the existence of some real American mental quality." On February 13 James wrote to his brother in reply that he meant "to write as good a novel one of these days (perhaps) as *The House of the Seven Gables*," *The James Family*, pp. 319–20.

2. *The American Novels and Stories of Henry James* (New York: Knopf, 1947).

3. *Grasping Imagination* (Toronto: Univ. of Toronto Press, 1970), pp. 3, 108, 159.

4. *The Selected Letters of Henry James*, ed. Leon Edel (New York: Farrar, 1955), p. 23.

5. *The American Henry James* (New Brunswick, N.J.: Rutgers Univ. Press, 1957), p. 348.

6. *Saturday Review*, 46 (Feb. 2, 1963), 15.

7. *Art of the Novel*, p. 4.

8. *Roderick Hudson* (Boston, 1876), 3:79. All citations from *Hudson* refer to this edition.

9. Cf. Buitenhuis: "In writing *Roderick Hudson* he [James] began, in a real sense, where Hawthorne left off in his last completed novel, *The Marble Faun*" (*Grasping Imagination*, p. 81).

10. *Art of the Novel*, p. 13.

11. *The Europeans* (Boston, 1879), 6:125. All citations from *The Europeans* refer to this edition.

12. *Literary Reviews*, p. 211.

13. Crozier, *Novels*, pp. 132–33.

14. James to William Dean Howells, March 30 [1877], *Selected Letters*, p. 70.

15. James to Mary Walsh James, March 15, [1878], *Selected Letters*, p. 53.

16. James to Howells, March 30, [1877], *Selected Letters*, p. 70.

17. Cf. Buitenhuis: "Gertrude is . . . a member of the line of New England women that culminates in the hard ruthlessness of Olive Chancellor in *The Bostonians*" (*Grasping Imagination*, p. 99).

18. "Henry James" in *The Shock of Recognition*, ed. Edmund Wilson (New York: Modern Library, [c.1955]), p. 859. Eliot includes "Margaret Fuller and her crew" in his list of nineteenth-century representatives of the "New England genius." Yvor Winters has argued persuasively that the origins of James's moral vision are to be traced to New England and its heritage of Calvinism, and he offers a brief survey of the relevant background of intellectual history. He omits, however, any consideration of transcendentalism, although he cites Joseph Warren Beach's observation that the Jamesian morality is "essentially the morality of the New England of Emerson and Thoreau" (p. 335). See "Maule's Well, or Henry James and the Relation of Morals to Manners," in *In Defense of Reason* (New York: Swallow, 1947), pp. 300–343.

19. *The Bostonians* (New York: Modern Library, [c.1956]), 20:180.

20. Ibid., 11:87.

21. *The Portrait of a Lady* (Boston, 1882 [1881]), 6:43.

22. *American Essays*, p. 70.

23. Ibid., p. 62.

24. *American Essays*, pp. 19, 13. Note that the date of the introduction to Hawthorne is incorrectly printed in this edition: it should be 1897, not 1879.

25. In *Hawthorne*, James said of Zenobia's suicide, "There is indeed nothing so tragical in all Hawthorne" (5:527).

26. *American Essays*, p. 19.

27. *The Blithedale Romance*, 25:218.

28. *Art of the Novel*, p. 67.

29. *The Complex Fate,* p. 33.
30. *American Essays,* p. 56.

CHAPTER 6

1. *Art of the Novel,* pp. 48, 51.
2. Richard Chase strongly supports this identification of the consciousness of Isabel Archer in his fine essay on *The Portrait of a Lady* in *The American Novel and Its Tradition* (Garden City, N.Y.: Doubleday, 1957). Of her "vision of things" he writes: "It emphatically is that of the romance associated with the American tradition of puritanism and transcendentalism. Isabel subscribes to the American romance of the self" (p. 131). He recognizes "the moral world shared by Isabel and Osmond" as "that of the high Emersonian self-culture" (p. 134).
3. *The Portrait of a Lady* (Boston, 1882 [1881]), 12:89. All citations from *Portrait* refer to this edition.
4. *Margaret Fuller,* ed. Miller, p. ix.
5. Philip Rahv cites this passage as a "revelation of Isabel's shining beneficent Emersonianism" in *Image and Idea: Fourteen Essays on Literary Themes* (New York: New Directions, 1949), p. 53. "She is," he observes, "truly the Young American so grandly pictured by the Concord idealist" (p. 52). While he affirms that James's heroine is "a young lady of an Emersonian cast of mind," he suggests that "her affinity as a fictional character is rather with those heroines of Turgenev in whose nature an extreme tenderness is conjoined with unusual strength of purpose" (p. 51). More recently, Richard Poirier, in *The Comic Sense of Henry James* (London: Chatto and Windus, 1960), has described Isabel's "mental processes" as "authentically Emersonian" (p. 219), and he defines her idealism as an effort at "self-creation" (p. 224). Interestingly, he suggests that Osmond may be viewed as "a mock version of the transcendentalist" (p. 219).
6. Cf. James's paraphrase of Emerson on this issue in *Hawthorne:* "He urged that a man should await his call, his finding the thing to do which he should really believe in doing, and not be urged by the world's opinion to do simply the world's work. 'If no call should come for years, for centuries, then I know that the want of the Universe is the attestation of faith by my abstinence. . . . If I cannot work, at least I need not lie!'" (4:491).
7. To my knowledge, A. D. Moody, in a searching essay entitled

"James's Portrait of an Ideal" in *The Melbourne Critical Review*, No. 4 (1961), 77–92, was the first critic who sought to interpret *The Portrait of a Lady* primarily in terms of Isabel's imagination. He makes no effort, however, to define the nature and background of Isabel's idealism as anything more substantial than a vague romanticism, and he does not explore the operation of the girl's imagination as the controlling force in her moral consciousness. Charles R. Anderson, in his important essay "Person, Place and Thing in James's *The Portrait of a Lady*," shares my view that "what Isabel sees and *how* she sees . . . these are essential to any understanding of her story" (p. 181). Printed in *Essays on American Literature in Honor of Jay B. Hubbell*, ed. Clarence Gohdes (Durham, N.C.: Duke Univ. Press, 1967), pp. 164–82.

    8. *Hawthorne*, 4:489.

    9. In his essay *Nature*, on the basis of his proposition that "the whole of nature is a metaphor of the human mind," Emerson argued that "the laws of moral nature answer to those of matter as face to face in a glass" (*Collected Works*, p. 21).

    10. In his discussion of "a noble doubt" in the chapter on "Idealism" in his *Nature*, Emerson openly acknowledged a problematical strain of solipsism in his thought to which Isabel gives ample if unconscious testimony in her self-indulgent reflections.

    11. "Emerson," *American Essays*, pp. 56–57.

    12. Cf. the high-minded fastidiousness of Isabel's reflections on "the disagreeable" in 4:26. Christopher Pearse Cranch captured Isabel's simplistic moral posture in his witty illustration for the conclusion of Emerson's *Nature*. His cartoon shows a seated Emerson banishing "disagreeable things" like swine, spiders, snakes, madhouses, and prisons from a universe designed to meet his own specifications. The cartoon is reproduced in *Emerson's* Nature: *Origin, Growth, Meaning*, ed. Merton M. Sealts, Jr., and Alfred R. Ferguson (New York: Dodd, 1969), p. 36.

    13. *Art of the Novel*, p. 48.

    14. *Hawthorne*, 4:491–92.

    15. *Hawthorne*, 4:487.

    16. *Art of the Novel*, p. 57.

    17. *The Blithedale Romance*, 3:21.

    18. Poirier interprets Isabel's decision to return to Osmond as "absolutely within the logic of her Emersonian idealism, so much so that the logic takes its vengeance" (*Comic Sense*, p. 246).

    19. Chase formulates the connection between Isabel Archer and

Olive Chancellor as follows: "[James gives Isabel] an element of perverse Yankee idealism of the sort that he was shortly to portray in the
more exacerbated form of positively perverted idealism in Olive Chancellor in *The Bostonians*" (*American Novel*, p. 121).

CHAPTER 7

1. *The Shock of Recognition*, pp. 566–67.
2. January 24, 1886, quoted in Virginia Harlow, "Thomas Sargeant
Perry and Henry James," *Boston Public Library Quarterly*, 1 (1949),
54–55.
3. *Hawthorne*, 4:491.
4. *The Notebooks of Henry James*, ed. F. O. Matthiessen and Kenneth B. Murdock (New York: Oxford Univ. Press, 1961), p. 47.
5. *Hawthorne*, 3:479.
6. *The Bostonians* (New York: Modern Library, [c.1956]), 3:20–21.
All citations from *The Bostonians* refer to this edition.
7. Quoted in *The James Family*, p. 327.
8. For another reading of the relationship between James's conception of his heroine and Hawthorne's of his pair, see Marius Bewley,
The Complex Fate, pp. 19–28 passim, esp. pp. 26–27.
9. *William Wetmore Story and His Friends*, I, 128.
10. In the summer of 1879 Howells wrote to James describing the
story of *The Undiscovered Country*, and James reported that he found
Howells's subject "real, actual & American." When James wrote to
Howells on July 20, 1880, after he had read the novel, his response was
clearly a mixed one. He still felt that the interest of the book resided
in the subject itself, "a larger & heavier one than you have yet tried,"
but one senses his disappointment that Howells had not managed to
fulfill the promise of his original conception. Kenneth S. Lynn, *William
Dean Howells: An American Life* (New York: Harcourt, 1970), pp.
243–44. Letter from HJ to WDH, July 20, 1880, quoted by permission
of the Harvard College Library and Mr. Alexander R. James.
11. *The Undiscovered Country*, 7:109–10. The network of connections that link *The Bostonians* with *The Undiscovered Country*, *The
Blithedale Romance*, and James's own "Professor Fargo" has been
given considerable attention recently by a number of critics, including
Martha Banta, Howard Kerr, and Lyall Powers. Banta speaks of this
network as constituting a "literary tradition," and her review of the
material is characteristic of the interest now shown in this "striking

collection" of works. See Banta, *Henry James and the Occult: The Great Extension* (Bloomington: Indiana Univ. Press, 1972), pp. 89–100.

12. One contemporary reviewer, e.g., speculated that "Mr. James may have had an indefinite image of the Priscilla of Hawthorne's The Blithedale Romance floating in his mind when he built this impossible Verena." *Atlantic Monthly,* 57 (June, 1886), 851–52.

13. Quoted in *The James Family,* p. 326.

14. *Hawthorne,* 5:534.

15. Ibid., 5:536. John Goode writes: "Certainly *The Bostonians* develops out of the historical commitment. It is an attempt to render the historical forces at work in the society of the United States in the period of reconstruction, and although it is a presentation in terms of highly specific social intercourse, the whole novel is controlled by the visit of Ransom and Verena to the Harvard Memorial, and is dominated therefore by the catastrophe of the Civil War." "The Art of Fiction: Walter Besant and Henry James," in *Tradition and Tolerance in Nineteenth-Century Fiction,* ed. David Howard et al. (New York: Barnes and Noble, 1967), p. 268.

16. Richard Poirier has suggested that Olive and Verena represent different aspects of the personality of Isabel Archer (*Comic Sense,* pp. 251–52).

17. Introd. *Margaret Fuller,* p. xxvii.

18. *Hawthorne,* 5:529.

19. *Memoirs of Margaret Fuller Ossoli,* ii, 37.

20. There are interesting similarities between this passage and one in the *Memoirs* of Margaret Fuller (ii, 8) which I suggested in my discussion of the latter in chapter 5. W. H. Channing wrote of Fuller's lively response to another young woman in their circle that she "seemed to long, as it were, to transfuse with her force this nymph-like form, and to fill her to glowing with her own lyric fire."

21. The comparison with the passage from Margaret Fuller's *Memoirs* (ii, 8) is suggestive: "No drop of envy tainted the sisterly love, with which she sought by genial sympathy thus to live in another's experience, to be her guardian-angel, to shield her from contact with the unworthy, to rouse each generous impulse, to invigorate thought by truth incarnate in beauty, and with unfelt ministry to weave bright threads in her web of fate." W. H. Channing writes here under the spell of Fuller's ideal, while James probes "the deeper psychology" that lies behind it. Cf. note 20.

22. In discussing Hester Prynne's subversive speculations which pro-

jected a total reform of society and of the relations between the sexes, Hawthorne observed, "Woman cannot take advantage of these preliminary reforms, until she herself shall have undergone a still mightier change; in which perhaps, the ethereal essence, wherein she has her truest life, will be found to have evaporated" (*The Scarlet Letter*, 13:165–66). Basil Ransom would have eagerly endorsed the truth of Hawthorne's statement.

CONCLUSION

1. *Errand into the Wilderness*, p. 198.
2. *Literature and Life*, pp. 278, 281.
3. *American Essays*, pp. 12–13.
4. *Literature and Life*, pp. 279–80, 283.

Index

Index